The Napoleonic Wars:

1792–1815
an illustrated history

THE NAPOLEONIC WARS:

an illustrated history 1792-1815

MICHAEL GLOVER

B. T. Batsford Ltd, *London*

First published 1979
Reprinted 1982
Copyright © 1979 by Michael Glover

ISBN 07134 1723 4

1. France - History, Military, 1789-1815
2. Napoleonic Wars 1810 - 1814

Filmset by Keyspools Limited, Golborne, Lancs.
Printed in Great Britain by The Anchor Press Limited, Tiptree, Essex
for the publishers B. T. Batsford Ltd
4 Fitzhardinge Street, London W1H 0AH

CONTENTS

ILLUSTRATIONS

COLOUR ILLUSTRATIONS

(between pages 136 and 137)

MAPS

ACKNOWLEDGMENTS

Illustrations 10, 23, 25, 26, 29, 30, 33, 35, 36, 58, 72, 82, 87, 91 and 95 are reproduced by Gracious Permission of Her Majesty the Queen. The Author and Publishers also thank the following for their kind permission to reproduce copyright illustrations as indicated: Bibliothèque Marmottan, 97; Bibliothèque Nationale, 40; the British Library, 56, 75, 85; Anne S. K. Brown Military Collection, 31, 32, 34, 50, 51, 60, 71, 73, 74, 76, 79, 80, 81, 83, 88, 92; Lord Cottesloe, 45; John R. Freeman & Co (Photographers) Ltd, 37; Giraudon, 78, 90, 97; Guildhall Library, 89; Lauros-Giraudon, 40, 63; the Mansell Collection, 11, 18, 27, 43, 54; Mary Evans Picture Library, 24; Musée de l'Armée, Paris, 52, 78; Musée Massena, Nice, 63; National Army Museum, 9, 19, 68; the National Gallery, 8; the National Gallery of Art, Washington, 67; the National Maritime Museum, 1, 2, 3, 13, 16, 17, 21, 46, 47, 49, 65, 66, 69, 70; the National Portrait Gallery, 20, 59, 61; the Parker Gallery, 64, 77, 96; Photographie Bulloz, 14, 28, 43, 52, 57, 62; Radio Times Hulton Picture Library, 15, 39, 53; the Victoria and Albert Museum, 38, 41, 42, 48, 55, 84. The diagrams on pages 4, 5, 6 and 7 are taken from *1815 The Armies at Waterloo* by Ugo Pericoli, and are reproduced by kind permission of the Publisher, Seeley Service & Co.

INTRODUCTION

The war which followed the French Revolution lasted, with two short intermissions, for more than 23 years and it has been no easy task to compress the four main threads of the story—naval, military, economic and diplomatic—into the space available. Inevitably this book must deal primarily with strategy, with the broad sweep of campaigns rather than with the details of individual battles, but since strategy is meaningless unless it is converted into victory or defeat—naval, military, economic or diplomatic—by tactics, I have tried to give examples of the tactics used at points where they are significant for the narrative as a whole.

Given the comparatively short length of the book, it may be asked why, since its title is *The Napoleonic Wars*, I have chosen to devote one third of the space available to what is generally known as the French Revolutionary War instead of beginning at the commonly accepted date of 1803, the end of the Peace of Amiens. The reasons are, first, that the short-lived peace was no more than a punctuation mark in the middle of what was for all practical purposes a single war. Secondly, that Bonaparte (as Napoleon was then known) was the dominant figure in the war from the time, early in 1796, when he assumed command of the *Armée de l'Italie* and the previous four years would in any case have had to be sketched in. I have, however, made no attempt to describe or discuss the causes or course of the French Revolution except so far as they affect the progress of the war.

Some may think that I have devoted a disproportionate amount of space to the struggle between France and Britain, since in terms of the land war Britain's contribution was comparatively small. To this I would reply that between 1792 and 1814 Britain was at war with France for 240 months, while among the great powers, Austria was at war with France for only 108 months, Prussia for 58 months and Russia for 55. These three were also at war with Britain for various periods, although not to the extent of actual fighting except when the Russian battleship *Sewolod* (74) was captured and burned by the Royal Navy in the Baltic in 1808. There can be no doubt that throughout the war Napoleon regarded Britain as France's main opponent, 'the most powerful and most constant . . . of my enemies.'

I must apologize to my Irish readers for using the term 'Britain' for what became in 1801 the United Kingdom but Scottish and Welsh readers will expect no apology from me because Napoleon habitually referred to the whole of the United Kingdom as 'England'. It may be said in his defence that in his day most educated Scotsmen, Welshmen and Irishmen did the same.

A few points in the text require explanation. In the vexed question of place-names, I have used the contemporary version and the spelling most usual in English. Where the name has changed in the last century and a half the modern name is given in brackets on the first occasion the name occurs (e.g. Austerlitz (Slavkov)) and both names will be found in the index.

The names of warships also cause confusion. Apart from names which occur in several navies (there was a *Phoenix* in each of the British, French and Dutch fleets), captured ships were usually taken into the navies of their captors under their original names and it is disconcerting to find the *Ça-Ira* and the *Peuple Souverain* fighting against the French. The situation was particularly confusing at Trafalgar where there was a *Swiftsure* and an *Achille* on each side, while the British line included *Téméraire*, *Spartiate*, *Belleîle* and *Tonnant* and the French fleet included the *Berwick*. To avoid this trouble I have adopted the usage devised, I believe, by Mr James Henderson, of giving the names of British ships in small capitals, e.g. SWIFTSURE, and of foreign ships in italics, e.g. *Swiftsure*.

The numerical strength of armies and the numbers of casualties present an almost insuperable problem. Some of the difficulty arises from the way in which returns were rendered. A French return, for example, gives a total which includes officers, NCOs and private soldiers; while a British return would give only the weapon strength, the corporals and privates, and would exclude officers, sergeants and drummers, who would increase the strength by one eighth. From the total in the returns must be deducted the sick, the missing and those detached (although some of the detached may be with the army if not actually with their regiments), and further allowance must be made for those who have fallen by the wayside since the last return was rendered. No confidence can ever be placed in any estimate of casualties suffered by an enemy and little confidence should be given to any statement by a French commander of the casualties suffered by his own army. When Napoleon announced that his army lost 4,100 men at Aspern-Essling (when the real total was over 40,000), it is no surprise to learn that '*To lie like a bulletin*' became a proverb in France. Subordinate French generals followed the example set by the Emperor until it was difficult for Paris to discover, especially from Soult, how many casualties had occurred. The figures given in this book are, therefore, the best estimates that I can make. The reader should assume that any round figure, e.g. 44,000 or 750,

1 A frigate. *Painting by W. I. Pocock*

2 HMS REVENGE, third rate (two-decker). *Painting by H. Robinson*

3 HMS HIBERNIA, first rate (three-decker). *Painting by H. Julia*

is an approximation. Any exact figure, e.g. 449, is, to the best of my belief, correct.

To give a full bibliography would consume more space than could be justified. Apart from a few basic sources, such as *Correspondance de Napoléon 1er*, the titles given in my select list are those of books which, from their own bibliographies, will show the interested reader where he or she can find more detailed information.

NOTE ON TYPES OF WARSHIPS

Ships of all nations were classified, 'rated', according to the number of long guns mounted in their two broadsides. No account was taken of additional ordnance deployed on the poop, quarterdeck or fo'c's'le.

The figures below refer to the Royal Navy but with minor differences apply to all fleets.

TYPE	NUMBER OF BROADSIDE GUNS	APPROX. TONNAGE	APPROX. COMPLEMENT[1]
Ships of the line (i.e. battleships)			
Three-deckers (i.e. with broadside guns mounted on three decks)			
First rate	100–120	2,500	840
Second rate	82–98	2,000	750
Two-deckers			
Third rate	64–80	1,750	600
Fourth rate[2]	50–60	1,250	400
Ships below the line (Single-deckers)			
Fifth rate	26–48	900	280
Frigates (fifth rate)	32–44	900	280
Sixth rate	20–24	5–600	275
Frigates/sloops (sixth rate)	28	500	250
Unrated (brigs, bombs, cutters)	4–18	80–400	—

[1] French warships normally had a crew up to a third larger than their British equivalents.

[2] Fourth rates and, except in the Dutch navy, the smaller third rates (64s), were no longer considered sufficiently powerful to take their place in the line of battle and, like the non-frigate fifth rates, were used principally as convoy escorts.

PROLOGUE

(i) EUROPE AT THE TIME OF THE FRENCH REVOLUTION

Even in the last quarter of the twentieth century there are an irritating number of delays for passport controls and custom posts when travelling overland across Europe. The situation was far worse in 1790, particularly east of the Rhine when the Continent was a jigsaw of tiny states each clinging to a sovereignty it could barely afford. France was something of an exception. With a population of 27 million she was the most powerful and homogeneous nation in Europe, with frontiers closely resembling those she holds today except in the south east where Savoy and Nice belonged to the Kingdom of Sardinia. Even France was not free from one of the besetting complications of political geography at the time—the presence of enclaves of foreign territories within her frontiers. The most conspicuous was Papal Avignon but there were other tracts on the west bank of the Rhine which belonged to some of the multifarious states of the Holy Roman Empire. Though she had lost Canada, her largest overseas possession, in 1763, France was still a considerable colonial power. She had trading posts in India and west Africa, the islands now known as Mauritius and Réunion in the Indian Ocean, and several substantial holdings, notably Martinique, Guadaloupe and San Domingue (Haiti), in the Caribbean. The wealth extracted from the West Indian sugar islands went some way to stave off the financial collapse, brought about by Bourbon extravagance and incompetence together with recurring wars, which caused the revolution which started in 1789.

Austria was second among the powers. Her population equalled that of France but lacked homogeneity—seven languages and a number of dialects were spoken in her army—while her political institutions lacked any form of coherence. Austria is, in fact, a convenient misnomer for what were really the Hapsburg lands. Austria herself comprised most of the modern state of that name, except the independent bishopric of Salzburg, but with

5

the addition of western Czechoslovakia, the Slovene area of Yugoslavia, and Trieste. Hungary was joined to Austria by a common sovereign but had a separate and different form of government. Apart from the modern state of that name, the kingdom of Hungary included eastern Czechoslovakia, western Romania (Transylvania), Croatia and the Vojvodina (now in Yugoslavia) and the Polish province of Galicia, which had been annexed in 1772. Austria and Hungary formed a contiguous territorial block but the Hapsburg lands also included the duchies of Milan and Mantua in Italy, a number of enclaves in Germany, and the Austrian Netherlands which consisted of Luxemburg and Belgium except for the bishopric of Liège. The Netherlands were a possession the Hapsburgs did not prize and for some decades they had been trying to persuade the Elector of Bavaria to take them in exchange for his domains round Munich. The Belgians on their side did not relish Austrian rule and in 1789 had succeeded in driving the garrison into Luxemburg where they had to wait for a year before gathering sufficient strength to reoccupy the country.

The Hapsburg sovereign was also, by a long tradition, the nominal overlord of Germany under the title of Holy Roman Emperor. This empire was little more than an anachronistic survival of earlier centuries. It consisted of more than 300 independent territories, many of them tiny, and few of which paid more than lip-service to their Emperor. It also included territories belonging to sovereigns outside the imperial boundaries. The Emperor himself held Austria and the Netherlands inside the empire while Hungary and the Italian duchies were outside. The King of England was an imperial elector by virtue of his Hanoverian possessions and the Stadtholder of Holland was an imperial dignitary as Duke of Nassau. The second power in Germany was represented within the empire by the Elector of Brandenburg, who was better known as the King of Prussia.

The rise of Prussia was one of the phenomena of eighteenth-century Europe. Two remarkable men, Frederick William, the Great Elector, and Frederick the Great, had raised her from a poverty-stricken electorate round Berlin with a detached province east of Danzig (which was outside the Holy Roman Empire) to the most formidable military power in Europe. In the process she had wrested Silesia from Austria, most of Pomerania from Sweden and, from the Poles, a strip of land connecting Brandenburg with East Prussia. She had also acquired Cleves-Geldres, astride the lower Rhine, Emden and East Friedland, Mark (which included most of the modern Ruhr district) and two duchies in south Germany. She remained, nevertheless, a poor country and most of her inadequate revenue was devoted to the upkeep of her army. She was viewed with the deepest distrust by the neighbours she had robbed.

Another eighteenth-century *parvenu* was Russia. Within a hundred years she had swelled from a small and landlocked Grand Duchy around Moscow to a vast empire. By 1790 her population was estimated at 40 millions and she had outlets on the Baltic and the Black Sea. Her western frontier ran from Riga through Kiev to Odessa, then a port still in the process of construction. Diderot had described her as 'a giant with feet of clay', but it remained to be seen whether the drastic steps taken by Peter the Great and Catherine the Great had brought Russia close enough to the standards of the west for her to be considered as a great power.

Squeezed between Austria, Prussia and Russia was Poland. She still had access to the sea between Memel (Prussian) and Riga (Russian) but her frontiers were indefensible, her internal factions bitter and her constitution unworkable. Her continued existence was a standing temptation to her neighbours who had, in 1772, seized strips from her territory.

Scandinavia consisted of only two states; the more important was Sweden which then included the whole of Finland, a possession which put her under constant threat from Russia, who did not relish the presence of a foreign power so close to her new capital of St Petersburg. Sweden also retained a small strip on the southern shore of the Baltic, including the fortress town of Stralsund; and, as Russia coveted Finland, so Prussia wanted Swedish Pomerania. Sweden in her turn was anxious to acquire Norway, then linked by a common crown to Denmark. Denmark was larger than she is in the twentieth century, holding the duchies of Schleswig and Holstein (both within the Holy Roman Empire) and the island of Heligoland. She was also a colonial power inasmuch as she owned the Caribbean island of Ste Croix.

A more substantial colonial power was Holland, more properly known as the United Provinces. She drew great wealth from her East Indian possessions (now Indonesia) and she also held the Cape of Good Hope (then important only as a staging-post for ships on passage to the east), Ceylon, a number of West Indian islands and Guiana on the mainland of Latin America. Although wealthy and the most important financial centre on the Continent, Holland was torn with internal dissension. The Stadtholder, William V, was one of the least inspiring members of the House of Orange and in 1787 a republican faction had seized much of the country only to be suppressed by Prussian troops acting at the instigation and at the expense of Britain. Britain was the guarantor of Dutch independence. There were long-standing dynastic and commercial links between the two countries and the most constant tenet of British foreign policy was that the potential naval base of Antwerp should not fall into hostile hands. Antwerp itself was in the Austrian Netherlands but the approaches to the port, the estuary of the Scheldt, lay in Dutch territory.

Portugal, while far less wealthy than Holland, was in a not dissimilar position. Although she had large overseas possessions, including Brazil and trading-posts in India, China and Africa, she was so dependent on her trade with Britain that economically speaking she was a British colony in all but name. Her government was weak and she was under constant threat from Spain who would undoubtedly have attempted to reabsorb her had Britain not been determined to preserve the deep all-weather harbour of Lisbon in friendly hands.

If Portugal felt threatened by Spain, no other country did so. In the seventeenth century Spain had been as powerful as any country in Europe but since that time she had stagnated. She was still the greatest colonial power. Except for Brazil and Guiana all Latin America was hers and her sovereignty extended to more of North America, Florida and all the land west of the Mississippi, than the United States claimed to rule. She also owned many of the Caribbean islands (including Cuba, Santo Domingo and Trinidad), and the Philippines. Despite these great possessions, Spain was the most backward state in western Europe. Her government, dominated by the deplorable Godoy, was corrupt and inefficient, her trade stagnant, her large navy for the most part unseaworthy and her army, though it dreamed of past glories, unfit for war.

Metternich was very near the truth when he remarked that Italy was no more than a geographical expression. Although less Balkanized than Germany, the peninsula was a jumble of small states. To the north west was the Kingdom of Sardinia, comprising Piedmont, Savoy, Nice and the little-considered island of Sardinia itself. This ramshackle realm controlled all the roads from France into Italy except those which ran through Switzerland, a disunited conglomeration of cantons which combined a professional neutrality with a profitable business in renting battalions to France, Spain and Austria. The Sardinian kingdom had as its eastern neighbour the Austrian duchies and, to the south east, the moribund republic of Genoa. The largest state in Italy was Naples, which was joined by a common crown to Sicily. Naples stretched as far north as the river Sangro and her king was an ineffective Bourbon whose queen, an active and malevolent woman, was an Austrian archduchess, sister to Marie-Antoinette.

North of Naples were the Papal States, which sprawled from the Sangro to the Po and even by contemporary Italian standards were notably misgoverned. The Pope also held two enclaves in Neapolitan territory, Benevento and Pontecorvo; while Naples had enclaves in the Grand Duchy of Tuscany, which was ruled by an Austrian archduke with his capital at Florence and, like the tiny republic of San Marino, was embedded in Papal territory. The other large political unit in Italy was the decaying republic of Venice which extended inland as far as the Adige river, and thus stood between Austria itself and the Austrian duchies of Milan and Mantua. On the east Venice held Istria, Dalmatia and the Ionian islands from Corfu off the coast of Albania, to Cerigo (Kithera) off the south coast of Greece. Wedged into the interstices of northern Italy were the duchies of Parma, Modena and Massa, and Piombino, together with the republics of Lucca and Noli.

There was one more continental power, the Ottoman Empire, which, apart from its heartland in Turkey, claimed suzerainty over all the eastern and southern shores of the Mediterranean. In Europe she governed the whole of south-eastern Europe up to the line of the Sava river, including the southern part of modern Yugoslavia, the whole of Greece, all Bulgaria, Romania (except for Hapsburg Transylvania) and Moldavia, which is now in the Soviet Union. Turkey was in a constant state of war or near war with Russia and between 1789 and 1791 was also fighting Austria. Swallowed up in European Turkey was the small but independent kingdom of Montenegro which had the unique distinction among European states that she never abandoned her neutrality in the long wars which followed the French Revolution.

Britain was far from considering herself a European power. Military intervention on the Continent, even in defence of the king's Hanoverian electorate, was traditionally unpopular and was most unlikely to be undertaken except to secure her paramount interests, the security of Antwerp or, possibly, Lisbon. Only six years before the French Revolution she had been humiliated by the loss of her American colonies in the face of a coalition which included almost the whole of Europe, even including Holland. She was, in consequence, widely under-rated by the continental states not only because of her poor military showing in America but because she was a small country with a population in Great Britain of only ten million, to which could be added four million Irish who were generally reckoned to be a source more of weakness to Britain than of strength.

In fact though her army was small, Britain had strengths unsuspected by her neighbours. Ireland, for instance, though turbulence there caused much concern and distraction in London, was always a principal reservoir of recruits for the British army. Britain's first advantage was her island position which insured her against invasion. This insurance was guaranteed by her possession of the largest and most efficient fleet in the world and behind the shield of her warships her immense merchant fleet could, even in wartime, ply with comparative security. Although she had lost the Thirteen Colonies, they remained her largest single trading partner, and her colonial possessions were still considerable. In America she still held Canada, Newfoundland, British Honduras; Jamaica and many other West Indian islands were hers; and in India she held Bengal, Bihar, Bombay, Surat, Madras and much of the east coast. All these possessions brought her wealth but she had also great resources in her own islands where her clear lead in the techniques of industrialization were being exploited to an extent undreamed of on the Continent. The output of her coalmines was twenty times that of the French, and her wealth, earned at home and by trade, was consolidated and increased by her development of viable economic institutions, of the mechanism of credit, on a scale and with a security that only Holland could, in a smaller way, hope to rival. The

9

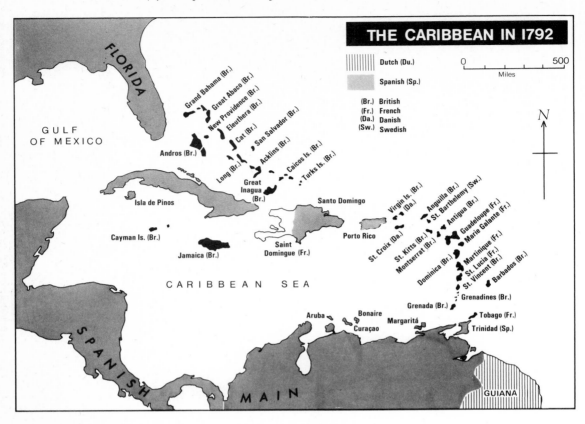

THE CARIBBEAN IN 1792

|||||| Dutch (Du.)

▨ Spanish (Sp.)

(Br.) **British**
(Fr.) **French**
(Da.) **Danish**
(Sw.) **Swedish**

0   500
Miles

N

FLORIDA

GULF
OF MEXICO

Grand Bahama (Br.)
Great Abaco (Br.)
New Providence (Br.)
Eleuthera (Br.)
Cat (Br.)
San Salvador (Br.)
Andros (Br.)
Long (Br.)
Acklins (Br.)
Caicos Is. (Br.)
Great
Inagua
(Br.)
Turks Is. (Br.)

Isla de Pinos

Santo Domingo

Virgin Is. (Br.)
St. Croix (Da.)
Anguilla (Br.)
St. Barthelemy (Sw.)
Antigua (Br.)
Guadeloupe (Fr.)
Marie Galante (Fr.)
St. Kitts (Br.)
Montserrat (Br.)
Dominica (Br.)
Martinique (Fr.)
St. Lucia (Br.)
St. Vincent (Br.)
Barbados (Br.)

Cayman Is. (Br.)

Jamaica (Br.)

Saint
Domingue (Fr.)

Porto Rico

CARIBBEAN   SEA

Grenadines (Br.)
Grenada (Br.)
Tobago (Fr.)
Trinidad (Sp.)

Aruba
Bonaire
Curaçao
Margaritá

SPANISH

MAIN

GUIANA

financial strains of the American war had been eased by the careful financial management of the younger Pitt who had been able to make a start on reducing the National Debt; and even if Pitt's economies had largely been achieved at the expense of the armed forces, Britain was in good shape to wage and win economic warfare.

(ii) THE WEAPONS OF WAR

In the last quarter of the twentieth century when weapons of increasing complexity become obsolete before they have left the drawing-board, it is difficult to comprehend how static was the weaponry of the end of the eighteenth century. In all armies the infantryman's musket was of a type that had been introduced around 1700, when the flintlock method of ignition had superseded the matchlock. With minor modifications the same types were in service at Waterloo. The cavalry fought with weapons centuries old and the only new development between 1792 and 1815 was the introduction, after a century of disuse, of the spear under the designation of lance. Artillery evolved slowly. During the eighteenth century the mobility of guns was improved, marginally better gunpowder

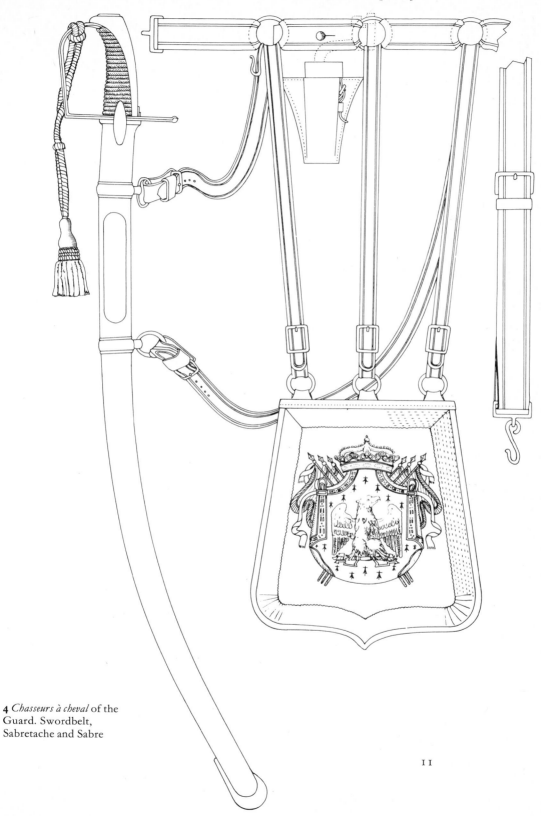

4 *Chasseurs à cheval* of the
Guard. Swordbelt,
Sabretache and Sabre

5 The Baker Rifle (British)

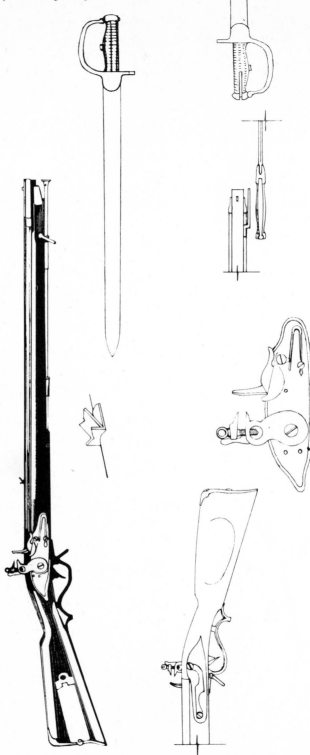

became available, grapeshot (canister) and the 'common shell' were introduced, but the design of cannon remained almost unchanged between the wars of Louis XIV and those of Napoleon. In 1811 Wellington undertook a siege using guns dated between 1620 and 1653 and the only reason why the battering fire was less effective than it would have been with guns of later date was that the bores were badly worn with heavy use.

Warships also had a long life. H.M.S. VICTORY was 40 years old at Trafalgar and continued in service for many more years. This longevity was fortunate since the raw material for the construction of warships— oak—was slow-growing and required in vast quantities. To build a 74-gun ship, a third-rate, called for 1,977 loads of oak, each load being 50 cubic feet or all the usable timber from a full-grown oak tree. Besides the oak such a ship needed 570 loads of elm, 139 of fir, and 2,500 of deal. In 1794 the Royal Navy had 71 of these third-raters in commission and 24 more in reserve or under repair. More difficult to obtain than the ships' timbers were the masts. A 74's mainmast was 108 feet long and a yard in diameter and while a few trees of this kind could be obtained in New Brunswick or New England the majority came from Norway or Russia. The 120-foot mainmasts of first- and second-raters, ships with up to 120 guns, could come only from the Baltic.

All forms of warfare were dependent on natural factors. It was impossible to fight a land battle in heavy rain. All infantry weapons were fired by a spark from a flint igniting a pinch of powder in an open flash pan. Even in fine weather the misfire rate was two rounds in thirteen and in a downpour there could be no firing at all. Artillery pieces, which on land were fired by a slow match or linstock being applied to powder in the touch-hole, were more likely to fire in bad weather than muskets; but sodden ground would make the guns immovable, a serious drawback as they had to be dragged back into position after the recoil of each round, and this would make roundshot and common shell largely ineffective.

At sea even the most powerful fleet was at the mercy of the wind. Dead calm and gale equally made all naval operations impossible and no ship could engage an unwilling adversary unless blessed by a favourable breeze. Natural and accidental hazards were far more dangerous to ships than the guns of the enemy. Between 1793 and 1814 the Royal Navy lost 32 ships of the line. Of these five were captured by the enemy (three were subsequently recaptured) and of the remainder 19 were wrecked or foundered at sea while eight were accidentally burned.

Communications were another problem. On land messages could only travel as fast as a horse could move—12 mph over short distances and little more than 60 miles a day on long journeys. At sea communication depended on being in visual touch. On a clear day signals could be read, masthead to masthead, at about 15 miles. At night or in fog it was difficult to transmit a message further than a man's voice would carry, although at night simple messages could be sent by an arrangement of lanterns. Even in daylight it was hard to send a message of any complexity at least until Captain Home Popham's 'Marine Vocabulary', the first comprehensive code of signals, was adopted by the Admiralty in 1803.

Both on land and on sea battles resolved themselves into pounding matches, with victory going to the side which fired fastest and most accurately and which had a commander who could put his forces into a position where their fire could tell most effectively. Nelson laid down that 'No captain can do very wrong if he places his ship alongside that of an enemy', and he meant literally what he said. Naval engagements were fought out at 'half pistol shot', about 20 yards, even when the ships were not actually touching each other with their guns pounding away while their muzzles were within inches of the enemy's sides.

By army standards warships were very heavily armed. H.M.S. MARS, rated a 74-gun ship, carried 28 32-pounders, 30 24-pounders and 16 9-pounders in her two broadsides, while she had two 9-pounder and six 24-pounder carronades on her poop and quarterdeck. The weight of shot from one of her broadsides, 37 long guns, was 880 lbs, a quarter more than could be fired by all Wellington's guns for an army of 70,000 men at the Battle of Vitoria. Nevertheless such was the strength of their oak construction that it was very rare for a battleship to be sunk in action. Of the 20 French battleships destroyed (as opposed to captured, wrecked, foundered or accidentally burned) only one, *L'Orient* (120), actually sank during a battle when she was set on fire and exploded in the Nile. The remainder were ignited by fireships, fired by their own crews to avoid capture, or driven on to rocks. Against this 60 French battleships were captured, most of them having been battered into such a state that their crews could no longer fight.

Military artillery was, by comparison, puny. The heaviest gun which could be moved about the country was the 24-pounder siege gun. This threw a non-explosive iron ball to an effective range of less than a mile and a half at the rate of one aimed round every two minutes. On good roads and in fine weather it took five pairs of bullocks to move the gun seven miles a day. Even the largest field pieces, Napoleon's 12-pounder *belles filles*, were only half this size and a more typical field gun was the 9-pounder, weighing, with its limber, two tons. This could fire three aimed rounds a minute with canister (which was effective only up to 300 yards) or two rounds of solid shot which had an effective range of 1,400 yards.

In land fighting the musket was the predominant weapon. There was little to choose between the muskets used by the various powers, the British being marginally the best while the Prussian was certainly the worst. All of them threw a lead ball weighing about an ounce and were capable of discharging five or six rounds a minute, although anything more than two or possibly three rounds a minute could only be achieved with a great loss of accuracy and at best accuracy could only be defined as the ability to hit a

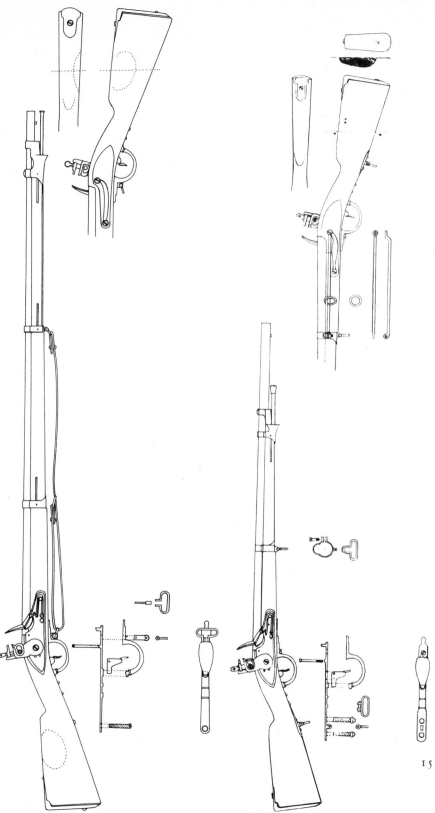

6 French infantry musket
7 French cavalry carbine

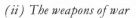

man-sized target at 80 yards.

Using so inefficient a weapon an attacking enemy could only be halted by discharging a vast mass of musket balls so that a large number of them were bound to find a target. This could be achieved by volley-firing carried out by men packed as closely as possible while still able to fire their weapons. Thus they were arranged in a line, usually three deep, with the files 'lightly touching, but without crouding [*sic*]; each man will then occupy a space of 22 inches.' Since only the front two ranks could fire there would be one musket on every eleven inches of front.

Even volley-firing was not necessarily efficient. Tests carried out by the Prussian army showed that a section (platoon) firing volleys at a range of 120 yards would score only 46.6% of hits on a target ten foot square. This Prussian experience was to some extent a special case. Frederick the Great, the supreme military figure of the eighteenth century, had laid down that 'battles are won by fire superiority. Infantry firing more rapidly will undoubtedly defeat infantry firing more slowly.' Believing that the rate of fire was more important than any other factor, he forbade his soldiers to aim, making them fire their muskets from the hip. To ensure that this order was obeyed, he supplied them with muskets with straight stocks, making aiming impossible, and these remained the standard weapon of the Prussian army until after their shattering defeat at Jena in 1806.

Other nations did not embrace the Frederican doctrine to the full but they still had to contend with the ineffectiveness of the musket and acknowledged that fighting in line was the best way of countering its defects. The line, however, was extremely difficult to manoeuvre. To advance and wheel, as Frederick did on occasions, with a line of men three deep and six miles long required a very high standard of foot drill, a standard attainable only by long-term professionals. In the eighteenth century this was acceptable since armies were small, difficult to recruit, and harder to feed by conventional means. The wars in which they engaged were in consequence limited affairs, and care was taken not to waste irreplaceable manpower. Decisive battles were rare and commanders usually limited their aims to capturing fortresses, towns or islands which would be useful as bargaining counters at the inevitable peace conference. As Count Guibert, one of a new generation of French military thinkers, wrote in 1772:

> *What can be the result of our wars? The countries involved have neither treasure nor superfluous population. Even in peacetime their expenditure exceeds their revenue. They go to war with armies they can neither pay nor recruit. The winners exhaust themselves as fast as the losers. The national debts grow larger. Credit is unobtainable and coin is not to be had. Recruiting fails. On both sides governments are forced to the conference table. Peace is made and a few colonies, a province or two, change hands.*

Five years after that was published France went to war with Britain and was, on paper, victorious. Britain was forced to grant independence to her American colonies. France regained Tobago (which she had lost 20 years earlier) but her war expenditure brought about the final collapse of the Bourbon government.

Guibert foresaw a time when limited warfare would be abandoned:

It remains to be seen whether a general of genius, leading an army trained to patience and sobriety, to greatness and strength, will not circumvent [the frontier fortresses] and carry the war into the interior of enemy countries, even to their capitals.

His general of genius would ignore any strong position held by his enemy and would adopt the 'strategy of the indirect approach', falling on the flanks and rear of the opposing army and striking at the vitals of his country. Such a strategy would cause a supply problem. Fighting troops could by-pass fortresses, but supply waggons would be tied to the roads which fortresses were designed to dominate.

There was only one logical answer to this problem and Guibert advocated adopting it. The supply columns must be sacrificed. Quoting Cato's adage that 'War must supply war', he asserted that in Roman times,

As soon as an army set foot on enemy territory it was the general's task to see that it was supplied. The best servant of the state was the general who, while triumphing in his campaign, not only supplied his army liberally but who brought home much [enemy] money to the Treasury.

The adoption of such teaching changed the nature of war. In future those who thought as Guibert did were to aim for the total defeat of the enemy, the occupation of his country for both the subsistence of the conquering army and the enrichment of the victorious state. The consequence of implementing this doctrine was not foreseen. Guibert was thinking in terms of small professional armies and failed to realize that even with such a force the occupation of another country and the pillaging of its food stocks must lead to popular resistance. However cooperative or apathetic the peasant is to an occupying army he is bound to fight against it by any means available rather than see his family starve. Popular resistance means that more occupying troops must be brought in to guard the lines of communication and this inevitably increases the drain on the food stocks, stiffening popular resistance. Guibert remarked: 'It is astonishing how much a competent commissary can extract from the resources of a country. I speak of a populous and fertile country such as Flanders and much of Germany.' He did not speak of Spain, Portugal, Poland, Russia and southern Italy. Nor did he appreciate that even Flanders and Germany must, under pressure from constant requisitions and the disruption that war always imposes on agriculture, become less fertile and less able to support a foreign army.

This factor was exaggerated by the enormous growth in the size of armies. The wars which started in 1792 were not fought by armies of modest size and consisting of professionals who were highly trained and under tight discipline. Instead, in all the continental armies, there arose huge conscripted forces. The general of genius, whose coming Guibert prophesied, did appear and he trained his army to greatness and strength but not to patience and sobriety. Napoleon's troops could never be persuaded to rely for their food on official requisitions. Few soldiers can be persuaded not to loot and the armies of revolutionary and imperial France set new standards in pillaging. They made enemies of every man, woman and child they robbed.

The scale of conscripted armies raised tactical problems. The linear tactics of the eighteenth century necessitated a very high standard of training which could not be drilled into hastily raised recruits. Other methods of achieving victory had to be devised and, more from necessity than conviction, the French put their faith in shock action rather than firepower. They subordinated everything to the attempt to rupture the opposing line by bursting through it with a mass of men ready to accept heavy casualties (which could be replaced by conscription) and determined to achieve a crushing victory. This technique proved highly successful (especially against under-trained troops fighting in line) and, in combination with other factors which the French were quick and well-adapted to exploit, made the armies of Napoleon the model for every other army in Europe with one exception. The exception was Britain which, having no conscription, could not afford to adopt tactics which demanded heavy casualties. Her army clung to the belief that firepower properly deployed could halt any attack. When Wellington was asked what he thought of the French system of shock action, his answer was unhesitating: 'I think it is a false one against steady troops.' Events were to prove him right but only because he was able always to lead a relatively small army trained to the old professional standards and one which, though by no means free from private pillaging, always rejected requisitioning, and paid albeit belatedly for the supplies it took from the countryside, thus ensuring at least the passivity and frequently the active assistance of the population among whom it fought.

While the French were revolutionizing tactics on land, the British were doing the same at sea. Eighteenth-century sea battles were as linear as those on land. The opposing fleets were drawn out in lines and each ship hammered her opposite number until one or the other could board and capture her opponent. Since there was little to choose between the ships of the various naval powers, such a battle was unlikely to prove decisive but for as long as they were prepared to risk fleet actions, the post-revolutionary French navy clung to linear tactics. The British, on the other hand, were looking for the kind of crushing victory that Guibert had foreshadowed on land. As a First Lord of the Admiralty wrote: 'It is annihilation that the country wants, and not merely a splendid victory, honourable to the parties concerned, but absolutely useless in the extended scale to bring Buonaparte to his marrow bones.' Nelson realized that annihilation could not be achieved in a linear battle. He wrote before Trafalgar:

> *No day can be long enough to arrange a couple of fleets, and fight a decisive battle according to the old system. When we meet … I shall form the fleet into three divisions in three lines. One division I shall put under an officer who, I am sure will employ them in the manner I wish, if possible. … With the remaining part of the fleet, I shall go at them at once, about a third of their line from their leading ship. … It will surprise and confound the enemy. They won't know what I am about. It will bring on a pell-mell battle, and that is what I want.*

This was precisely what the French generals were trying to achieve on land with their massive columns of attack but their reasons were the exact opposite of Nelson's. They were compensating for their troops' lack of training by surprising and confusing the enemy and bringing on a pell-mell battle. Nelson on the other hand was exploiting the superlative training of his crews and the skill of his captains who could fight pell-mell while the fleets against which he fought, normally confined to the harbours by the British blockade, found it easier to fight on the old linear formation.

The long wars from 1792 to 1815 saw fighting in almost every corner of Europe, in the Middle East, South Africa, the West Indies, the Indian Ocean and Latin America. Every country in Europe, except Montenegro, was involved at one time or another and almost every belligerent state at one time or another was in alliance or at war with both France and Britain (though at no time was Switzerland allied to Britain). Such was the reversal of customary alliances that in 1795 Protestant Britain landed her Twelfth Light Dragoons at Civitavecchia to protect her arch-enemy the Pope. At bottom, however, it was a war between France and Britain. The latter was not prepared to tolerate the domination of any one power over the European continent. France knew that all her victories over the continental powers were useless as long as Britain was undefeated. These two antagonists had difficulty in coming to grips with each other. One was preponderant on the land; the other on the sea. In the end the victory went to sea power. Unless France could overwhelm the Royal Navy she could only win by destroying British trade, and she could only do this by closing all the ports of Europe to British ships. In attempting to do so she had to extend her army from Moscow to Lisbon, from Jutland to Calabria. In the event she over-reached herself. 'Napoleon', said Wellington, 'never in his life had the patience for a defensive war.' Had he been prepared to wait, had he postponed the Russian expedition for a few years, he must have won the war. The French calculated, and the Admiralty in London would not have

19

disagreed, that, 'We shall be able to make peace with safety when we have 150 ships of the line.' They meant that with a three to two superiority at sea the invasion of Britain would be a safe and successful operation. Napoleon never lost sight of this target. To attain it would at last allow his army to achieve the task which the Straits of Dover had always frustrated. At the time of his first abdication the French navy had 102 battleships and every dockyard in France and occupied Europe was adding to the number. The British knew that time was not on their side. The First Lord of the Admiralty admitted that Buonaparte must eventually 'have sent forth such powerful fleets that our navy must have been destroyed.'

CHAPTER I

1792–1797

The Republic finds a General

'Rich provinces, opulent towns, all shall be at your disposal.'
GENERAL BONAPARTE, 29 MARCH 1796

Revolutionary France needed a war. When in 1789 her finances finally collapsed and democratic government was introduced her first need was for measures to avert bankruptcy, but the first three years after the collapse of the *ancien régime* were filled with words, high-minded sentiments and vain strivings after an ideal state. Even the Bourbons would have tried to do something to improve the state of the country but the moderate idealists who undertook the government could only mouth their worthy platitudes. When it became clear that having coined the phrase *Liberté, Fraternité, Egalité*, they could not find food for the population of Paris, the moderates were discarded and extremists, some of them honest men, took their places. They were more notable orators but no better at financial reconstruction.

If the new form of government was to be preserved public attention must be focussed on external dangers but the European powers showed distressingly little inclination to intervene in France's internal affairs. The Austrian Emperor did go so far as to issue a declaration calling for a government in France which would give proper rights to both the King and the people. As brother to the Queen of France, he could scarcely do less but within a few weeks he withdrew even this declaration on hearing that Louis XVI had accepted the Constitution of 1791.

The indifference of the powers seemed likely to be disastrous to the French government. Jacques Pierre Brissot, the Minister for Foreign Affairs, declared that 'War is a national benefit: the only calamity to be feared is that we should have no war.' Every provocation was offered to Austria but neither the Emperor Leopold nor his son, Francis, who succeeded him in 1792, would react. On 20 April 1792 the French Assembly was reduced to declaring war on Austria and a month later on Sardinia.

France was in no condition to go to war. Not only was there no money to pay the armed forces but the Revolution had debilitated both the army and the navy. Egalitarian slogans had eroded discipline. Mutiny had gone unpunished; on occasions it had been commended as a demonstration of revolutionary fervour. There was a desperate shortage of officers. 593 generals had been cashiered or forced to resign between January 1791 and July 1792. Since the fall of the Bastille, 5,500 out of 9,578 officers had left the service. Some were driven out because of their noble blood. Many more resigned because it was impossible to act as officers when their men were encouraged to disobey them. Many in the ranks followed their example. In 1789 the army had consisted of 160,000 regulars, all of them volunteers, and 110,000 militia (including coast defence companies) recruited by ballot. Since then the 10,000 men of the Household troops had been disbanded except for the *Cent Suisses* who were left to be murdered on 10 August 1792. The militia was abolished and the 46 foreign battalions—Flemish, German, Irish, Scots and Swiss—who comprised a quarter of the infantry of the line, disbanded themselves. In the regular regiments, composed of Frenchmen, desertion was rife and when war broke out scarcely 50,000 men could be put in the field.

Mistrusting the regular army, the government called for volunteers. The first batch, 101,000 men formed into 169 battalions, were of good quality. They were for the most part former militiamen and were leavened by former members of the Household troops. They were allowed to choose their own officers but those elected must have had previous service as officers or *sous-officiers* in the regulars or the militia. Two further batches of volunteers, raised in 1792, were of much poorer quality.

The weakness of an improvised army consisting of demoralized regulars and untrained volunteers showed from the start. Three French columns invaded the Austrian Netherlands on 29 April 1792. They met only the lightest opposition but it was more than sufficient. All three columns immediately retreated, two of them in blind panic. There were few casualties except three French generals, shot by their own troops.

There followed a pause which lasted well into the summer before the government could at last use in earnest the cry they had been mouthing hopefully for months—*La patrie en danger!* A Prussian army with some Austrian support entered France at Longwy. There was nothing to stop them marching directly on Paris and dictating peace, but it was in fact a very tentative invasion. Its commander, Ferdinand of Brunswick, had been a hero of the Seven Years' War but he utterly disapproved of his new mission. Having reached the Meuse he halted, declaring further advance impossible, and only the unsolicited surrender of Verdun shamed him into a further move forward.

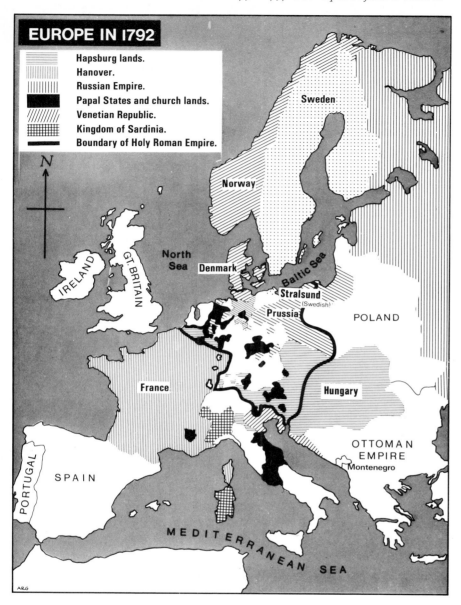

EUROPE IN 1792

- ≡ Hapsburg lands.
- ⦀ Hanover.
- ‖‖ Russian Empire.
- ▓ Papal States and church lands.
- ⧄ Venetian Republic.
- ⊞ Kingdom of Sardinia.
- ▬ Boundary of Holy Roman Empire.

N

Norway

Sweden

North Sea

Denmark

IRELAND

GT. BRITAIN

Baltic Sea

Stralsund (Swedish)

Prussia

POLAND

France

Hungary

OTTOMAN EMPIRE

Montenegro

PORTUGAL

SPAIN

MEDITERRANEAN SEA

A hundred miles from Paris he was confronted with 36,000 ill-disciplined Frenchmen at Valmy. He marched out to attack them on the morning of 20 September and came under fire from French guns. As it happened the artillery was the arm of the Bourbon army least affected by the Revolution and it was undiluted with volunteers. At Valmy their fire was impressive but not notably damaging, inflicting only 184 casualties throughout the day. The Prussian guns caused four times as much loss but they could not silence the French artillery. Seizing his chance to break off

23

8 The cannonade at Valmy, where French Revolutionary troops held the Prussian army, saving Paris and the Revolution. *Painting by Horace Vernet*

the campaign, Ferdinand declared the French position impregnable and ordered his men back to camp. His opponent, Dumouriez, was so alarmed by the unsteadiness of his own infantry that on the following day he sent to propose an armistice. Ferdinand did not wait to reply but retired across the frontier.

The cannonade of Valmy was a miraculous deliverance for France. To the emotion stirred by the cry of *La patrie en danger!* could be added the boost to national pride caused by the defeat of 'the veterans of Frederick the Great'. At the same time French troops occupied Savoy and Nice, where they met no resistance, and General Custine marched to the Rhine at Speyer and Worms. The government saw its opportunity and proclaimed a republic. 22 September was declared to be the first day of Year I in the revolutionary calendar and the royal family was imprisoned. At the same time all royal and ecclesiastical property was expropriated, thus easing, temporarily, the chronic shortage of cash.

Elections followed. Every adult male was eligible to vote but only one in ten did so, to produce a National Convention which at once declared that until the end of the war government must be 'revolutionary', and in consequence it made over all its effective functions to the Committees of Public Safety and General Security (10 December). Already the republic could point to great victories. Custine took Mainz and crossed the Rhine to occupy Frankfurt (from which he was ignominiously chased back before the end of the year); and Dumouriez invaded Belgium and drove out the

24

Austrians after his victory at Jemappes on 6 November. When the news of this triumph reached Paris the government declared that France would offer 'fraternity and aid to all nations who wished to regain their freedom.'

The victory at Jemappes and several that followed require explanation. How could a makeshift army defeat good regular troops? The answer lies partly in the incompetence of the enemy and partly in the adoption of the doctrines of Guibert and his fellow theorists (see p. 16). The Austrian and Prussian armies were hamstrung by their supply trains which, in the Austrian army, always carried rations for nine days and included a vast assemblage of carts loaded with the officers' baggage. With such a tail any movement must be cumbersome and the minds of the generals, many of them septuagenarians, were not fashioned to move at any great speed.

The French, living from the countryside, were plagued with no baggage trains, nor were their generals elderly. They could and did out-manoeuvre their opponents and they improvised a way of overcoming the massed fire of infantry in line. Their own requirement for fire power was deputed to their admirable artillery which was supplemented by the independent musketry of a swarm of skirmishers—*tirailleurs*. Behind this preparation the main body of the infantry was formed into heavy columns in some of which 5,000 men formed with a front of 170. When the artillery and the *tirailleurs* had sufficiently shaken the enemy line, columns were launched at its weaker points, and frequently they managed to fracture it, making a gap through which cavalry could be poured to complete the enemy's discomfiture.

Such a system should have proved disastrous and would have done so if the conventional armies had been capable of keeping the *tirailleurs* at a distance. The fire power of the line was certain to triumph over the bayonets of the column, provided that the line's volleys were reserved until they could be brought to bear on the main strength of the enemy. It was the misfortune of both the Austrian and Prussian armies that they had no trained skirmishers of their own who could keep the *tirailleurs* at a distance. A Prussian observer at the Battle of Kaiserlautern (26-28 November 1793) wrote that 'thousands of skirmishers attacked in open formation—*en débandade*—through woods, along creeks, over meadows and marshland, but were repeatedly driven back by the volleys and counter-attacks of our line.' This was true, but the Prussian line exhausted and disarrayed itself in fighting off the attacks of the *tirailleurs*. They were still realigning themselves and reloading when they were struck by the whirlwind advances of the French columns.

In the Netherlands the French task was made easier by a strikingly pernicious doctrine fashionable among the Austrian commanders—the cordon system. This was an attempt to be equally strong on all sectors of the front and the effect of the doctrine was that the army practising it was always outnumbered at any point where the enemy chose to concentrate.

9 William Pitt as Colonel
of the Cinque Port
Volunteers

*Sarjeat I desire you will back upon that Old
Woman facing the front rank the glare of her
red cloak will put the Gentlemen out.*

To make matters worse, no Austrian general could resist the lure of a
fortress, then a common feature of the Belgian landscape. It was
inconceivable to them that any advance should not be interrupted for a few
weeks while some fortress, which might at some future date threaten the
army's communication, was reduced according to the strict conventions of
siegecraft. There was nothing wrong with the Austrian and Prussian
soldiers but their commanders were thinking in terms that were no longer
relevant.

*   *   *

Heartened by the conquest of Belgium, the French decided to widen the
war. Britain had viewed the Revolution with equanimity and, despite the
elegant diatribes of Edmund Burke, not without sympathy. Pitt's
government was pledged to peace and financial reconstruction and was
even prepared to tolerate the French seizure of Antwerp and her
declaration that the estuary of the Scheldt (in Dutch territory) was open to
the ships of all nations. Pitt would not react further than to restate Britain's
guarantee of the neutrality of Holland. Holland, however, was an obvious
target for French aggression. It was the richest country on the Continent
and the republic was in increasingly difficult financial straits. On 1 February
1793, eight days after the execution of Louis XVI, France declared war on
both Britain and Holland, gratuitously adding Spain to her enemies on 9
March.

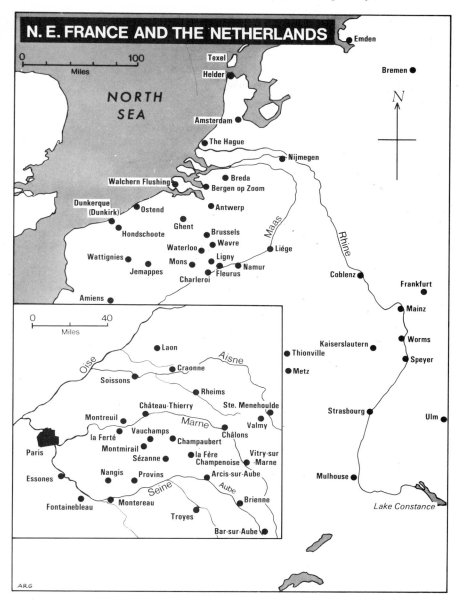

N. E. FRANCE AND THE NETHERLANDS

NORTH SEA

Emden
Bremen
Texel
Helder
Amsterdam
The Hague
Nijmegen
Breda
Bergen op Zoom
Walchern Flushing
Antwerp
Dunkerque (Dunkirk)
Ostend
Ghent
Hondschoote
Brussels
Waterloo
Wavre
Wattignies
Ligny
Liége
Mons
Namur
Jemappes
Fleurus
Charleroi
Amiens
Maas
Rhine
Coblenz
Frankfurt
Mainz
Kaiserslautern
Worms
Thionville
Speyer
Metz
Strasbourg
Ulm
Mulhouse
Lake Constance

Laon
Aisne
Craonne
Soissons
Rheims
Château-Thierry
Ste. Menehoulde
Montreuil
Marne
Valmy
Vauchamps
Châlons
la Ferté
Champaubert
Montmirail
Vitry-sur-Marne
Paris
Sézanne
la Fère Champenoise
Nangis
Provins
Arcis-sur-Aube
Essones
Seine
Aube
Brienne
Fontainebleau
Montereau
Troyes
Bar-sur-Aube

ARG

The British army was no great asset to the allied forces in the Netherlands. It might have been expected that they would have been experienced in the problem of dealing with *tirailleurs* since they had faced this form of attack in the American War of Independence. During that war Britain had raised and trained excellent light infantry, some of them armed with rifles, which would have performed valuable service in the new war had they not all been disbanded under the pressure of peacetime economy. This also accounted for the entire British army being extremely small, and

27

what there was of it was for the most part devoted to garrisoning the overseas possessions. Since Pitt intended to follow the practice of his father, the great Earl of Chatham, and devote his main war effort to the 'filching of sugar islands' from the French, there was little left over for the Netherlands. Britain's initial contribution to the allied army consisted of 2,000 men of the Brigade of Guards who were without artillery, transport, medical supplies or reserve ammunition. Some time later a further brigade, composed 'of nothing but undisciplined and raw recruits', followed the Guards and in time some cavalry and artillery were added but the contingent never became a balanced force and it was always under Austrian commanders and subject to their pernicious strategy.

What Britain could provide was a fleet which could blockade French ports and halt her overseas trade. She could also provide the money needed to build a coalition of the powers, all of which were on the verge of bankruptcy. This First Coalition was constructed piecemeal by the British government between March and September 1793 and consisted on the one hand of the great powers—Austria, Prussia and Spain—who made their independent contributions to the war, and on the other of smaller states— Sardinia, Naples, Portugal, Hanover, Baden and the two Hesses—who acted as auxiliaries to the British at sea or on land. Holland, financially strong but militarily impotent, acted as joint paymaster to the coalition, which was joined by Russia as a sleeping partner. On paper it was a most imposing combination of states; in practice it was useless since it neither attempted to define its aims nor to coordinate its military activities. Austria and Prussia both insisted that they should be compensated for their expenses not only by subsidies from Britain and Holland but by the annexation of parts of French territory, and even Britain fleetingly considered that her exertions entitled her to acquire Dunkirk.

The fighting in the Netherlands reflected little credit on the generals of either side. Both sides had their victories. A French invasion of Holland was crushed at Neerwinden (18 March 1793), and Belgium was for the time being cleared of the revolutionary army. At such minor actions as Villers-en-Cauchies (24 April 1794), where one Austrian and one British squadron of light horse, 272 rank and file in all, rode through a French division, captured three guns and inflicted by the French estimate 1,200 casualties, the immense superiority of trained troops over hastily raised levies was clearly demonstrated. The Austrians took a number of fortresses but the main trend of the war was in favour of the French. The great battles, Hondschoote (8 September 1793), Wattignies (15-16 October 1793), Kaiserlautern (26-28 November 1793) and above all Fleurus (26 June 1794) were all French victories, won by the enthusiasm and *élan* of their infantry and the bold deployment of their artillery, which were more than a match for the plodding tactics of the Austrian and Prussian generals.

Poland, prostrate though she was, was France's most effective ally. The

greed to divide her remaining territory kept Russian troops from fighting in the west, although Catherine the Great regularly contributed expressions of warm support. Prussia, in receipt of a British subsidy of £50,000 a month, steadily withdrew her men from the Rhine to have them ready on the Vistula. This prompted Austria, always suspicious of Prussian motives, to withhold 60,000 men from the Netherlands to watch her northern borders. The other allies did not have their hearts in the campaign in the Netherlands. The Dutch were lethargic in all their movements and the British, although they supplied Hanoverian and Hessian auxiliaries, were primarily interested in the West Indies.

France's greatest asset was the emergence of an organizer of genius. This was Lazare Carnot, an engineer officer who became Minister of War. He knew exactly what armies could achieve and had a talent for conjuring something more from them. He provided troops, arms and supplies when lesser men believed it to be impossible to do so. By his presence he inspired mediocre generals to win great victories, notably at Fleurus where he abandoned the plan prepared by the commander, General Jourdan, substituted his own and led the attack, sword in hand, in civilian clothes.

Without Carnot even the bungling of the allies would not have enabled the French to win a clear-cut victory. The Committees in Paris developed a

10 The French army using an observation balloon at the Battle of Fleurus. The use of balloons was discontinued soon after. *Painting by D. Langendyk*

29

deep distrust of all generals, a suspicion dating from the day when, after his defeat at Neerwinden, Dumouriez had defected to the Austrians, taking with him the then Minister of War and three deputies who had been sent to arrest him. Henceforward every general knew that even a minor reverse would be considered as treason, and to see that he did not forget the fact a *représantant en mission*, usually ignorant of war, was attached to his headquarters. The experience of General Houchard, the victor of Hondschoote, is typical. In August 1793 he was appointed to command the *Armée du Nord* and, on reaching his headquarters, he found that the *représantant* had arrested every member of the staff and had impounded all the army's papers for examination in Paris. Houchard suffered a minor setback later in the year and despite Hondschoote was sent back to Paris and executed.

Before the end of 1794 the Austrians, though maintaining a large army in Alsace, evacuated the Netherlands. The Dutch Texel fleet of 14 ships of the line was captured on 23 January 1794 while fixed in the ice, by a lieutenant-colonel with a squadron of French hussars who had a company of infantry riding pillion behind them. The British were driven into Germany in an increasingly disorderly retreat. They re-embarked at Hamburg on 14 April 1795.

Holland made peace as best she could. She had to pay a huge financial indemnity to France and ceded to her Maastricht, Venlo and all her territory south of the Scheldt, while her navy was put at the disposition of the French. The Austrian Netherlands vanished and in Paris the Convention decreed that Belgium, Limburg, Liège and Luxemburg were '*parties intégrantes et inséparables de la République Française.*' Prussia made peace with France on 5 April 1795 and Spain followed her example on 22 July.

*   *   *

By declaring war on Britain the republic had introduced another element— the sea—into the struggle. Neither Austria nor Prussia had significant fleets but Britain was indisputably the supreme naval power, having 115 ships of the line (of which only 26 were in commission when the war broke out) and 88 frigates. To these Holland could add 49 battleships, most of them small, and Spain had a strength, on paper, of 76 ships of the line although only half of them proved to be seaworthy. Naples and Portugal added a further 10 battleships between them to the naval strength of the coalition.

The French navy had reached its apogee during the American War of Independence when it produced a fine crop of admirals and, almost for the only time, could fight the British, ship for ship and squadron for squadron, on equal terms. The design of French ships was the finest in the world and her warships sailed faster, handled better and carried a heavier armament than their British counterparts. At the time of the Revolution, the French

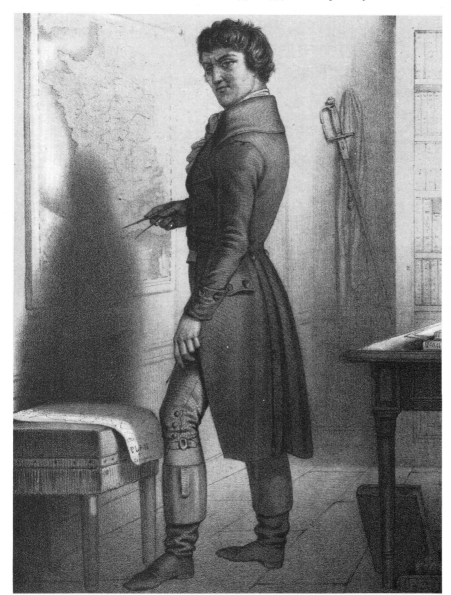

11 Lazare Hippolyte Carnot planning the defence of France. *Engraving after a painting by A. Lacauhie*

navy consisted of 246 ships, of which 82 (with four more nearing completion) were of the line and 79 were frigates. This was a very formidable fleet, the more so since Britain had to deploy a considerable portion of her fleet to protect her overseas possessions and guard her trade routes. (France had three third rates and six frigates in the Caribbean and five frigates in the Indian Ocean.)

In fact the French were never able to make a serious challenge to the Royal Navy. The Revolution destroyed the discipline of the French fleet to

12 Ships of the French fleet in the inner basin of the port of Brest. *Painting by J. F. Hue*

an extent from which it never wholly recovered. Insubordination and mutiny were as widespread as in the army but the consequences were more serious. While the army could replace the strict training of the three-deep line with the glorious improvisations of the *tirailleurs* and the charging column, the working of a warship depended on the disciplined coordination of experienced seamen. No amount of revolutionary or patriotic fervour could replace hard-learned skills applied with precision. To make matters worse, the corps of marine gunners, a body of non-commissioned officers, was abolished on the grounds that it smacked of aristocracy. The Minister of Marine responsible justified this disastrous act by asserting that 'disdaining skilful evolutions, our seamen will think it more fitting to try those boarding actions in which our Frenchman was always a conqueror.' It was perhaps ironic that one of the French battleships noted as unserviceable in 1794 was named *Citoyen*.

The French navy also suffered from a disadvantage that was the fault of no government. The main naval base was at Brest, the obvious tactical location in a war against England since until Antwerp was secured, there was no large safe harbour further up-channel. More than half the battle fleet, 47 of the line, were stationed there in 1793 and there was no place in France more difficult to supply. Generations of shipbuilders had stripped the countryside within a hundred miles of the port of every piece of timber suitable for use in ships and all stores had to be brought to Brest over many miles of the worst roads in France. Once a ship came damaged into Brest it was likely to be a long job to get her to sea again.

The bare statistics of the first three years of the naval war must have made depressing reading at the French Admiralty. They lost 33 ships of the line of which 26 were lost due to enemy action (one of them being subsequently recaptured) while seven were wrecked, foundered or were accidentally burned. In addition 38 frigates were lost to the enemy (two of them to the Spanish navy) and two more were wrecked. The corresponding figures for the Royal Navy were three of the line captured (one of them being CENSEUR which had been taken from the French six months earlier), four accidentally burned and one wrecked. Six British frigates were captured (one of which was almost immediately recaptured) and two were wrecked. These losses were more than made good by 15 of the line and 27 frigates captured from the French and taken into the British service.

The French navy did perform one vital service to the republic. At the beginning of 1794 France was in serious danger of famine. The harvest of the previous year had been bad and agriculture was much disrupted by war. The future of France was dependent on the import of grain. This the United States were happy to sell and there were a large number of French merchantmen in the West Indies which could carry the grain if the Royal Navy's blockade could be evaded. The Committee of Public Safety, now headed by Robespierre, decided that the risk must be taken and 117 ships loaded with corn were assembled in Chesapeake Bay. Four battleships were slipped across the Atlantic to act as a close escort.

The task of warding off the British Channel Fleet under Lord Howe was entrusted to the Brest squadron and Robespierre instructed Admiral Villaret-Joyeuse that he was 'at his peril, not to let the great convoy to fall into the hands of Lord Howe. If he did so, his head should answer for it under the guillotine.' To make the point absolutely clear the Minister of Marine embarked in the flagship, the 120-gun *Montagne* (formerly *États de Bourgogne* and later to be renamed successively *Peuple* and *L'Océan*). The Minister was Jean Bon Saint-André, the man who had advocated boarding as an alternative to gunnery. He had been a preacher and his knowledge of the sea was confined to two trips on board merchant ships.

The outlook for Villaret-Joyeuse was bleak, not least because it would be as difficult for him to find Howe's fleet in the vastness of the Atlantic as it would be for Howe to find the great convoy. Nor could the admiral, though a competent and gallant sailor, be said to be fully qualified for his task. Three years earlier he had been no more than *lieutenant de vaisseau* and he had had no subsequent opportunity to practise the complicated task of manoeuvring a fleet at sea. The same was true of his subordinates. The two junior French admirals had in 1791 been respectively a lieutenant and a sub-lieutenant. Of the 26 captains in the fleet, three had been lieutenants, eleven sub-lieutenants, nine masters of merchantmen, one a boatswain and one an able seaman. The previous occupation of the remaining captain is unknown but it is certain that in 1791 he was not in the navy.

It is greatly to the credit of Villaret-Joyeuse, his officers and his ships' companies that when, after some weeks of groping for each other, the two fleets, 26 ships on each side, met in a series of engagements between 28 May and 1 June, only seven French ships were captured, one of which, *Vengeur*, was so badly damaged that she sank almost immediately. Saint-André went below as soon as the action was joined but as soon as the guns ceased to fire he emerged to write a report highly critical of Villaret-Joyeuse's handling of his fleet.

The Glorious First of June was much acclaimed in England when the six surviving prizes and 3,500 prisoners were brought into port. King George presented Howe with a diamond-hilted sword on the quarterdeck of his flagship. There were gold chains for the admirals, gold medals for most of the captains and prize money for all ranks, but though the battle had been a tactical victory it was a strategic defeat. On 14 June the great convoy entered Brest having lost only one ship which had foundered. France was safe from famine. It was a deliverance equal to the cannonade at Valmy. Villaret-Joyeuse's head was safe on his shoulders. It was, he said, 'well worth half a dozen rotten old hulks.'

Fleet actions formed only a very small part of the Royal Navy's task. The ships spent most of their time engaged in blockading French ports and in preventing the enemy fleet from putting to sea. It was to be several years before this wearisome task was performed with any great efficiency, since Howe and his immediate successor believed that it was more important to preserve their ships from the ravages of the weather than to keep a constant watch on the French fleet. Thus for long periods the bulk of the Channel Fleet lay no closer to Brest than Spithead and it was often possible for French warships to slip out to escort reinforcements to the West Indies and to prey on British shipping. In the winter of 1794–5, 70 British merchantmen were captured before the fleet left Spithead. Nevertheless, French trading vessels became rarities on the high seas and French imports shrank to those which the British were prepared to license.

It was under cover of the Royal Navy that the British carried out their principal military operations. Pondicherry, St Pierre and Miquelon were taken. Tobago, France's only gain from the American war, returned to Britain and St Domingue (Haiti) passed from French control, though Britain despite a lavish expenditure of lives was unable to secure it. Martinique was captured at the second attempt but the forces which took St

Lucia and Guadaloupe were soon dispossessed by French counter-attacks.

There were few battle casualties in these operations but disease took a terrible toll. Out of 400 officers who took part in the capture of Martinique, 27 were killed in action or died of wounds, 170 died of disease. In 1795 alone 12,000 British soldiers and sailors died in the West Indies. It was a form of warfare which earned Britain the scorn of her continental allies but although the cost in lives was undoubtedly much inflated by inefficiency, lack of sanitary precautions and the prevalence of cheap rum, it paid a handsome dividend in the long term. The capture of each French island reduced by one the number of French bases from which warships and privateers could attack British shipping, and it was the continued and expanding trade that made it possible for Britain to finance not only her own war efforts but those of her allies. Holland's conversion into a French satellite, following her defeat in 1795, further strengthened Britain's

13 King George III presenting a diamond-hilted sword to Admiral Lord Howe on his own quarterdeck after the Glorious First of June. *Painting by H. Briggs*

35

economic position. Amsterdam, previously one of the great financial centres of the world, stagnated, and its business was transferred to London; and a start was made in securing the Dutch colonies. The Cape of Good Hope, a permanent threat to the Indian trade route, was taken, together with a squadron of two ships of the line and four frigates, when the governor surrendered to a British expedition in September 1795. His only stipulation was that Britain should underwrite the paper currency he had issued. In the previous month a landing had been made on Ceylon which capitulated on 16 February 1796.

* * *

The third, and perhaps the most fortunate of all the deliverances of the French republic was that from counter-revolution. The revolution had never been popular everywhere in France and as the extremists gained control in Paris, the republic became widely hated. Monarchism remained strong in the south and the west and many who had supported the events of 1789 opposed the Revolution once the constitution of 1791, with its provision for limited monarchy, was superseded. The persecution of the church, with priests being hunted by troops and mobs, made the new order detested in many districts; but the spark that set off the first major rising was the introduction of conscription. The demands of a war on four fronts—in the Netherlands, on the Rhine, in the Pyrenees and in the Maritime Alps—and the number of men required, and expended, by the new tactics, forced the government to call for more and more troops. On 23 February 1793 the compulsory enlistment of 300,000 men was decreed. On 10 March a riot against troops trying to enforce this decree at St Florent-le-Viel in La Vendée flared into rebellion. Within a month 30,000 men were under arms and much of western France was lost to the government. If Britain could have given effective support, the Vendéan movement, which had its parallels on a smaller scale in other parts of France, might have paralysed the republic. At the very least it should have been possible for the British, with the widespread local support, to have seized Brest and secured the main French fleet. The opportunity was missed. It was not until September that London began even to consider what could be done to help, and it was 2 December before a derisory force of 4,000 British infantry and 100 gunners arrived off the Cotentin peninsula where it had been arranged that they should meet the main Vendéan army, led by Jean-Nicholas Stofflet, a gamekeeper who had shown himself to be a natural general. He, however, had underestimated Whitehall's capacity for delay and had brought his men to the coast too early. They had been defeated at Granville on 12 November and, when no sign of the British appeared, they had gone back to their own country where they were further defeated near St Nazaire on 23 December.

For a time the Vendéan rebellion was suppressed but it burst into flame again in 1795 when the British landed 3,500 *émigré* troops in Quiberon Bay. Since almost half of these men had been hastily recruited from prisoner-of-war camps it was unwise to rely too far on their loyalty and the expedition went down to early disaster. There were savage reprisals, 600 *émigrés* being massacred in a single batch, and the Vendéans were left to fight to a hopeless finish. Stofflet was executed on 25 February 1796 but their resistance was never finally crushed and they were still in arms to distract Napoleon in 1815.

The Vendéan rising was not the only golden opportunity that the British failed to grasp in 1793. Other rebellions had broken out in Lyons, Marseilles and Toulon and while the first two were quickly and brutally suppressed, Toulon turned to the British for help. It was with the deepest misgivings that Lord Hood, commanding the Mediterranean Fleet, accepted the port in trust for King Louis XVII (then a sickly prisoner in Paris). Hood knew that he had insufficient troops to defend the place but he dared not refuse to try since it was the second largest fleet base in France, containing 30 ships of the line and 20 smaller warships. On 28 August he therefore landed every man he could spare—1,200 soldiers who were serving as marines, and 300 seamen—while sending ships to all the allied ports in the Mediterranean to collect troops. As the time passed he collected a Sardinian battalion, several thousand undisciplined Spaniards and a wholly useless Neapolitan contingent. 750 British troops arrived from Gibraltar and more sailors were landed, every ship being reduced to the state where it was only just possible to handle her. Nelson's AGAMEMNON (74), which had a complement of 550, was left with only 345 on board. So many sailors were sent to man the defences that it was impossible to find crews to sail the French ships out of the harbour. The French sailors proved strongly republican and posed such a threat to the garrison that 5,000 of them had to be embarked in the three least usable battleships and ordered to sail for Rochefort. Five frigates were transferred to the Sardinians but the remaining ships had to remain in the harbour while 14,000 men of all nationalities guarded a perimeter ten miles long. The British government was consistently unhelpful. Dundas, the Secretary for War, wrote several times to Hood accusing him of making unnecessary difficulties and on one occasion ordered him to send one of his British battalions to the West Indies. Hood refused to obey and continued to hold his perilous position in the hope that something would turn up.

Unfortunately what did turn up was a French army of 38,000 men among whom was a 24-year-old captain of artillery called Buonaparte. He was the son of a Corsican count who had no money but could produce the sixteen quarterings of nobility, albeit Genoese nobility, which were necessary before his son could receive a free place at the Royal Cadet School at Brienne, from where he proceeded to the *École Militaire* in Paris. In September 1785 Napoleone Buonaparte had been gazetted a second lieutenant of artillery. His presence before Toulon was fortuitous. His job was the overseeing of the coast defences further to the east. He had been called to the siege when another officer was wounded and became the effective head of the artillery because the actual commander was confined to his bed. He had never been on a battlefield before but with an instinct which for many years was to prove unerring, he saw that if one single post, Fort Mulgrave, could be captured the allied fleet would have to leave the harbour and the town must fall. It took time to convince his superiors of this point and even longer to persuade Paris, where a concentric attack by columns totalling 160,000 men was being planned. It was not until mid-November that Buonaparte, by that time promoted to major, had his plan approved and it took him three weeks to collect the necessary artillery.

On 17 December, after 48 hours of bombardment, 6,000 Frenchmen attacked Fort Mulgrave. The Spanish garrison fled as soon as they saw the onslaught, leaving the defence to a captain's detachment of redcoats who were, inevitably, overwhelmed. In the fighting a private of the Eighteenth (Royal Irish) Foot drove his bayonet into the thigh of Major Buonaparte who had led the assault. Next day the allies evacuated Toulon. Four French battleships sailed, nine more were burned by the British, but fifteen, whose destruction had been confided to the Spaniards, were left intact.

The only consolation the British could take from the counter-revolution in France was in Corsica. The island had been a French possession only since 1768, when the Republic of Genoa had sold it to Louis XV. This had offended many Corsicans and at the Revolution their great patriot leader, Paoli, had offered the sovereignty to George III. A British force had landed in February 1794 and having captured Bastia in May, proclaimed the island as one of the King's dominions, although it was 10 August before the garrison of Calvi was reduced to surrender. In consequence, Buonaparte, promoted *général de brigade* for his services at Toulon, became technically a British subject.

*   *   *

By the beginning of 1796 the French republic's external crisis was over. She had lost Corsica but she had gained Holland, the Austrian Netherlands, Nice and Savoy. She had made peace with Spain and Prussia and, although she was still at war with Austria, Britain and a number of smaller states, military operations had stagnated despite the presence of Austrian armies on the left bank of the Rhine and in Piedmont. At home the situation was far less stable. Civil war had been suppressed but there was much banditry in country districts. No widely acceptable form of government had emerged from the stress of external and internal war. The pressures of the counter-revolution had driven the Committee of Public Safety to draconian measures of repression justified by Robespierre's phrase that 'Without virtue, terror is useless; without terror, virtue is powerless.'

14 Recapture of Toulon, British troops assisting with the embarkation of refugees

From March 1793 suspects were being detained without trial and by September imprisonment had been decreed for defined categories of men and women irrespective of the views and actions of the individuals concerned. 17,000 suspects were condemned to death but 40,000 were executed by one means or another.

The *coup d'état* of 9 Thermidor Year II (27 July 1794) and the execution of Robespierre ended the left-wing Reign of Terror, substituting a short sharp purge of its instigators. Even Buonaparte was imprisoned at Antibes for ten days since he had had associations with Robespierre and his brother. France searched for a stable form of government and the economy continued to plunge downwards. The paper currency, the *assignats*, became all but worthless. A hundred-franc note was worth only 80 centimes and in Paris a pound of bread cost 50 francs in *assignats* or 35 centimes in coin. It was the rise of the price of bread to 20 centimes which had sparked off the events of 1789. A new constitution, the third in four years, was promulgated on 30 October 1795 and was confirmed by a referendum in which five out of six of the voters abstained. The new form of government was a Directory of five men with two legislative houses, the lower of which was elected by those who could prove that they owned a substantial amount of property. Food riots and *coups d'état* merged into each other and, on 13 Vendémiaire (4-5 October), a right-wing coup was only frustrated when Brigadier-General Buonaparte, serving as Director of Military Plans at the *Bureau Topographique*, sent young Captain Joachim Murat galloping off for some guns with which to administer 'a whiff of grape-shot'. This earned Buonaparte the rank of *général de division* and he was given command of the *Armée de l'Interieur*. This, however, was an insufficient reward for an ambitious and capable soldier to whom the Directory owed much. Perhaps, too, they felt that he was too dynamic a man to command the force which alone kept them in power. They sought for a reward which would both express their gratitude and keep him away from the centre of government. On 2 March 1796 General Buonaparte was appointed Commander-in-Chief of the *Armée de l'Italie*. He was 27 and had seen action only at Toulon.

Peace would have given the republic time to consolidate itself but the army called for war and a successful war would unite the people and bring plunder to the Treasury. Lazare Carnot, one of the five Directors, planned an aggressive campaign on the grandest scale. A vast pincer movement was to encircle Switzerland and the main Austrian armies. The main blow was to be struck across the Rhine with two French armies. General Jourdan with the *Armée de la Sambre et Meuse* was to capture Mainz and advance to the area Bayreuth-Ansbach-Wurzburg. On Jourdan's right Moreau with the *Armée du Rhin et de la Moselle* was to mask Mannheim ('circumventing the frontier fortresses') and drive into Swabia (roughly the area now known as Baden-Württemberg). Each of these armies had a nominal strength of 70,000 men. The *Armée de l'Italie* was said to be 63,000 strong and was cast in a subsidiary rôle, as the anvil to the hammers of Jourdan and Moreau. Buonaparte was ordered to do his best to detach Sardinia from her Austrian alliance by diplomatic means and having done so to drive the Austrians back across Lombardy as far as the Adige. Then he was to swing left to Trento and break through the mountains into the Tyrol where, it was hoped, he would meet Moreau's men coming south. He made his preparations by changing his name to Bonaparte, married the former mistress of the most influential of the Directors, and joined his new headquarters at Nice on 26 March.

He found the *Armée de l'Italie* holding a position facing north, with its right close to Genoa and its left at Nice. The advanced posts were on the Ligurian Apennines. There were only 37,000 men fit for duty and even these were in poor condition. Some units were without muskets, many without boots. 200 mules comprised the entire transport of the army and men, horses and mules were on reduced rations. Pay was weeks in arrears and two units had mutinied in the month the new commander-in-chief arrived. With all these defects the army still had a greater potential than the forces which had fought in Belgium three years earlier. By the *Amalgame*, promulgated in January 1794 and finally implemented by the end of 1795, the regulars and volunteers had been brigaded together and wore the national uniform of blue, previously worn only by the new levies while the regulars had continued in the white of the Bourbons. There had been time

40

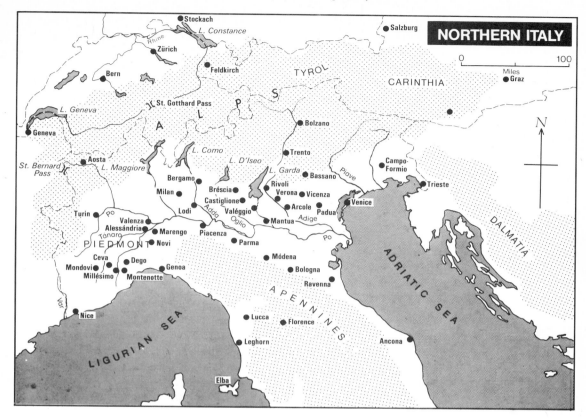

to train the volunteers and a common tactical doctrine had been evolved. It was now possible for all parts of the army to fight in line but with the memory of recent successes, the use of the column was still much favoured. Bonaparte favoured a combination of both systems—the *ordre mixte*. Under this tactic a battalion (or brigade) in line was flanked on each side by a battalion (or brigade) in column, thus combining the fire power of the line with the impetus and solidity of the column.

The arrival of a new commander-in-chief was greeted with little pleasure by the three divisional commanders. Two were 11 years older than Bonaparte, the third had been 26 when the new general was born. The troops, however, responded favourably when they found that he had brought with him an issue of pay, and were roused to enthusiasm by his proclamation in which, according to his own subsequent (and suspect) account, he promised: 'I will lead you into the most fertile plains on earth. Rich provinces, opulent towns, all shall be at your disposal; there you will find honour, glory and riches.' Generals and troops alike were impressed by his immediate grasp of the situation, by his restless eagerness and by his confident assertion that the campaign would open on 15 April.

Facing the *Armée de l'Italie* were three armies under the command of the

41

72-year-old General Beaulieu. Opposite the French left was a force of 20,000 Piedmontese, stiffened by 5,000 Austrians, and commanded by General Colli, also an Austrian. The French right was opposed by 11,000 Austrians under Argenteau. Both these forward armies held the crests of the Ligurian Apennines and their combined front stretched 80 miles. In reserve, under Beaulieu's own hand were 20,000 Austrians of whom half were required as garrisons for Alessandria and other strongpoints.

It was Beaulieu who opened the campaign by moving his disposable reserve to the extreme left of his line in order to frustrate an imaginary French move against Genoa, which was still tenuously neutral. This forced Bonaparte to attack earlier than he intended and on 12 April he struck at the junction between the two opposing armies. At Montenotte he shattered Argenteau's right so thoroughly that only 700 of the 6,000 Austrians present escaped as an organized body. The French were able to make up their deficiencies in muskets and boots on the battlefield.

Having interposed his men between the Austrians and the Piedmontese, Bonaparte unhesitatingly exploited his advantage. On 13 April he launched Augereau's division westward. Despite a gallant Austrian defence of Millesimo, the Piedmontese were driven back to Ceva. Riding back to Montenotte, Bonaparte sent Massena's division against Argenteau, whom he defeated at Dego (14 August). An Austrian counter-attack on the following day was almost disastrous and was held only by the courage and skill of Massena, but when it was beaten off Argenteau had to retreat, having lost 6,000 men and 30 guns in two days' fighting. Beaulieu, reporting that his army was reduced to 'barely 16,000 men', fell back on Alessandria and Bonaparte was able to turn his full strength against the Piedmontese. They eluded him at the Tanaro river (18 April) but they were pinned down and routed at Mondovi on the 21st. The French had broken through to the plains and Bonaparte started to march for Turin. Late on 21 April, Colli asked for an armistice.

Soldiers! In fifteen days you have won six victories, taken twenty-one colours, fifty-five guns, several fortresses, and conquered the richest regions of Piedmont; you have taken 15,000 prisoners, killed or wounded more than 10,000 men.

In those 15 days Bonaparte had risen from obscurity to fame as the first general in Europe.

The collapse of Piedmont made it possible for the *Armée de l'Italie* to be reinforced from the *Armée des Alpes*, stationed in Savoy. This brought Bonaparte's numbers up to 40,000 and enabled him to set off in pursuit of Beaulieu who with little more than 20,000, including his garrison troops, fell back behind the Po in an attempt to protect Milan. His opponent was not deterred by the broad river. Feinting at Valenza, Bonaparte threw a picked force under Colonel Jean Lannes across the river at Piacenza, 50 miles downstream, and sent the main body of the army over behind them.

Piacenza was in neutral Parma, but this did not worry Bonaparte. He forced the Duke to send 20 paintings by Correggio and Michelangelo to Paris, besides contributing £80,000 to the French military chest. A similar exaction was made at Modena.

With the French advancing from Piacenza, Beaulieu could only fall back eastward as fast as his troops could march. He crossed the Adda in safety and left a rearguard to delay the French at Lodi. The bridge there was 170 yards long and was approached by a causeway on each side. Six Austrian guns, backed by three battalions, faced directly across the bridge, while three more guns were sited on either flank to sweep the approaches. After a close reconnaissance, Bonaparte brought up 24 guns and under their fire launched a column of grenadiers across the bridge. A storm of grapeshot stopped them before they were half-way across, but a second column, led by Massena and Berthier, the chief of staff, completed the crossing and, having been reinforced, withstood a strong counter-attack. The French lost 350 killed and wounded but took 1,700 prisoners and the Austrian guns.

The action at Lodi was showmanship. No strategic or tactical purpose was served as the Austrians were intent on retreat and Bonaparte did not intend to continue the pursuit, having decided to move next on Milan. As

15 Generals Massena and Berthier leading the French columns across the bridge at Lodi. The bridge was 170 yards long. *Engraving by Carle Vernet*

43

an exercise in public relations it was a triumphant success. The bridge at Lodi became a symbol of victory to the French army and the general who directed the attack became for the first time a hero to his men and to France. It also enabled him to defy an order from Paris that he should hand over half his army to Kellermann, hitherto commanding the *Armée des Alpes*, who was to march on Rome. Flushed with success, Bonaparte offered his resignation.

> *To divide the command between Kellermann and myself is to plan disaster. I cannot bring myself to serve with a man who considers himself the first general in Europe. I believe it is better to have one bad general than two good ones.*

Lodi convinced the Directory that he could not be superseded. 'Immortal glory to the conqueror of Lodi. . . . Your plan must be followed.' Before this answer could be received the army had marched into Milan (15 May). Bonaparte levied a contribution of £800,000 from the city which was also extensively looted, both officially and unofficially.

Beaulieu, who had scraped together 30,000 men, tried to hold a line on the river Mincio between Lake Garda and Mantua, but from this he was easily manoeuvred and by the beginning of June he was invested in Mantua with 14,000 men, the rest of his army retreating to the north.

Mantua, being almost surrounded by a lagoon formed by the Mincio, is very difficult to besiege, and while the preparations were being made Bonaparte undertook a fund-raising expedition against the neutral states. Tuscany and Genoa were both mulcted of large sums and forced to send works of art to Paris, while the Pope was so intimidated by a march to the south that he not only paid a vast indemnity in cash, pictures and sculpture but ceded Bologna, Ferrara and Ancona to France. These provinces, together with Modena and Reggio, were established as the Cispadine Republic.

It was at this time that Bonaparte formed a personal bodyguard. At the end of May he had been dining in the village of Vallegio, near Brescia, when a troop of Austrian cavalry galloped into the main street, causing the general to decamp over a wall wearing only one boot. To ensure that this did not recur a squadron of 200 *guides à cheval* under Captain Jean-Baptiste Bessières was attached to him, and soon afterwards they were augmented by two battalions of grenadiers under Colonel Lannes. This force was in time expanded to become the Imperial Guard.

The Austrians were determined to relieve Mantua and thanks to the passivity of Jourdan and Moreau, could make large detachments from their army in Germany. Their first attempt by 47,000 men under the 72-year-old Marshal Würmser achieved some initial success. Although defeated at Castiglione (5 August), Würmser was able to capture 179 French siege guns and to put reinforcements and supplies into Mantua. However, on 8

September, the marshal was heavily defeated at Bassano and with 9,000 of his men he was forced to join Beaulieu in Mantua.

Heartened by events in Germany where the Archduke Charles had beaten Jourdan at Wurzburg, the Austrians tried again. Marshal Alvinsky, only 61 years old, attacked in two columns down the valleys of the Piave and the Adige. Having been narrowly held in the three-day battle of Arcole (15-17 November), Alvinsky withdrew and made a second attempt early in the new year. This time he attacked in three columns but his largest force was driven back from Rivoli, losing a quarter of his strength, on 10-14 January. A smaller force got to within signalling distance of Mantua before it was surrounded at La Favorita on the 16th. On 2 February, worn down by disease and starvation, Würmser surrendered Mantua and the 16,000 survivors of the garrison.

This was the end of Austrian resistance in Italy. Sending Massena to pursue the remainder of their army over the passes, Bonaparte invaded neutral Venice and levied the usual vast indemnity. Massena reached Klagenfurt on 28 March and was only 90 miles from Vienna when on 11 April Austria asked for an armistice.

The defeat of Austria was an unparalleled personal triumph for Bonaparte, who had received very little assistance from the French armies in Germany. The speed of the victory made it unique among campaigns up to that time. He had added little to the art of tactics. His favourite manoeuvre, a holding attack in front to divert attention from the main blow struck by a flanking column, was as old as war itself, but the speed and flexibility with which he deployed his divisions was something quite new and faced the elderly Austrian generals with their lumbering supply trains and their pedantic staff officers, with problems they were unable to solve. The Austrians fought well and there was nothing to choose between them and the French in courage and steadiness, but the lightning speed with which Bonaparte switched troops from one sector to another left his opponents in a state of bewilderment which led to defeat after defeat.

*   *   *

The war between Britain and France developed in a way that gave little satisfaction to either side. October 1796 was a particularly bad month for Britain since Naples was frightened into making peace with France and Spain was coerced into declaring war on Britain. Joined to Bonaparte's occupation of northern Italy, these two events meant that the Mediterranean Fleet could henceforward find shelter from the weather only in the bays of Sardinia and Corsica, neither of which had harbours of consequence. In November it was decided to withdraw the fleet to Gibraltar. Corsica and Elba were evacuated and the profitable Levant trade left without escort. Britain's only consolations were the smashing of the main Spanish fleet off Cape St Vincent (14 February 1797) and the capture of Trinidad (17 February 1797), two operations which cost Spain eight of her most seaworthy battleships, including two first-rates mounting 112 guns each.

Possession of the Dutch fleet gave France the possibility, given adequate luck, of invading Britain and dictating peace in London. As a preliminary she decided to capture Ireland, and at the end of December 1796 18,000 troops set out from Brest, carried in and escorted by 17 ships of the line, 19 frigates and 7 transports. The operation showed the ineffectiveness of the British blockade. Lord Bridport and the Channel Fleet were lying at Spithead and the offshore squadron did not notice that the French fleet had sailed until 48 hours had passed and even then no effective dispositions were made to hamper the invasion force. Most of the French ships reached Bantry Bay on 20 December and it was bad weather, not the Royal Navy, that prevented a landing which could scarcely have failed to capture Ireland.

In February 1797 French troops actually landed on British soil. A force of 1,800, recruited from gaols, was despatched to sail up the Avon, burn Bristol, re-embark for Cardiff and march from there to Liverpool. The commander of this sanguine venture was an American, Colonel Tate, and several of his officers were Irishmen including one, Joseph Wall, an ex-governor of Goree who had fled to France in 1784 to avoid prosecution for illegally flogging a sergeant to death. The expedition succeeded in burning some shipping in Ilfracombe Bay and then turned aside from its prescribed task to land at Pencaern near Fishguard. There on 22 February they surrendered to the Pembrokeshire Yeomanry, making that unit the only regiment to be awarded a battle honour for an engagement fought on British soil. Wall escaped but was later captured and hanged. Even this melodramatic and ineffective foray had its result. News of a French landing caused such a run on gold that Pitt, despite the advice of all the fashionable economists and the deplorable example of the *assignats* in France, introduced the paper currency which has survived to this day.

In April an even more serious danger threatened Britain. The seamen of the Channel Fleet mutinied at Spithead and refused to put to sea. They demanded increased pay, better food and medical care and occasional shore leave. When these were granted the men returned to their duty but in May a very serious outbreak occurred at the Nore. Here a more desperate line was taken by the mutineers who threatened to blockade London. Their leader, Richard Parker, formerly a midshipman court-martialled for insubordination, entitled himself President and claimed that the crews had the right to elect their officers. In so doing he over-reached himself and lost the support of most of the seamen. The mutiny collapsed and Parker and 28 of the ringleaders were hanged.

Two things were remarkable about these mutinies. The first was that the soldiers, regular and militia alike, remained firmly loyal to the government

although they suffered many of the intolerable grievances of which the Spithead men complained. The second was the attitude of the sailors who, especially at Spithead, maintained the strictest naval discipline among themselves and repeatedly asserted that should the enemy threaten, they would take the fleet to sea and defeat them. In October the North Sea Fleet, which contained a high proportion of ex-mutineers from the Nore, gave certain proof of their loyalty when, led by Admiral Duncan, they attacked the Dutch fleet off Camperdown and captured seven ships of the line. A separate mutiny occurred in September 1797 on the other side of the Atlantic when the crew of the frigate HERMIONE (32), having suffered under an exceptionally brutal captain, murdered him and his lieutenants and handed the ship over to the Spaniards.

France was having her own internal troubles. The elections of 1795 had produced a majority of moderates which was becoming monarchist in tone. By 1797 even the Directory was split, with three Directors, led by Barras, a

16 The Battle of Camperdown. Admiral Duncan defeated the Dutch fleet, although many of his crew had recently taken part in the Nore Mutiny. *Painting by P. J. de Loutherbourg.*

Admiral
Visct DUNCAN.

ci-devant marquess, standing for republicanism and continued war, while two, Carnot and Barthélemy, supported a return to a constitutional monarchy and peace. They had, moreover, the backing of General Pichegru, a former commander of the *Armée de la Sambre et Meuse* who was in touch with agents of the exiled Bourbons. Barras saw that only force could break the deadlock and asked Bonaparte to supply a general to command the Paris military region. The appointment was given to Augereau, a hero of the *Armée de l'Italie*, a ruthless man devoid of political ambition. On the night of 3-4 September (18 Fructidor) he put the city under martial law and arrested Barthélemy and Pichegru. Together with 42 deputies and 11 members of the upper house (*Conseil des Anciens*) they were transported to Guiana, but Carnot managed to escape to Switzerland. The remaining Directors then annulled the elections of 49 *départements* and curtailed the representation from others, so that they were able to continue to govern with suitable democratic and revolutionary support from the legislature.

The position of the purged Directory was further strengthened when on 17 October 1797 peace was signed with Austria. The terms of the Treaty of Campo Formio were, however, settled by General Bonaparte who paid little attention to the instructions sent him by his nominal masters in Paris. Under the treaty Austria surrendered all her rights to Belgium, Luxemburg and her possessions on the west bank of the Rhine. She also relinquished Milan and Mantua and agreed that this territory, together with that of the short-lived Cispadine Republic, should become the French-dominated Cisalpine Republic. In return Austria acquired the mainland territory of neutral Venice east of the Adige. The Dodecanese Islands, however, passed to France. With all northern Italy in her possession, the Adriatic a French lake, and outlets into the Ionian sea, France was more than the predominant power in Europe. She was on her way to becoming the rapacious landlord of the whole continent.

17 *Opposite Page* Admiral Lord Duncan. *Painting by John Singleton Copley*

CHAPTER II
1798–1801

The Consul

'It is no longer the frontiers of the republic you are called upon to defend.
We must invade the territories of our enemies!'
GENERAL BONAPARTE, CONSUL, 25 DECEMBER 1799

The Treaty of Campo Formio brought France face to face with her basic dilemma. She now had only one open and substantial enemy against her—Britain—and the time available to defeat her might not be long. Austria was temporarily out of the fight but she was unlikely to remain quiet. There were new monarchs in both Russia and Prussia who might not be content to follow the passive rôle of their predecessors. Paul, the new Czar, was known to be of an unpredictable disposition and it was certain that the attention of Russia would no longer be focussed on annexing parts of Poland. Since the third partition of 1795 Poland no longer existed.

When the Directory objected that harsher terms could have been exacted from Austria, Bonaparte pointed out that there were more urgent priorities than humiliating the Hapsburgs.

The Austrians are a clumsy and grasping nation; no state is less subtle and less likely to be a threat to our internal affairs. On the other hand, the English are courageous, meddling and energetic. We must pull down the English monarchy. . . . Let us concentrate our efforts on building up our fleet and on destroying England. Once that is done Europe is at our feet.

The problem of how Britain was to be destroyed remained. Direct invasion was for the time being an unpromising prospect. The heavy losses suffered by the Dutch and Spanish navies in 1797—15 ships of the line in all—threw the main responsibility for invasion back to the French and they had not had a good year at sea. In January the new battleship *Droits de*

18 Paul I, Czar of all the Russias

l'homme (74) had been attacked by Sir Edward Pellew with two frigates and driven on to the rocks of Audierne Bay with the loss of 900 out of her complement of 1,750 (including 1,000 soldiers). It was small consolation that one of the attacking frigates, AMAZON (36) also struck the rocks and was lost although only six of her crew were drowned. 1798 also started badly when *Hercule* (74) surrendered to MARS (74) off Brest in April. The Directory were nevertheless determined to try invasion and on 27 October 1797 they had appointed their star general to command the *Armée de l'Angleterre* which was assembling round the Channel ports.

Had the French been able to get across the Straits of Dover there would have been little the British could do to stop the French army conquering England. The regular army was in a chaotic state owing to the manic expansion that had taken place in the early years of the war. Recruiting was

51

19 Privates, First Foot
Guards, United Kingdom,
1812. *After a painting by C.
Hamilton Smith*

poor, scarcely sufficient to cover the insatiable demands caused by fever in the West Indies. The only striking force available was a body of 6,000 men (of whom 4,000 were enlisted foreigners) which, for no very clear reason, was stationed at Lisbon. There were few regulars in Britain and its defence rested almost wholly on the militia which, whatever its virtues, was completely untried. Behind them stood the Volunteers, a huge body of patriots whose enthusiasm for the military life was fanned by the knowledge that the slight demands made on them by their regiments exempted them from the ballot by which the militia was recruited. Some Volunteer regiments were serviceable but little could be looked for from the Somerset House Volunteers, commanded by Richard Brinsley Sheridan, whose terms of service insisted that they could not be required to fight outside the confines of Somerset House. At least in the 1st Royal Edinburgh Volunteers there was a keen interest in the health of all ranks. 'The lieutenant-colonel assures the regiment that he will not permit a single gentleman, officer or private, to march out of Edinburgh unless he is provided with a flannel underdress.'

Since the defence of Britain rested solely on the Royal Navy, it required considerable courage on the part of the government to send orders to Admiral Lord St Vincent, commanding the blockade of Cadiz, to detach Rear-Admiral Nelson with three of the line, two frigates and a brig, to pass the Straits of Gibraltar and discover what was happening at Toulon.

This instruction was despatched on 29 April 1798. 17 days earlier Bonaparte had been transferred from the Channel coast to command the *Armée de l'Orient*. After making a careful inspection of the military and naval resources available for the invasion he had had to report:

Whatever efforts we make, we cannot gain naval supremacy for some years to come. To invade England without such supremacy would be to embark on the most daring and difficult task ever undertaken. . . . If, in view of the present state of our navy, it seems impossible to obtain the promptness of execution which is essential, we can only abandon the expedition, while maintaining a pretence of it, and concentrate our attention and resource on the Rhine in order to deprive England of Hanover and Hamburg. . . . Alternatively we could undertake an eastern expedition to threaten England's trade with the Indies. If none of these projects is practicable, I see no alternative to making peace.

This realistic assessment stated clearly the problem that was to face France until 1814. She could only achieve her aim of dominating Europe by defeating Britain and this could be done either by outbuilding the Royal Navy or by ruining British trade. Bonaparte persisted in pursuing both these courses and in doing so brought about his own downfall.

In 1798, however, the Directory, while agreeing that the invasion of Britain was not practicable, were not prepared to risk striking a serious blow at British trade. As Bonaparte had suggested, the seizure of Hanover and Hamburg would certainly be a damaging blow to Britain but any move by French troops in this direction would be likely to bring Austria back into the war and Prussia would almost certainly resist French expansion so near her own territory. It was decided therefore that the most damaging blow against Britain could be struck in the Mediterranean. The occupation of Egypt would close the Levant to British trade and would threaten Britain's most profitable market, India. It might even be possible to intervene directly in the sub-continent.

The withdrawal of the Royal Navy from the Mediterranean made an attack on Egypt a practical proposition since the Toulon fleet could now move at will east of Gibraltar. It had been strengthened by some Venetian ships, although most of the Most Serene Republic's fleet was found to be too leaky to put to sea. Almost the whole of Italy was available as a base. The Cisalpine and Ligurian (Genoan) Republics provided the ports of Genoa, Leghorn and Ancona and in February 1798, Civitavecchia became available when General Berthier occupied Rome, deported the Pope and established the Roman Republic. To secure communications between France and Italy, Switzerland was occupied in March and converted into the *République Helvétique*. Geneva, commanding the approaches to the St Bernard Pass, was annexed to France.

Ten million Swiss francs paid for the preparations for the Egyptian expedition, and during the spring troops were assembled at Toulon, Genoa and Civitavecchia. On 9 May General Bonaparte arrived at Toulon to oversee the final preparations, and on the previous day Nelson and his squadron sailed east from Gibraltar. They captured a French corvette on the 17th and learned from her that a large armament was collecting at Toulon although they gathered no indication of its destination. Nelson steered for Toulon and it is possible that had he reached the approaches to the port the expedition would never have sailed. Admiral Brueys, who commanded the French fleet, believed the operation to be unwise and might well have used the presence of even a small British force as an excuse to cancel it.

As it happened, the weather frustrated Nelson. On 20 May a north-westerly gale dismasted his flagship, VANGUARD (74), and all but drove her on to the Sardinian shore. She was towed to safety by her consorts but before she could be repaired two misfortunes befell her admiral. Bonaparte sailed and passed unseen close to the British squadron, while Nelson's two frigates, believing that VANGUARD must retire to Gibraltar for repairs, took themselves off to that port and did not reappear during the campaign. Although Nelson was joined by ten more of the line on 7 June his scouting force was reduced to a single brig, the MUTINE (18). Somewhere in the Mediterranean was Bonaparte, who once he had picked up his detachments from Italy and Corsica had with him an army of 31,000 men distributed in 300 transports and escorted by 15 of the line (two of them Venetian 64s

with most of their guns removed), seven frigates, eight brigs, four bomb-ketches and 14 gun boats. Nelson had no way of finding him.

One of the reasons why the Admiralty had ordered St Vincent to send Nelson into the Mediterranean was the belief that the Toulon expedition was bound for Ireland and this thought was one of the factors that made Nelson's search more difficult. There was no doubt that French help was expected in Ireland, for a rebellion broke out in two places there in late June. The most serious rising was in the south east where 15,000 armed men seized Wexford, and it was not until 21 June that General Lake was able to defeat this rebel army at Vinegar Hill. By that time the parallel rising in Ulster had been put down and the rebellion sank into brigandage. The aftermath was made horrible by the barbarity practised by both sides, many of the government troops being Irish militia who, said John Moore, 'except that they are clothed with more uniformity are as much a rabble as those that oppose them.' A Welsh unit, the Ancient British Fencibles, earned itself a reputation for behaving as brutally as the native Irish.

Nelson, meanwhile, was groping round the Mediterranean for the great French convoy. He heard on 22 June from the skipper of a Genoese merchantman that the French had been to Malta and had left there six days earlier, bound, it was thought, for Sicily. In fact Bonaparte, who had accepted the precipitate surrender of the Knights of St John on 12 June, had not sailed again until the 19th and was heading for Alexandria. Nelson guessed his destination correctly but believing that the French had three more days' start than was actually the case, made such good speed to the Egyptian coast that he found Alexandria roads empty when he reached them on 28 June. Without his frigates he had been unable to scout on a sufficiently wide front to discover that Bonaparte had kept a more northerly course and had been delayed for 24 hours by a gale off the coast of Crete. When on 1 July the French reached Alexandria, Nelson was searching the coasts of Asia Minor and, finding no sign of the enemy, turned back to Sicily. He did not return to Egyptian waters until 1 August.

In the intervening month Bonaparte had conquered Egypt. In the first three days of July the army landed on the open beach at Marabout and quickly seized Alexandria with no more trouble than might be expected for an army that had had to march eight miles under a blazing Egyptian sun without water-bottles. Two battles against the Mamelukes, the second of them under the shadow of the Pyramids (21 July), gave the French possession of Cairo and, sending out detachments to drive away the remnants of the Mameluke army, Bonaparte set about colonizing the country. He opened hospitals, created a postal service, established the first printing press the Egyptians had ever seen, reopened neglected canals and tried to enforce sanitary regulations to guard against the endemic plague. Street lighting was introduced into Cairo, windmills were built and, with the help of a number of *savants* imported with the army, the beginnings of higher education were launched. More lastingly, the study of Egyptian archaeology was begun.

Unfortunately Bonaparte was less constructive in giving orders to Admiral Brueys. As battleships could not enter the harbour of Alexandria, the admiral anchored his larger ships in Aboukir (Abu Q'ir) Bay while he waited for the general to make up his mind. Batteries were erected on Aboukir Island to protect the fleet but Brueys anchored his ships in line where the nearest was 3,200 yards from the shore guns and thus out of their effective range. Since he was also insistent that his ships should have at least six fathoms of water under their keels, the admiral succeeded in getting his line in such a position that there was a passage between them and the shore.

On the afternoon of 1 August the lookout of H.M.S. ZEALOUS (74) reported that the mastheads of the French fleet were in sight. Nelson, who for some days had been so sick with worry that he had not eaten and had scarcely slept, sent the hands to dinner and ordered a meal for himself. He had 14 of the line, all 74s, and a 50-gun ship and was determined to lose no more time in bringing the French to battle. Brueys had 13 of the line but two of them were 80-gun ships and his flagship *L'Orient* (formerly *Dauphin Royal* and later, for a short time, *Sans-culottes*) carried 120 guns in her broadsides. Since he was accompanied by four frigates, two of 40 and two of 36 guns, there was little to choose between the two fleets in weight of metal. The French, however, were unprepared. Many of their men were ashore digging wells, their inshore gunports were closed and blocked with stores, and their admiral, something of a defeatist, was disinclined to believe that even Nelson would start a battle so shortly before daylight ended. Nevertheless, according to Captain Foley's log,

> *At 15 minutes past 6, the* GOLIATH, *being the leading ship, crossed the van of the enemy's line and commenced the action: having crossed, anchored with the sheet anchor out of the gun-room port, and brought up alongside the 2nd ship.*

Four ships followed GOLIATH inside the French line and then Nelson in VANGUARD turned and engaged the French from the outside, the rest of the fleet following her. When darkness fell the whole of the French van and centre was engaged from both sides. The French fought as bravely as they always did but the odds were heavily against them. The fiercest of the fight was around *L'Orient* and on one of the ships engaging her, SWIFTSURE, Midshipman John Theophilus Lee remembered that

> *the incessant flashes of the numerous guns, discharged at nearly the same instant, were so vivid at times as to enable each party to distinguish clearly not only the colours of the respective contestants, but the disastrous results of battle upon them.... The brave Brueys, having lost both his legs, was seated with torniquets [sic] on the stumps in an armchair facing his enemies; and giving directions for extinguishing the fire [which had started near the mizzen chains], when a cannon ball from the* SWIFTSURE *put a period to his gallant life by nearly cutting him in two.*

21 *L'Orient* blowing up at the Battle of the Nile. *Painting by T. Whitcome*

The fire in the French flagship soon gained an undeniable hold and became so hot that SWIFTSURE, engaging her from fine on her bow, found that the pitch was running out of her own seams. At 10 pm *L'Orient* blew up, carrying with her to the bottom £3 million in bullion which had been looted from Malta.

By morning the French Mediterranean fleet consisted of two battleships and two frigates making the best speed they could away from Nelson's battered squadron. Two 80s and seven 74s were British prizes. *L'Orient* had sunk and *Le Timoléon* (74) ran aground and was fired by her own crew to avoid capture. 2,000 French sailors were killed or seriously wounded and 3,225 were taken prisoner. The British loss was 218 killed and 677 wounded. The French had one small compensating success. Nelson sent LEANDER (50) with his despatch for Lord St Vincent off Cadiz. On 18 August she had the bad luck to fall in with *Généreux* (74), one of the French survivors, and was battered into surrender.

The Battle of the Nile was one of the most crushing naval victories of all time. On 1 May the Mediterranean had been a French lake with no British warship sailing east of Gibraltar. On 2 August the Royal Navy had complete mastery. The only remaining French ships of the line were flying for refuge, one to Corfu, one to Malta. An army of veterans commanded by France's most brilliant general was stranded in an inhospitable country with no means of regaining France except in small numbers.

Five days after the victory, on 6 August, another French squadron slipped to sea from Rochefort. It consisted only of three frigates but they carried 1,019 soldiers and three field pieces. Its destination was Ireland and its aim was to keep British attention fixed at home and prevent her from reinforcing the Mediterranean. Unlike the Fishguard expedition the troops were of excellent quality, many of them veterans of the *Armée de l'Italie*, and their commander, General Humbert, was a skilful and resolute officer.

On 22 August they landed in Killalla Bay, Co Mayo, and drawing their guns with carriage horses marched 40 miles southward. At Castlebar they found themselves opposed by 1,700 men with 11 guns (27 August) and most of their Irish adherents melted away under the cannonade. The French regulars, however, fixed their bayonets and charged. Apart from the gunners and a small party of regular infantry, the defenders took to their heels, among them a complete regiment of regular cavalrymen, the Sixth (Irish) Dragoon Guards.

Despite this victory Humbert's foray could not last long, the more so since he found little Irish support in Connaught. He was brought to bay at Ballinamuck on 8 September and had to surrender. He and his troops had distinguished themselves not only by their bravery but by their discipline, a virtue in which they were in marked contrast to their opponents, mostly

22 The Battle of the Nile

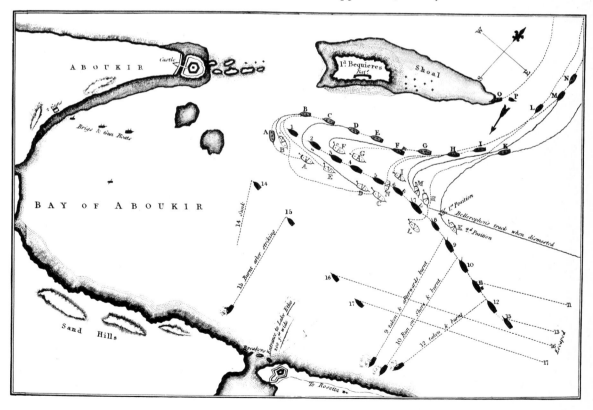

Irish militia but including some Scottish troops. When the fighting was over the government found it necessary to disband both the Fifth (Royal Irish) Dragoons and the Perthshire Fencibles. Humbert was making no great exaggeration when he reported to the Directory that with 2,000 more French troops he could have conquered all Ireland. There is no doubt that had the French fleet been able to face the Royal Navy the conquest of Ireland would have been a simple matter. This, however, continued to be the stumbling block. In September of the same year 3,000 more soldiers were despatched with an escort of one ship of the line and eight frigates. They were intercepted by Commodore Warren off Tory Island, Donegal, on 11 October and lost the battleship and three frigates.

*   *   *

Nelson's victory in Aboukir Bay had set all Europe aflame and a Second Coalition came into being almost of its own accord. Turkey declared war on France on 2 November. Naples followed her example in November and made the first military moves on the continent. Urged on by Nelson, Neapolitan troops under the Austrian General Mack occupied Rome but the French soon ejected them, and in January 1799, the French occupied Naples and proclaimed that it had become the Parthenopian Republic. Meanwhile Russia allied herself with Turkey and Britain, and British troops seized Minorca, thus securing a much needed naval base in the Mediterranean. The King of Naples fled to Sicily under Nelson's convoy and the Maltese rose against the French garrison, which was penned up within the fortifications of Valletta. In March Austria belatedly joined the Coalition. Only Prussia stood aside.

Faced with most of Europe in arms against them, the Directory ordered an offensive on all fronts regardless of the fact that their armies were everywhere under strength and their commissariat was rotten with corruption. Three armies were launched against the Austrians. The most northerly of these, under Jourdan, marched eastward through the Black Forest only to meet the Archduke Charles at Stockach, near Lake Constance, on 25 March. Jourdan was heavily defeated and within a fortnight was back on the west bank of the Rhine. In the centre Massena was ordered east from Switzerland to join hands with Jourdan on the Inn. After some initial success he was checked at Feldkirk and with Jourdan in retreat and the Swiss rising against their occupiers, he was forced back to Zurich. Unable to hold the city, Massena took up a strong position on the hills to the north and on the river Limmat.

It was the southern offensive which met with the greatest misfortune. The *Armée de l'Italie* under Schérer had been ordered to cross the Mincio and force its way up the Valtellina to support Massena's right. The plan miscarried from the start. Schérer was defeated near Verona on 26 March and falling back was defeated again at Magnana (5 April). Moreau

23 An officer of the 24th Infantry Regiment, Prussia, 1800. *Painting by J. A. Langendyke*

superseded Schérer but the Austrians were reinforced by 20,000 Russians, and with the 69-year-old Suvarov in supreme command drove westward, reaching Milan on 28 April.

The allied advance made the French position in southern Italy untenable and on 7 May General Macdonald, a Frenchman of Scottish descent, evacuated Naples. Picking up the garrison of Rome on his way, he hurried north to avoid being cut off. Had Macdonald concentrated on joining the *Armée de l'Italie* the situation might have been stabilized but he took it into his head to try to relieve the garrison of Mantua. Suvarov caught him on the river Trebbia near Piacenza and inflicted 10,000 casualties, a third of his strength (17–19 June). Moreau was in his turn superseded by Joubert but he was defeated and killed at Novi on 10 August. By the middle of that month only Genoa remained of Bonaparte's Italian conquests and the invasion of France was only prevented by 35,000 dispirited men in the Ligurian Alps and the redoubtable Massena near Zurich.

The French situation was little better at the eastern end of the Mediterranean. Bonaparte had succeeded in putting down an Egyptian rising—'Here in Cairo, I have cut heads off at the rate of five or six a day'—but he heard that a Turkish army was being massed in Palestine for the reconquest of Egypt. In February 1799 he set out to throttle this menace at its source. He stormed Jaffa (Yafo) on 7 March. The garrison of the citadel, 2,500 strong, surrendered as prisoners of war. Thinking it difficult to feed them, he mustered them in the presence of a division of infantry. 'A signal gun was fired. Vollies of musquetry and grape instantly played against them.' None survived. When the French plundered Jaffa the plague got a hold among the army. Soon thirty Frenchmen were dying each day.

The Turkish army had its base at Acre, a Crusader fortress built on a rocky peninsula, which Bonaparte attempted to capture. Unfortunately his siege guns, transported by sea, were captured by the Royal Navy, and even the crumbling battlements of Acre were proof against field guns. Moreover Commodore Sidney Smith landed seamen and Royal Marines to reinforce the defence which was brilliantly organized by Colonel de Phélippeaux, an *emigré* artillery officer who had been a fellow pupil of Bonaparte at Brienne. The siege lasted from 17 March until 20 May but Phélippeaux's skill and the traditional toughness of the Turkish infantry in defence were too much for Bonaparte who retreated to Egypt. His army had lost 2,200 dead but Phélippeaux died of exhaustion and plague. The Turkish invasion of Egypt also failed. 8,000 men were landed at Aboukir but Bonaparte attacked them on 25 July and thanks largely to a brilliant cavalry charge led by Brigadier Murat drove them into the sea.

Despite their other preoccupations the Directory were doing their best to support their general in Egypt. They ordered the Brest fleet to sea and told its commander, Admiral Bruix, to collect the Spanish fleet from Cadiz, pass the Straits of Gibraltar, and clear the fleets of Britain, Russia, Turkey

Bosselman sc.

and Portugal from the Mediterranean. He was also to embark 3,000 soldiers on the Riviera and to employ them in relieving the garrisons of Corfu, Malta and Egypt. In fact, Corfu, together with *Généreux* and her prize LEANDER, fell to a Russo-Turkish expedition seven weeks before Bruix put to sea.

Bruix, although like so many of his colleagues inclined to be pessimistic about the result of any encounter between the French and British fleets, was a very competent sea officer, and despite the over-sanguine tone of his orders stood a chance of being able to bring overwhelming numbers to any battle. There was no difficulty in slipping out of Brest. Lord Bridport's blockade was so lax that the lugger *Rebecca*, which Bruix sent to sea with false despatches and orders to have herself captured, had to spend three days cruising before she could find a British frigate to whom she could surrender. On 25 April 25 of the line left Brest. It was 24 hours before the British realized that they had left and even then Bridport ordered his ships to concentrate on the approaches to Ireland.

On 4 May the French fleet was off Cadiz, but rather than face Lord Keith with 15 of the line Bruix decided to leave his allies to follow, and to make for the Straits. There he met his first setback when a gale damaged several ships, one of which managed to slip back into Cadiz, and on the following night three of his ships collided. With Keith now in pursuit, Bruix decided to make for Toulon which he reached on 13 May with eight ships in need of repair. On the previous night the Spanish fleet—17 battleships—finding Cadiz unguarded, put to sea. Like Bruix, they met a gale in the Straits which brought down one or more masts on nine of their ships. They put into Cartagena, where there were five more battleships ready for sea. Keith, meanwhile, put into Tetuan to re-provision his 15 ships.

The balance of naval power in the Mediterranean had now swung sharply. The Franco-Spanish strength in ships of the line had risen from six (five at Cartagena, one at Malta) to 47 although 17 of them were in need of at least some repair. Against them the British had 29 but these were widely scattered. Apart from Keith's 15 at Tetuan, there were two off the Palestinian coast, three at Malta, five, under Nelson, off Sicily and four at Minorca. The two in the Levant were too distant to recall but, as it happened, Keith could only rally his own ships and those at Minorca, 19 in all. The three from Malta joined Nelson's squadron but he refused to cooperate with the rest of the fleet, and besotted with Lady Hamilton and dazzled by the flattery of the Queen of Naples kept his eight battleships engaged in petty Neapolitan expeditions.

Bruix, therefore, had the ability to bring at least 30 of the line against Keith's 19, odds that should have guaranteed him success, but partly because the Spaniards were markedly disinclined to risk a battle, he declined to take the chance. Instead he made a short expedition to take supplies to the battered *Armée de l'Italie* at Genoa and then sailed for Cartagena which he reached on 16 June. Finding that he could muster 37 of the line (22 French and 15 Spanish), he still declined to attempt a battle and sailed the combined fleet back to Brest, arriving on 13 August. He had achieved nothing and had lost a squadron of three frigates which fell in with Keith's fleet on 18 June.

Later in the year the Spaniards lost two frigates off Cape Finisterre when *Thetis* (34) and *Santa Brigida* (34), both loaded with coin and other valuables, were taken by four British frigates. This was the kind of capture which was every seaman's dream, the hope that kept men of all ranks at sea despite the almost intolerable conditions on board a warship. In the

25 Russian infantry, 1799.
Painting by W. van Kobell

division of the prize money each of the four captains received £40,730 18s while the lieutenants got £5,091 7s 3d, the warrant officers £2,468 10s 9½d, the midshipmen £791 17s 0¼d and the seamen and marines £182 4s 9½d.

However badly things were going in Italy, the Directory had little trouble with the Coalition's other land campaign. The Czar had agreed to provide 16,000 Russian soldiers to cooperate with the British in northern Europe. Once hopes of Prussian assistance had faded it was decided to land in Holland where it was believed that the population were ready to rise against the French. In Britain the generals were unanimously opposed to the whole concept but Pitt and Dundas insisted that a landing should be made, with the twin aim of capturing the Dutch Texel squadron and invading France through Flanders. No amount of argument would persuade the Cabinet that the two aims were incompatible since the Texel at the northern tip of Holland was the worst possible part of the country on which to base a march into Flanders.

26 A skirmish between French infantry and British light dragoons during the Helder expedition in 1799. *Painting by J. A. Langendyk*

By permitting militiamen to volunteer for the regulars, a move hitherto illegal, a British army of 36,000 was scraped together and a landing was made on 27 August 1799. At first there was some success. The Texel squadron, 24 ships of 24 guns or more, surrendered with alacrity and a French counter attack was beaten off. From that time everything went wrong. There was no Dutch rising, the Russians were difficult allies, the British were, as usual, almost without transport, the ex-militiamen were scarcely trained, the navy was unhelpful, the LUTINE (36) carrying the army's paychest of £140,000 was wrecked on the Dutch coast and a vast consignment of rations bought in north Germany remained windbound in the Elbe. At the beginning of October the allies, reduced to two days' rations, were happy to make a convention with the French which allowed them to evacuate the country. The most powerful part of the Dutch fleet, including 14 third-rates, was still secure in the ports of South Holland.

By that time the situation in south Europe had changed. The Austrians had given Suvarov the command in Italy but they constantly interfered with his operations, and instead of permitting him to invade France through Provence they insisted that he participate in a complicated three-pronged attack on Massena at Zurich. While the preliminary moves were being made Massena, who had been strongly reinforced, struck at the force immediately to his front and routed them. Suvarov tried to fight his way through the mountains but was trapped in the Reuss valley and had to force his way eastward with the loss of 10,000 men and all his artillery. By 1 October Switzerland was clear of the allies.

Soon afterwards an even more significant event occurred. The French army in Egypt had never been wholly isolated. It had always been possible for frigates to slip in and out of Alexandria and Damietta and on 23 August Bonaparte with his principal staff officers—Berthier, Lannes, Murat, Bessières and Marmont—embarked on *Muiron* (28) and put to sea. He handed command of the *Armée de l'Egypte*, still 20,000 strong, to General Kléber, who was informed of his elevation only by letter. On 9 October Bonaparte landed at Fréjus, near Cannes.

*   *   *

Bonaparte's return to France came at a time when the Directory was tottering towards dissolution. Although Massena's Swiss victory had averted the worst threat to France, the armies of the republic were shrinking in numbers, desperate for supplies, and apparently directed with utter irresponsibility. Never popular, the Directors had overdrawn on such public support as they had by a compulsory loan, by the withholding of the salaries of public officials, and by the abolition of all exemptions from conscription. It could be only a matter of weeks before the Directory collapsed and the far left with its ally, the Paris mob, took over—a change that must lead to France's defeat through sheer ineptitude. Three amoral but clear-sighted politicians, Sieyès, a Director himself, Talleyrand and

27 Charles Maurice de Talleyrand

Fouché, were planning a *coup d'état* and searching with mounting desperation for a soldier who could implement it. For them Bonaparte's reappearance was providential. By 9 November Paris was swarming with troops, commanded by officers returned from Egypt, and a story of a terrorist plot was used as a pretext to move the two legislative chambers out of Paris. At the same time three of the Directors were put under house arrest.

28 *Opposite Page* Bonaparte as First Consul. *Painting by Baron François Pascal Simon Gérard*

Next day, 18 Brumaire, the lower chamber, the Council of Five Hundred, met at St Cloud. Their president, Lucien Bonaparte, called on his victorious brother to address them. The general lost his nerve, and ranted at the deputies, rousing them to fury. Blows were exchanged and a smear of blood was seen on Bonaparte's cheek. Lucien called for troops and Murat, ordering the drums to beat, led a file of grenadiers into the chamber, ejecting those deputies who had not jumped out of the windows. Later a rump of carefully chosen deputies was readmitted to elect Bonaparte, Sieyès and one Roger Ducos as Consuls. Lucien Bonaparte became Minister of the Interior and Berthier Minister for War. The French Revolution was over and 15 years of personal absolutism had begun.

A new constitution was proclaimed a month later in which Bonaparte was nominated as First Consul and equipped with the reality, if not the form, of absolute power. Sieyès and Ducos were replaced by nonentities with wholly ceremonial functions. The Consular Guard was inaugurated— a battalion of grenadiers, a company of *chasseurs à pied*, three squadrons of light horse and a battery—a force which in time would swell to the 40,000 men of the Imperial Guard.

On Christmas Day the new First Consul sent messages to the Emperor of Austria and the King of England proposing peace on the basis of the *status quo* except that Austria would give up her new conquests in Lombardy and Piedmont. Both sovereigns refused to consider the proposal. It had not escaped their notice that on the same day that Bonaparte had proposed peace he had announced to his army: 'Soldiers! It is no longer the frontiers of the republic which you are called upon to defend. We must invade the territories of our enemies!'

There was no need for France to propose peace to the Russians. Czar Paul, whose mental stability was crumbling, had become disenchanted with his allies. He pulled his troops back from western Europe, retaining only Corfu as a warm-water base for his fleet. England became anathema to him and he planned an attack on India. 20,000 Cossacks were assembled in the southern Urals and to their commander he wrote: 'It is four months' march from your headquarters. . . . I enclose the only map I could find here [although] I find it goes no further than Khiva. God bless you.' The last phrase was the most helpful. It was 1,500 miles from Khiva in Uzbekistan to the nearest British settlement in India.

Britain's military aid to the disintegrating Coalition was not such as to

29 Private, Consular Guard,
France, 1803. *Painting by
J. H. Turner*

A Private of the Consular Guard

cause much distress to the First Consul. Malta eventually fell to her in September 1800 but during the rest of that year the British army confined its attention to a series of abortive operations on the Atlantic coast. In June they decided to seize Belleisle, off St Nazaire. No suitable boats for the landing could be procured and the idea was abandoned at the last moment. In August 12,000 men were put ashore near Ferrol. A reconnaissance of the fortifications reported, wrongly, that they were very strong. The troops were re-embarked and, having taken a despairing look at the defences of Vigo, sailed on to Gibraltar. In September the whole charade was repeated at Cadiz. There 5,000 men were actually in their landing craft when the admiral remarked casually to the general that it would be several hours before a second wave could be landed. The force sailed back to Gibraltar. By the end of the year a force of 16,000 men had been accumulated at Gibraltar but the government could not decide what to do with them. Had they arrived earlier they might have given valuable help to the Austrians in Italy.

The Consulate was anxious to gain a great victory to consolidate its position and two Austrian armies were in a position to threaten France. In south Germany Kray commanded 140,000 men facing the upper Rhine, and in Italy Melas had 95,000 men in Piedmont. The French armies opposing them were the *Armée du Rhin*, 120,000 men between Switzerland and Mainz, under the command of Moreau, and the *Armée de l'Italie*, now under Massena. This had a strength, on paper, of 150,000, but its

30 Austrian dragoons.
Painting by J. B. Seele

71

commander reported that only 36,000 were present, of whom 28,000 were fit for duty. They were defending a front of 180 miles of which the main bastion was Genoa.

Between these two armies Bonaparte ordered an *Armée de la Réserve* to be collected at Dijon. This was intended to consist of 60,000 men but since sufficient waggons could not be horsed for its transport the eventual strength was only 40,000. The consular constitution forbade any of the consuls to command armies, so the nominal command of the *Armée de la Réserve* went to Berthier who was replaced by Carnot at the Ministry for War. Pay for all the armies was procured from the merchants of Amsterdam who loaned 12 million francs at 12%, secured against forests of timber in France.

Bonaparte planned to have the main blow struck by the *Armée du Rhin* which was to attack Kray's right and interpose itself between that army and Vienna. When this scheme was put to Moreau he raised every kind of difficulty, whereupon Bonaparte decided that instead he would march the Armée de la Réserve across the Alps and cut Melas's communications. These were lengthened when the Austrians attacked Massena on 5 April and split the *Armée de l'Italie* in two. Half, under Gabriel Suchet, retreated into France where it clung tenuously to the line of the Var, west of Nice. The remainder fell back to Genoa and by 2 May Massena was confined within the city under bombardment by the Austrians from the land and the Royal Navy from the sea.

This Austrian initiative took Bonaparte by surprise. The *Armée de la Réserve* was not ready to move and it was not until 14 May that its advance guard began to approach the Great St Bernard Pass. Nine days earlier Moreau had been ordered to detach 25,000 men who were to enter Italy by the St Gotthard and Simplon passes. It was clearly going to be a near-run thing for, as Bonaparte wrote to Berthier, 'If Massena is forced to surrender, General Melas only needs eight days to move from Genoa to Aosta and if he gets there before you he will be able to prevent you breaking out into Italy.' Everything depended on Massena's iron determination. If Berthier could not get clear of the passes the campaign would be, at best, a fiasco. Bonaparte wrote to Massena, 'What reassures me is that it is *you* who are holding Genoa,' and the general did not let him down. It was not until 4 June that Massena, down to his last rations, with a civilian revolt within the typhus-ridden city and with only 8,110 men fit to stand, surrendered. By that time Bonaparte and the *Armée de la Réserve* had reached Milan. A week later a corps which Melas had detached had been defeated by Lannes at Montebello and Bonaparte was across the Po and between Melas and Austria. Equally Melas was between Bonaparte and France.

Having put himself in this advantageous position by a brilliant strategic stroke, the First Consul, now openly commanding the army, showed himself as a deplorable tactician. With little idea of the strength or position of his opponent he fumbled his way towards the fortress city of Alessandria, leaving two corps north of the Po to secure his retreat. He was left with 31,000 men but of these he detached 5,300 under Desaix to guard against an imaginary threat from the direction of Genoa. Bonaparte was under the impression that Melas was retreating, whereas Melas, who had 28,500 men at Alessandria, was determined to break out eastward. On the morning of 14 June a further French division, 3,500 men under Lapoye, were sent away to the north of the main army. Bonaparte thus had only 22,000 against Melas's 28,500.

At 9 am on the morning of 14 June Melas drove eastward out of Alessandria in three columns. Throughout the morning the French tried to stand on a line between the villages of Marengo and Castel Ceriolo but with only 15 guns against 100 on the Austrian side, the position was desperate. Messages were sent to Desaix and Lapoye but the latter was not found until evening and Desaix, who was marching to the sound of the guns, was 12 miles from the battlefield. Marengo was lost and a counter-attack failed to retake it. Castel Ceriolo was lost, regained and lost again. During the afternoon the French fell back four and a half miles to San Giulano Vecchia. The last reserve, the Consular Guard, was put into the line and ammunition was almost exhausted.

It was 5 pm before Desaix arrived with his division and eight guns. Marmont brought together the ten guns remaining to the rest of the army and under their fire Desaix attacked the Austrian right, aiming for Marengo. He died at the head of his men but the Austrians fell back and Kellermann, son of the hero of Valmy, went at them with 500 horsemen. The Austrian right dissolved in panic and when the rest of Melas's army tried to retreat over the Bormida river into Alessandria, they found the three bridges jammed by a mass of struggling fugitives. The French were too exhausted to take advantage of the confusion and contented themselves with resuming their original line. They had suffered 5,835 casualties, the Austrians lost 9,400. Next day an armistice was signed. Melas agreed to retire unhindered to the Mincio and there was to be no more fighting in Italy until a general peace was agreed between France and Austria.

The Consulate had won the victory it needed but it had been won almost despite the First Consul. The real victors were Desaix, Marmont, Kellermann and, above all, Massena whose stubborn defence of Genoa had made the campaign possible. The Bulletin issued after the battle admitted that during the afternoon 'the battle appeared to be lost'. This view was, however, not permitted to go down to history. On Bonaparte's instructions the *Dépôt de la Guerre* reviewed the evidence and in 1803 and 1805 produced revised accounts of Marengo with the commander-in-chief's part in gaining the victory increasingly stressed. The final version was dictated by Napoleon himself at St Helena and this made the retreat of

31 The French army
crossing the Great St
Bernard Pass on the way
to the Marengo campaign.
Lithograph by H. C. Muller

32 Bonaparte dispatching an ADC with orders at the Battle of Marengo.
Painting by Pierre Martinet

the French army a deliberate manoeuvre designed to draw the Austrians on to the bayonets of Desaix's division. But if Bonaparte doctored the record he learned from his mistakes. At Austerlitz in 1805 he employed the manoeuvre of tempting forward one wing of the enemy army so that it could be smashed, to the greatest possible effect.

Five days after Marengo the Austrians were beaten in Germany. Moreau defeated Kray and the Archduke Charles at Höchstadt (19 June) and occupied Munich. Vienna, nevertheless, was not prepared to agree to a humiliating peace and negotiations dragged on until November when the armistices which had been agreed on both fronts were allowed to lapse. This time the main blow was struck by Moreau who crushed the northern Austrian army at Hohenlinden on 3 December while Macdonald, commanding a new *Armée de la Réserve*, made an epic winter march over the Splügen pass and reached Bolzano before the Austrians recognized the inevitable and asked for a further armistice. On 9 February 1801 a peace treaty was signed at Lunéville by which Austria agreed to confine her Italian possessions behind the Adige and to acknowledge as sovereign states the French puppets known as the Batavian (Dutch), Helvetian, Ligurian (Genoese) and Italian Republics, the last, an expansion of the

Cisalpine Republic, consisting of Lombardy, Parma, Modena and Tuscany.

Once again Britain was alone, apart from the peripheral support given by Naples and Sicily, Portugal and Turkey. Her position was even weaker than it had been in 1798 as Czar Paul was now an enemy in everything but name. In September 1800 all British property in Russia was sequestered and although it was restored a week later the Czar, following a precedent dating from the time of the American War of Independence, organized an Armed Neutrality by which Russia, Denmark and Sweden agreed to exclude British trade from the Baltic. This was a threat Britain could not afford to neglect; the loss of her Baltic trade would be serious, but worse was the cutting of of the timber supplies which kept the Royal Navy operational. The Danes bore the brunt of the British reaction. Her merchant ships were seized, her West Indian colony captured, and in March 1801 a British fleet under Sir Hyde Parker sailed for the Baltic. The moment was well chosen for the Russian fleet was still icebound and few Swedish ships were fit for the sea.

On 2 April Parker detached Nelson with ten ships of the line to deal with

33 The death of General Desaix at the Battle of Marengo, where his march to the sound of the guns saved Bonaparte from a serious defeat. *Painting by J. F. J. Schwebach*

34 French troops in 1800

the defences of Copenhagen which consisted of the great Trekroner fortress and a line of 19 armed hulks and floating batteries, supported by a small mobile battle squadron. That evening Nelson wrote in his journal:

> *Moderate breezes southerly; at 9 made the signal to engage the Danish line; the action lasted about 4 hours, when 17 out of the 18 of the Danish line were taken, burnt or sunk. Our ships suffered a good deal. At night went on board the* ST GEORGE *very unwell.*

Although it was still unknown at Copenhagen, the Armed Neutrality had already suffered a mortal blow. On 23 March Czar Paul had been murdered in a palace revolution at St Petersburg. His son, Alexander I, reversed his policy and in mid-June signed a convention with Britain.

Before that Britain had suffered further setbacks. At the end of March, Prussia, pursuing the jackal role in which she had cast herself since 1795, occupied Hanover, and a few weeks later Spain, encouraged and assisted by France, invaded Portugal. Although she had 16,000 men at Gibraltar, Britain refused to listen to Portuguese pleas for help. Instead she advised her ally to make peace as quickly as possible. Reluctantly Portugal agreed and signed the Treaty of Badajoz (6 June 1801) by which she ceded Olivenza to Spain besides paying a large indemnity and agreeing to close her ports to British trade (an agreement she could not afford to honour). The Spaniards were delighted by this quick victory and the treaty was approved by Lucien Bonaparte, then French ambassador to Madrid. The First Consul was highly displeased. He had counted on a long war which would draw off Britain's disposable troops and would end with a Franco-Spanish occupation of Portugal, thus effectively closing the ports of Lisbon and Oporto. Instead, British trade with Portugal continued almost unabated and Britain still had an expeditionary force in the Mediterranean which could interfere with French concerns.

The French concern most exposed to British interference was the army in Egypt. Kléber, on hearing that Bonaparte had abandoned the army, leaving it seven million francs in debt, had remarked, 'Ce bougre-là a laissé ici ses culottes pleines de merde'. He soon attempted to negotiate for an evacuation of Egypt in return for an unobstructed passage back to France but this came to nothing. Being a very good soldier and administrator, he continued Bonaparte's organization of the country and, in March 1800, defeated a Turkish army at Heliopolis. It was unfortunate for France that Kléber was assassinated by a Muslim fanatic on the day Marengo was fought, and his successor, Menou, who embraced Islam, was not his equal as a soldier. Bonaparte was meanwhile doing his best to send help from France.

In January 1801 Admiral Ganteaume put to sea with the available strength of the Brest squadron, seven of the line and two frigates, with orders to take 2,500 troops to Alexandria. They reached the Mediterranean

but captured a British sloop from which they learned that fourteen battleships were lying off Alexandria. Ganteaume was not to know that this was untrue and he judged it wiser to make for Toulon which he reached on 18 February. After a month's stay he put to sea again only to be driven back by a gale, but in mid-May he sailed with peremptory orders to go to Alexandria, bombarding Elba, then held by the Neapolitans, on his way. He did succeed in slipping a frigate into Alexandria but having sighted the British Mediterranean fleet he wisely decided to return to Toulon. On the way he was fortunate enough to capture the SWIFTSURE (74) which was sailing alone and was overpowered (24 June).

The Royal Navy lost another ship of the line in the following month when Rear-Admiral Saumarez attempted to attack a Franco-Spanish squadron under the guns of Algeciras. In a light and intermittent breeze the HANNIBAL (74) went aground. All efforts to refloat her failed and she was pounded into surrender, becoming the only British battleship in the entire war to be captured and not retaken. She was quickly avenged. On 13-14 July the enemy squadron, reinforced to nine ships, was at sea in the Straits of Gibraltar when Saumarez with six ships attacked them at night, destroyed two Spanish 80-gun ships and captured a 74.

35 The landing of the British army at Aboukir Bay in Egypt, 8 March 1801. *Painting by Edward Dayes*

The fate of Menou's army in Egypt had already been sealed. On 24 October 1800 General Sir Ralph Abercromby, commanding the expeditionary force at Gibraltar, had received the last of a long series of contradictory orders from London. He was to invade Egypt in cooperation with the Turks. He therefore took 15,000 men and landed them in Marmorice Bay on the Turkish coast, near the island of Rhodes. There Abercromby, a good but desponding soldier, set about ensuring that the expedition should succeed. He managed, unlike most of his fellow generals, to work well with his naval colleague, Lord Keith. Together they arranged a series of joint landing exercises so that every man in both services knew how to act. The final instructions for the landing, planned by John Moore for the army and Alexander Cochrane for the navy, were so well thought out that identical instructions were issued in 1854 when the Anglo-French army landed in the Crimea.

Abercromby's army landed against opposition in Aboukir Bay on 7 March 1801 and two weeks later the French were decisively beaten in the Battle of Alexandria (21 March) after which Menou allowed himself to be invested in that city. Unfortunately Abercromby was mortally wounded in the battle and the command fell to the intensely unpopular Major-General John Hely Hutchinson. The latter did, however, succeed in taking Rosetta and in June, Cairo, the French surrendering on condition that they be repatriated. Six weeks after Cairo fell, an Anglo-Indian division, which had landed at Kosseir on the Red Sea, reached the city after a remarkable march which included a stretch of more than a hundred miles across the desert.

It was 2 September before Menou surrendered Alexandria on the same terms as the other parts of his army and the French occupation of Egypt was finally at an end. This result could have been achieved 20 months earlier and without bloodshed had Kléber's proposals been allowed to succeed but the campaign had one important result. The Battle of Alexandria on 21 March 1801 was the first occasion since the war began on which a British force of all arms met and defeated a French army on equal terms. The self-confidence of the army, sapped by the defeat in America and by the disasters and fiascos of Flanders and Holland, began to revive. It was the beginning of a long road which was to lead through Maida, Vimeiro, Salamanca and Vitoria to the final triumph of Waterloo.

Before the news of the liberation of Egypt reached London the preliminaries of peace between Britain and France had been signed (1 October 1801). Both sides recognized that a stalemate had been reached; both needed a respite before continuing the struggle. The definitive treaty was signed at Amiens on 25 March 1802.

The Peace of Amiens

The two contracting parties signed the Treaty of Amiens with different opinions as to what peace might bring. Bonaparte saw peace as the continuation of war by other means. Four years earlier he had written that France would have to make peace if Britain could not be invaded, if her German and Baltic trade could not be stopped or if her Indian trade could not be threatened (see p. 53). The collapse of the Armed Neutrality and the French defeat in Egypt meant that the second and third options had been destroyed. The balance of naval power could be more easily altered in peace than in war. Bonaparte agreed to the treaty but put in hand the construction of 23 ships of the line.

Britain made peace because she could see no way in which she could effectively intervene on the Continent and because an end to the war would give her the opportunity to rebuild her economy which, it was widely believed, was on the brink of ruin. The Armed Neutrality had temporarily halted grain shipments from the Baltic and this, added to two successive bad harvests, had raised the price of wheat to 151s a quarter, three times the price in 1798. The import of grain from other markets had cost the country £24 million in gold, the Bank of England's reserves fell to £4½ million and the pound dropped 13% at Hamburg. Even those who believed that the war must eventually be renewed recognized that a pause would be valuable, and since William Pitt, whose determination to win the war had been matched only by his incapacity to direct it, had resigned (over Catholic Emancipation), the business of making peace was consigned to his successor, Henry Addington.

The negotiations leading to the Treaty were a French triumph. The British plenipotentiary, Lord Cornwallis, could not compete with the French delegate, Joseph Bonaparte, the First Consul's elder brother, and made concession after concession. All the French colonies, including even Tobago, were returned, while Minorca reverted to Spain and the Cape of Good Hope to the Batavian Republic. All that Britain retained were Trinidad and Ceylon. Thus Britain surrendered all the naval bases she had

so laboriously won with the single exception of Malta, though even here she showed no conception of the strategic importance of the island, being concerned only to keep it out of French hands. After much wrangling, in which both sides vied for the support of Russia, it was agreed that Malta should be handed back to the Knights Templar, of whom the Czar regarded himself as the protector. The tenure of the Knights was to be secured by a guarantee of all the powers and the island was to have a garrison of Neapolitan troops, who had recently demonstrated that they were the least reliable in Europe.

In return for the British concessions France agreed to evacuate Naples and the Papal States, knowing that she could reoccupy them at will. She also recovered from British prison camps the large number of prime seamen she badly needed, and managed to evade paying for their upkeep while they were prisoners, though this point occupied Cornwallis's attention almost to the exclusion of all other matters.

Having obtained this needlessly humiliating peace, Addington set about reducing government expenditure. In 1802 he was able proudly to announce that he had saved £25 million, having reduced the Secret Service Fund from £35,000 to £12,000, taken £2 million from the Navy Estimates, demobilized the militia and cut the regular army from 187,000 men (1800) to 95,000. It is fair to Addington to add that the new peace establishment of the army was twice that of 1792, although it was a puny figure compared with the 400,000 maintained by France. There were, however, signs that Britain was making progress in the long-needed task of making her army an effective force. The Duke of York, who had been appointed commander-in-chief in 1795, was a talented and conscientious administrator and was beginning to produce results. The under-qualified (and frequently under age) officers who had flooded into the army in 1793-4 were relegated to half pay or forced to do their duty. Over-rapid promotion was forbidden, a Staff College and a Military Academy for potential officers were founded. Greatcoats became a normal issue to the troops and a small increase in pay for those in the ranks was wrung from a reluctant House of Commons. A uniform system of battle drill was imposed on the regiments, and British units of light infantry and riflemen were trained on lines that were soon to prove them the best in the world. Nor was Alexandria the army's only victory. Far away in India any chance that France might have had of enlisting the aid of the native princes was wrecked by the destruction of the Mahratta Confederacy, notably at the battles of Assaye (23 September 1803) and Argaum (29 November 1803). At both the British commander was a major-general, born in the same year as Bonaparte, who had recently changed his name from Wesley to Wellesley.

The Royal Navy fared badly during the peace. Not only were the Estimates sharply cut but the First Lord of the Admiralty embarked on a crusade against corruption in the dockyards. Rightly believing that the

36 *Opposite Page* Hussars and a dragoon, France, 1802. *Painting by J. A. Langendyk*

timber merchants were holding the government to ransom, Lord St Vincent (who as Admiral Sir John Jervis had won the battle of that name) tried to force the price down by staying out of the market. His motives were admirable but the result could have been disastrous. By May 1802 the navy's reserve of timber, normally maintained at three years' supply, was less than peacetime consumption for a year. Simultaneously Bonaparte was requisitioning all the stocks of oak in France for his own shipbuilding programme.

While Britain was trying to get back to normal business, across the Channel Bonaparte was consolidating his hold. In 1802 a plebiscite made him Consul for life and France began to return to a monarchist, but not a Bourbon, form of government. At the Consular court life was regulated by a strict etiquette, exhumed from the great days at Versailles, which was soon to pass imperceptibly into imperial pomp. These deviations from the egalitarianism, proclaimed if seldom enforced since the Revolution, antagonized the strong minority of republicans and did nothing to endear the Consul to the rather larger minority of monarchists, but there was widespread and enthusiastic support for the new order among the mass of the French people. After 13 years of revolution, war, *coups d'état*, famine, terror, civil strife, inflation, and corruption, any government that could promise peace and stability was welcome. Another source of pleasure to the majority was the Concordat signed with the Pope whereby freedom for public worship was re-established and priests paid from public funds. The swing back to religion was confirmed when in 1802 the 15 August was marked in the church calendars as the hitherto uncelebrated feast of St Napoleon.

Bonaparte also brought prosperity to France, though much of it was based on the systematic robbery of the puppet states and the prohibition of their external trade. The French wool industry, for example, expanded fourfold between 1800 and 1812. Education made great strides forward. Every *commune* was required to have a primary school and every *département* at least one secondary school. The curricula were strictly controlled from Paris and the teaching of modern history was forbidden, being replaced by instruction on the times of Charlemagne. Work went forward on the reform and codification of the law. The civil code, the great *Code Napoléon*, was promulgated between 1802 and 1804, the commercial, criminal and penal codes following. The savage decrees against the *noblesse* were relaxed (save against 1,000 names still proscribed), and 40,000 *emigrés* returned to France. They were still liable to arrest by administrative decision but many of them played a full part, military or civil, in the imperial glories that were to come. As a first step towards the creation of a new aristocracy the *Légion d'honneur* was instituted (19 May 1802).

Yet another constitution was proclaimed but Bonaparte made it clear that it was not to be taken too seriously. As he told the Council of State in

1802, 'A constitution must not interfere with the process of government.... Every day brings the necessity to violate constitutional laws.' France, under a democratic façade, became a police state. The liberty of the subject was assured, provided that he did what he was told. An increasingly severe censorship was imposed on the press and the theatre. A steady stream of intellectuals began to leave the country, some of their own free will, some by consular order.

An attempt was made to restore France's colonial empire. Apart from the islands handed back by Britain, Bonaparte tried to restore French rule in St Domingue, a venture that resulted in the death of the army sent there, including its general, the Consul's brother-in-law, and was marked by a singularly squalid piece of treachery when the indigenous ruler, Toussaint L'Ouverture, was lured to his death in a French prison. The Spanish government was also induced to retrocede Louisiana, a name that then covered all the land between the Mississippi and the Rockies (except Texas) as far north as the present Canadian border. France, however, found this vast tract of America too much of a problem and Bonaparte sold it to the United States (3 May 1803) for 80 million francs (55 million net), a welcome addition to the reserves of the Bank of France which Bonaparte had caused to be founded in 1800.

Those in Britain who expected that peace would bring a return to prosperity were soon disillusioned. Although there was relief that Pitt's new-fangled income tax, introduced in December 1798, was abolished in 1802, there was dismay when it was found that Bonaparte would not permit British ships to trade with France or her satellites. Tempers ran particularly high when the packet-boat FAME, plying between Southampton and Jersey, was forced by a gale to shelter in Cherbourg. Under a law of 1794 by which ships carrying British goods were not permitted within four leagues of the French coast, FAME was impounded and her crew imprisoned. The total tonnage of shipping leaving British ports showed a steady decrease. In 1801, the last year of war, it had been 1,958,373 tons; in 1802 it fell, despite an early increase, to 1,895,116 and in 1803 to 1,788,768 tons.

While the trading community was discovering that peace was no better than war, French foreign policy was causing increasing disquiet. Bonaparte's acceptance of the presidency of the Italian Republic while negotiations were in progress at Amiens had not been a promising start and between August and September Elba, Piedmont and Parma were successively annexed to France. French intrigues in Turkey, Egypt, the Barbary States, the Ionian Isles and even as far away as Muscat, raised great alarm in England.

On her side Britain had fulfilled the whole of her obligations under the Treaty with the single exception of the evacuation of Malta. Since even the Czar was now urging Britain not to leave the island, it was decided to postpone the garrison's departure until the European situation was clarified. British protests in Paris about French moves in Italy and particularly the reoccupation of Switzerland were met with bland assertions that the Treaty of Amiens made no mention of Piedmont or Switzerland. These were coupled with increasingly strident denunciations about British perfidy over Malta.

The fact was that Britain and France held diametrically opposed views about how the treaty should be interpreted. The instructions given to the French ambassador in London stressed that it was his task 'to prevent on any occasion any intervention by the British government in continental affairs.' At the same time the British ambassador to Paris was authorized

> *to state most distinctly His Majesty's determination never to forego his right of interference in the affairs of the continent on every occasion in which the interests of his own dominions [which included Hanover] or those of Europe in general appear to require it.*

By the New Year of 1803 few in Britain believed that the peace could or should be maintained. In March the King's Speech drew Parliament's attention to the size of the French armaments and the Lords and Commons responded by approving the re-embodiment of the militia. The strength of the regular army was increased, at least on paper, to 120,000 and the establishment of the navy was raised from 30,000 to 50,000 seamen and marines. Bonaparte replied with a tirade, lasting two hours, against the British ambassador.

Despite her retention of Malta, Britain was sure of her moral ground and on 10 May made a last gesture to peace. The ambassador offered that Malta should be evacuated as soon as an alternative base could be constructed on Lampedusa. Britain would also recognize the Republic of Italy and the annexation of Piedmont, provided that compensation was found elsewhere for the King of Sardinia. In return she required that French troops should leave Holland and Switzerland.

Although Bonaparte and Talleyrand, his Foreign Minister, were anxious to postpone the renewal of the war until the 23 new battleships were ready, no reply was vouchsafed to this proposal and the ambassador set off for home. On 17 May Britain declared war and seized all merchantmen in British harbours. The first shots were fired on the following day when the frigate DORIS engaged a French convoy in the Channel.

CHAPTER III
1803–1807

Emperor of the French

'Glory can only be won where there is danger.'
NAPOLEON I, 14 NOVEMBER 1806

Britain's declaration of war caught Bonaparte on the wrong foot. He had overestimated the amount of provocation that Addington's government would tolerate and he had not been sufficiently accommodating to induce Britain to give up Malta, the vital base for naval operations in the Mediterranean. The French navy was in a depressed state. Only 13 of her 42 battleships were in commission and she had a squadron in the West Indies of which one third-rater and four frigates were captured before the end of 1803. Britain, by contrast, was more prepared than she customarily was at the outbreak of a war and had 55 ships of the line in commission.

Since France had an unassailable army and an inferior navy while Britain had a negligible army and an overwhelming navy, there was little belligerency in the first two years of the new war. Britain swept up St Lucia, Tobago, Surinam, Demerara and Essequibo (the last three being Dutch) in the West Indies. She also clamped a blockade on the French-held coasts and the new blockade was a far more effective affair than that maintained between 1793 and 1801. Now, under Admiral Cornwallis, there were heavy squadrons off the French bases. Only bad weather could drive them away and even then they made only the minimal withdrawal possible. The squadron watching Brest, for example, withdrew not to Spithead but only to the shelter of Torbay where they remained as short a time as possible.

There was little that France could do to hurt Britain but Mortier's corps was sent to occupy Hanover. This had only a small effect on British trade, which merely moved further east from the Hanoverian ports, but had the unforeseen advantage that it added to the British army 12,000 good troops of all arms, since the best of the Hanoverian army made its way to Britain and was formed into the King's German Legion. The closing of French-held ports to British trade caused some temporary loss of trade to Britain; exports fell from £25½ million to £20½ million in 1803 but with the Baltic and the Levant still open recovered to £23¼ million by 1805. At the same time a series of good harvests brought down the price of bread and obviated the need to buy much corn abroad.

The only way in which Bonaparte could defeat Britain, therefore, was to invade her and a month after the declaration of war he ordered the *Grande Armée* to assemble on the Channel coast and to begin training for a seaborne operation. Although work had begun on building a fleet of invasion craft before the Peace of Amiens, it had been stopped in 1801 and those craft already built had been allowed to decay. Only 28 *chaloupes-cannonières* (gun brigs) and 193 gunboats were found to be seaworthy, and having given his personal attention to suitable designs, the First Consul gave orders for the construction of 2,000 light craft.

If, as is sometimes suggested, Bonaparte had no intention of invading England but merely used the preparations to conceal his real intention of striking at Austria, it was certainly the most elaborate deception exercise in history. The harbours of Boulogne, Ambleteuse, Étaples and Wimereux were rebuilt and extended at enormous expense. Improvements in the roads between the Channel ports and Paris, where the second wave of invasion troops was assembled, cost 20 million francs, while no money was allocated to the roads which the army would need to march from the Channel to Germany. The expenditure in money and manpower on the building of landing craft was itself very considerable. By 8 August 1805 the number of boats, for the most part specially built, assembled at the Channel ports amounted to:

18 *prames* (3-masted ships, 110 ft long) each capable of transporting				120	soldiers
320 gun brigs	,,	,,	,,	130	,,
572 gun boats	,,	,,	,,	100	,,
349 pinnaces	,,	,,	,,	60	,,

In addition there were 405 horse transports, 10 *paquebots*, 81 converted fishing-boats and smaller numbers of bomb ketches, sloops and caiques. In all there was transport for 167,590 men and 9,149 horses in a single lift.

How this miscellaneous collection of vessels would have fared had it ever put to sea must be a matter for speculation. The best-known comment—that of Lord St Vincent—that 'I do not say that the French will not come. I only say they will not come by sea', is only what might be expected of a First Lord of the Admiralty speaking in public. Lord Keith, Commander-in-Chief in the North Sea and thus responsible for the defence of the Straits of Dover, was much less positive. Writing confidentially to

the Duke of York, he said that it was possible that:

37 View of the port and harbour of Boulogne on the departure of the fleet, 16 August 1803

a fleet or squadron may get out of Brest unperceived and watch for an opportunity for running up to the Downs or Margate roads, in which case it might be superior to our squadron long enough to cover the landing of any extent of force from the opposite coast.

Keith gave this opinion in October 1803 when the French navy was comparatively weak. By 1805, when the landing craft were ready and in position, France could call upon 70 or 80 ships of the line. As soon as the war had been resumed Bonaparte had called on Spain to provide him with 15 ships of the line under the terms of the Treaty of San Ildefonso (1796). Madrid was unwilling to comply and compromised by sending to France a monthly subsidy of £240,000. She could find this sum only by importing precious metals from her South American colonies. Britain, led once more by William Pitt, was determined to stop this massive aid to her enemy and in 1804 a force of frigates under Commodore Graham Moore, brother to Sir John, was despatched to intercept the annual convoy. On 5 October

38 Frederick Augustus, Duke of York. *Painting by Henry Wyatt*

Moore came up with the *flotta* and informed the Spanish admiral that 'his orders were to detain the squadron, and that it was his wish to execute these orders without bloodshed, but that the Spanish admiral's determination must be instantly made.' The Spanish answer being 'unsatisfactory', Moore opened fire and after one of the Spanish frigates had blown up the other three surrendered. Their cargo was valued at a million pounds, but since Britain was not at war with Spain it was ruled that prize money was not payable, the money going to the (British) Crown. Even after this high-handed action it took the Spanish government two months to decide to declare war on Britain. More than 30 ships of the line (of which more than 20 were fit for sea) were added to Bonaparte's fleet, giving it an effective strength of about 75 battleships and thus a force equal in numbers to that available to defend the British Isles.

Bonaparte's plan for concentrating his fleet in the West Indies so that it could be used *en masse* to escort the landing craft across the Straits of Dover has frequently been criticized as being a soldier's crude attempt to impose a landsman's thinking on his admirals. It is hard to see what other plan was open to him. He was faced with the problem of gathering together squadrons which were scattered as far apart as Toulon, Cartagena, Cadiz, Rochefort, Brest, Antwerp and the Texel and all of which were marked down by powerful British forces. His solution was to rely on the vastness of the oceans and the extremely poor communications available to his enemy. His hope was that while his own ships would concentrate, the Royal Navy would scatter and this hope was not altogether disappointed. It was frequently possible for his ships to slip out of their ports unobserved and once they had done so the British would have to search for them. There were a number of possible destinations for which any single French squadron might make—Ireland, Egypt, the West Indies, the North Sea, the English Channel, the Indian Ocean—and the decision as to which way to pursue them would have to be taken, on the slightest evidence, by the British commander on the spot, who would not be able to consult with either the Admiralty in London or the commanders of other squadrons at sea. It was inevitable that some of them would guess wrong, as Lord Bridport had done in 1796 when he concentrated the Channel Fleet on the approaches to Ireland while Bruix was making for the Mediterranean (see p. 46). Thus, while the French would be working to a prearranged plan and knew where they were to meet, the British were working on a number of unconcerted guesses of which some must, inevitably, be wrong and lead to a number of their ships searching vast stretches of empty sea. The fact that Bonaparte's plan did not work was partly bad luck and partly because at a vital moment his own nerve failed.

The first moves went well. Missiessy, with five of the line, got clean away from Rochefort in January 1805 and sailed to the West Indies where he was to wait for the Toulon squadron. The latter also put to sea under Admiral Villeneuve but was driven back to port by a gale while Nelson with the blockading squadron was vainly searching for him in the Levant. Villeneuve slipped out again in March and this time got through the Straits of Gibraltar (8 April), picked up some Spanish ships from Cadiz and by mid-May was at Martinique with 20 of the line and eight frigates. Unfortunately by that time Missiessy, thinking from the delay that Villeneuve was not going to the West Indies, had returned to the eastern Atlantic. On the other hand Nelson had again searched the Levant for the Toulon squadron and had returned to the west. It was not until 11 May that he learned from a British officer in the Portuguese service that Villeneuve had gone to the Caribbean.

39 Admiral P. C. J. B.
Villeneuve

By that time Bonaparte had lost his chance: 21 of the line under Admiral
Ganteaume were ready at Brest but their orders were to get to sea without
fighting an action. As it happened the Channel Fleet had had to detach ships
to escort a troop convoy and the blockading squadron off Brest consisted of
only 15 battleships. Ganteaume telegraphed (by semaphore) for permission
to engage. 'Success is not doubtful. I await your orders.' Bonaparte replied:
'A naval victory in existing circumstances could lead to nothing. Keep but
one end in view—to fulfil your mission. Get to sea without an action.' The
fleeting opportunity passed. The Channel Fleet was reinforced and the
Brest squadron was never again to have a chance to join in the great
combination.

Villeneuve achieved little in the West Indies. He captured 14 ships
loaded with sugar and seized 'H.M.S. Diamond Rock', a tiny island held by

the Royal Navy, a mile from the French island of Martinique. On 10 June he set sail for Europe when he heard that Nelson with ten of the line and three frigates had reached Barbados. Making for Ferrol, Villeneuve met a British squadron under Sir Robert Calder on 22 July. In a scrappy action fought in intermittent mist Calder, with 15 of the line against 20, captured two Spanish battleships and inflicted much damage, forcing the Combined Squadron into Vigo. From the British point of view it was far from being a discreditable affair and Calder believed that he had won a substantial victory. It was not enough for the navy or for public opinion in Britain. The admiral, a grasping and unpopular man, was brought before a court martial and sentenced to be severely reprimanded for 'not having done his utmost to renew the engagement, and to take and destroy every ship of the enemy.'

Villeneuve was ordered to pick up the Ferrol squadron, which would make his battleship strength up to 29, and sail northward to join five ships from Rochefort which were already at sea, and, if it could slip out, the Brest squadron. He was then to make his way round the north of Scotland and rendezvous with the ships from the Texel. He would thus, even without the Brest squadron, have more than 40 of the line which would be amply sufficient to overpower the 11 battleships with which Keith was defending the northern approaches to the invasion coast. On 16 July Bonaparte urged him to 'make yourself master of the Straits of Dover, even if it is only for four or five days.' Villeneuve actually succeeded in putting to sea with his own and the Ferrol squadron on 13 August, thus missing a further message from Bonaparte which enjoined him to 'Sail! Lose not a moment; enter the channel with my assembled squadrons. England is ours. We are all ready, everything is embarked. Show yourself for twenty-four hours and all will be over.'

Villeneuve failed to join the Rochefort squadron but he did meet a Danish merchant ship from which he gathered a story, carefully planted by a British officer, that a British fleet of 23 ships was bearing down on him. He took advantage of a discretionary clause in his orders and made for Cadiz. The Rochefort squadron stayed at sea for a time and caused much damage to British trading vessels. They also took the CALCUTTA (50), a converted Indiaman, which fought a hopeless battle to enable the convoy she was escorting to escape, but from the end of August the invasion of England was no longer a practicable operation.

*   *   *

While the invasion preparations were being made, Bonaparte was again altering the French constitution. Since August 1802 he had been Consul for life, an appointment ratified by plebiscite, and in the following year his effigy had appeared on the coinage. There was, however, no provision for a successor and the danger of France being plunged into anarchy should the

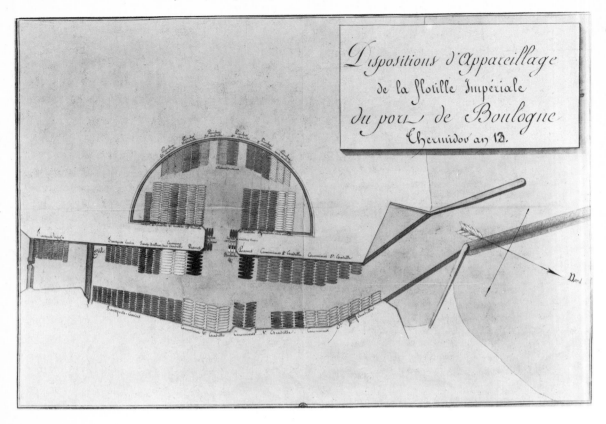

Dispositions d'Appareillage de la flotille Impériale du port de Boulogne Thermidor an 13.

40 Mooring plan of invasion craft in the port of Boulogne, 1804

Consul die was highlighted by the discovery of a conspiracy against his life in which the leading figure was Georges Cadoudal, a survivor from the Vendéan leaders. Although predominantly royalist, the plot had republican supporters, among them General Pichegru, who had returned secretly from exile. Cadoudal was executed, Pichegru was found strangled in his cell, and a determined attempt was made to implicate Moreau, the victor of Hohenlinden and Bonaparte's only rival for military fame. He was aquitted by a court but a new verdict was demanded and, reluctantly, a sentence of two years' imprisonment was substituted. The Consul altered this to banishment. This tampering with the courts was intensely unpopular, and to divert public attention Bonaparte invented another threat. He ordered the arrest of the Duc d'Enghien, great-grandson of the famous Prince de Condé and a cousin of the Bourbons, on the grounds that he was preparing to lead an *emigré* invasion of France. D'Enghien, who had neither the intention nor the means for such an operation, was quietly living with a lady at Etterheim in neutral Baden when troops and *gendarmes* sallied over the frontier, seized him and took him to Vincennes. After a hasty trial, he was shot at 2 am on 21 March 1803, an act so unprincipled that it shocked every government in Europe.

This demonstration of the transience of human life was used to persuade the Senate to suggest that the Consulship should become hereditary. Dissatisfied, Bonaparte replied by asking the Senate to 'make known the whole of its intentions'. The Senate took the hint and on 3 May 1804 proclaimed: 'The government of the republic is now entrusted to an emperor. Napoleon Bonaparte, first consul, is Emperor of the French.' On the following day 18 of the most notable generals were promoted to be Marshals of the Empire. Four years later most of them were created dukes.

In England Pitt was pondering the problem of how to defeat the new French empire. He realized that Britain could never win the war by her unaided efforts and that the main burden of land fighting must be borne by continental allies. France, drawing on a population of 30 million, had an army of 446,000 men. The United Kingdom, with a population of 15 million, had an army of only 160,000 and this could not be substantially increased since conscription was politically unthinkable and recruiting was certain to be poor because enlistment entailed a high risk of being sent to die of fever in the Caribbean. Since 65,000 British troops were required to garrison the colonies and as many more were needed to guard the home islands and keep the peace in endemically turbulent Ireland (which nevertheless provided a high proportion of the army's recruits), it was clear that no substantial expeditionary force could be employed on the Continent. Pitt, therefore, set about building a third coalition against France.

Czar Alexander was very ready to ally himself with Britain. He had been outraged by the murder of the Duc d'Enghien and already saw himself as the enlightened liberator of western Europe. Russia could produce an army of half a million men (including 100,000 Cossack irregulars) but could not afford to put them into the field. Pitt was quite willing to provide a substantial subsidy. Gustavus Adolphus IV of Sweden was also ready to fight the French. The king detested Napoleon in a way that was scarcely sane, indeed he was becoming increasingly unbalanced on a wide range of subjects. Unfortunately neither Russia nor Sweden had a common frontier with any French possession and it would be impossible to deploy their troops against France unless Austria and, if possible, Prussia could be induced to join the coalition.

After two humiliating defeats in the past decade many Austrians were unwilling to try conclusions with France again at least until the reform of the army was completed. Moreover the economic state of the empire was such that the military budget had been cut from 87 million florins (1801) to $34\frac{1}{2}$ million in 1804. It was not until Napoleon had affronted the Emperor by being crowned King of Italy at Milan (25 May) and annexing Genoa to France (4 June) that Francis decided to ally Austria with Russia and Britain on 9 August 1805. Britain agreed to pay the Austrians, as they had the Russians, $£1\frac{1}{4}$ million for every 100,000 men.

41 *Right* Alexander I, Czar of all the Russias. *Painting by Baron François Pascal Simon Gérard*

42 *Opposite Page* Francis II of the Holy Roman Empire, later Francis I of Austria. *Painting by A. Einslie*

Austria's adherence to the Third Coalition encouraged the Czar to make strategic plans on the grandest scale. On the right of the line a Russo-Swedish army of 36,000 men was to march westward from Swedish Pomerania. On their left 40,000 Russians would move parallel to them with the support of the Prussian army. 70,000 Austrians and 50,000 Russians were to advance up the Danube with their flanks guarded by a further 22,000 Austrians in the Tyrol. The main Austrian effort, however, was to be made in Italy where 90,000 men were to drive westward across the Adige and reconquer Lombardy in cooperation with a force of 25,000 Russians (from Corfu) and 9,000 British (from Malta) who were to march north from Naples.

In the unlikely event of the movements in this grandiose scheme being coordinated, France might have been overwhelmed but it was wrecked from the outset by the timidity of the King of Prussia who preferred to accept Hanover as a bribe from Napoleon rather than the uncertain fruits of war against France. Alexander's master plan was therefore reduced to the advance up the Danube and the two operations in Italy.

Napoleon was slow to believe that he was threatened by so massive an alliance. On 27 July 1805 he wrote to tell his viceroy in Italy that nothing was to be feared from Austria. On 22 August he was still reckoning on the arrival of Villeneuve's fleet in the Straits of Dover. It is certain that he would not still be intent on sending 160,000 men across the Channel if he expected to be attacked by Austria and Russia. The first hint of alarm came on 23 August when he received a demand from the Neapolitan court that French troops should evacuate their territory. At the same time he heard that 6,000 British troops had reached Malta. Since Britain and Naples alone could not take any effective action in Italy, they must have Austrian support. On 24 August Napoleon sent an ultimatum to Vienna requiring a reduction in the Austrian garrisons in Venetia and the Tyrol. Two days later orders were given for the *Grande Armée* to march to Germany.

The move of 176,000 men and 286 guns from the Channel coast to the upper Danube was an unparalleled administrative feat. No other army could have performed it with such speed and efficiency, although the problems were eased because only eight days' rations were carried on waggons and these were not issued until contact was made with the enemy. Up to that point the troops were fed by foraging. It was a movement inconceivable to the nearest Austrian commander. The 53-year-old General Mack had shown himself a competent staff officer in the Flanders campaign of 1792–4 but his only essay as an independent commander had been when he led the ill-starred Neapolitan foray to Rome in 1799. He had developed an over-riding belief in the importance of moving quickly, and at the head of 60,000 men he crossed the Austrian border into Bavaria, a French ally, on 10 September. Regardless of the promise of 100,000 Russians who were moving through Poland and Moravia to support him, he hustled his army to Ulm, 75 miles west of Munich, and took up a position on the Danube and Iller rivers. It had never occurred to him that the *Grande Armée* could be near him and he was astonished when on 8 October Murat's cavalry, supported by two corps of infantry, cut his communications with Vienna. His efforts to escape from the trap were largely unavailing. One division of 6,000 men slipped through before the French noose tightened and the Archduke Ferdinand fought his way out with 1,500 cavalry, but 8,000 surrendered at Nördlingen and 6,000 at Memmingen. The only serious fighting took place when Ney stormed the bridge at Elchingen where he captured 3,000 Austrians. By 15 October the remainder of Mack's army was penned into Ulm where, after four days' bombardment, they surrendered, 33,000 strong.

The disaster at Ulm finally ruptured the Czar's masterplan. There were only 48,000 Austrian troops to defend Vienna and as only 30,000 Russians, under Kutusov, were within even distant reach, a large draft had to be made on the 90,000 Austrians in Italy. This meant that the Anglo-Russian advance from Naples would have been abortive even had they succeeded in landing before 20 November. In the event they advanced to the line of the Garigliano where they stayed until the new year. They then re-embarked without having fired a shot. The Russians returned to Corfu, the British to garrison Sicily.

The adherence of Naples to the coalition did make one significant contribution to the course of the war. On 14 September Napoleon sent orders to Villeneuve to break out of Cadiz, pass Gibraltar, pick up the Cartagena squadron and transport French troops to Naples. Delayed by adverse winds, it was 18 October before the Franco-Spanish fleet could start to leave the harbour. They mustered 33 of the line (18 French and 15 Spanish) with five French frigates and two brigs. Outside lay Nelson with 27 of the line, four frigates, a schooner and a cutter. Nelson's intention was well-defined:

> *The business of an English Commander-in-Chief is first to bring the enemy's fleet to battle on the most advantageous terms to himself (I mean that of laying his ships well on board the enemy as expeditiously as possible), and secondly to continue them there without separating until the business is decided.*

On the morning of 21 October he wrote in his diary:

> *At daylight, saw the enemy's Combined Fleet from east to ESE; bore away: made the signal for Order of Sailing and Prepare for Battle . . . May the Great God whom I worship, grant my country, and for the benefit of Europe in general, a great and glorious victory; and may no misconduct in anyone tarnish it.*

As the Signal Officer wrote later:

> *At about a quarter to noon his lordship came up to me on the poop and said, 'I wish*

43 Napoleon receiving the surrender of General Mack at Ulm, 20 October 1805. *Painting by Charles Thévenin*

44 Plan of the commencement of the Battle of Trafalgar

*to say to the fleet "*ENGLAND CONFIDES THAT EVERY MAN WILL DO HIS DUTY*"'; and he added: 'You must be very quick, for I have one more to make, which is for Close Action.' I replied, 'If your lordship will permit me to substitute* expects *for* confides, *the signal will soon be completed, because the word "*expects*" is in the vocabulary and "*confides*" must be spelt.' His lordship replied, in haste and with seeming satisfaction: 'That will do, Pasco, make it directly.'*

When the message was seen in ROYAL SOVEREIGN, Vice-Admiral Collingwood remarked 'What is Nelson signalling about? We all know what we have to do.' By that time Nelson had ordered Lieutenant Pasco to 'make the signal for Close Action and *keep it up.*'

By nightfall the Combined Fleet was back in Cadiz reduced from 33 to 11 of the line. Four more had escaped to the south. Villeneuve was a prisoner on board CONQUEROR (74) but Nelson and 449 of his men were dead.

The British were only able to retain five of their prizes, one of these being *Swiftsure* (74), which had been captured by Ganteaume in 1801. Twelve more ships were destroyed by their captors, wrecked in the storm that followed or, in the case of *Achille* (74), caught fire and lost. One of the ships

45 *Above* The end of the action at Trafalgar. *Painted under the direction of G. Thomas, R N, who was present as an officer of HMS* NEPTUNE

46 *Left* HMS VICTORY breaking the Franco-Spanish line at the beginning of the Battle of Trafalgar. *Watercolour by N. Pocock*

47 The death of Nelson at the Battle of Trafalgar. *Painting by Denis Dighton*

wrecked was the *Berwick* which had been taken by the French in the Mediterranean in 1795.

A gallant counter-attack carried out on 22 October by three French and two Spanish ships recaptured the *Santa Ana* (112). On board her was a young officer, son of the Spanish rear-admiral, who ten years later as Major-General Don Miguel Alava was to be the only man to fight at both Trafalgar and Waterloo.

The four ships which succeeded in escaping to the south were unfortunate. Their commander, Rear-Admiral Dumanoir, decided to make for Rochefort where they could be repaired. On 2 November they fell in with the frigate PHOENIX (36) which cleverly led them on to a squadron of four British third-rates under Commodore Richard Strachan, thereafter known as 'the delighted Sir Dicky'. Dumanoir did all that he could to escape but on 4 November decided that he could only stand and fight. This he did with the utmost gallantry although all his ships had been seriously damaged at Trafalgar and his opponents were undamaged. As Strachan reported, 'The French fought to admiration and did not surrender until their ships were unmanageable.' All four were brought into Plymouth and taken into the Royal Navy where one of them, the *Duguay-Trouay* (74), renamed IMPLACABLE, survived until 1949.

Three months later the French navy suffered another blow. On 6 February 1806 Rear-Admiral Duckworth found a French squadron lying unprepared off St Domingue. By noon three ships of the line had surrendered and two more, one of them the *Impérial* (120), '*le plus fort et le plus beau vaisseau qui eût jamais été construit dans aucun pays du monde*', were on the rocks.

48 Don Miguel Alava, a midshipman at Trafalgar and a Major-General at Waterloo. *Painting by George Dawe*

49 Nelson's funeral procession on the River Thames. *Painting by D. Turner*

As the First Lord of the Admiralty wrote:

Thanks to Sir Robert Calder's action, the splendid victory off Trafalgar, the valiant achievement of Sir Richard Strachan [and] Sir John Duckworth's brilliant action off San Domingo . . . the enemy lost in the short space of six months 31 sail of the line, 5 frigates and 5 corvettes.

The French navy was reduced to 32 of the line and although 21 more were building and would be completed by 1809 it was clear that unless large numbers of ships could be acquired from other nations, the invasion of England would not be a practicable policy for some years to come.

* * *

Mack's surrender at Ulm left Napoleon with a quandary. His army, having marched 500 miles at a steady 15 miles a day, was tired and the weather, since it was already mid-October, was certain to deteriorate. There was a good case to be made for suspending the campaign until the following spring but to do so would sacrifice much of the advantage already gained. Although the northern Austrian army was now negligible, Russian strength was beginning to accumulate in the eastern parts of the Hapsburg Empire and delay would enable the Archduke Charles to bring a large detachment of the army in Italy round for the defence of Vienna. It was not impossible that Prussia would join the coalition since she had made bellicose gestures when some French troops had marched through her detached territory of Ansbach. Napoleon decided to press on.

With the assistance of large quantities of supplies captured at Ulm the *Grande Armée* marched eastward only a week after Mack's surrender. Corps were detached to hold the Alpine passes so that the Archduke would have to make a long detour to the east before he could join the northern army, but the main body advanced against Kutusov who with 27,000 Russians and 20,000 Austrians was on the line of the Inn to the north of Salzburg. Determined not to be trapped, the Russian general made a fighting withdrawal during which he succeeded in mauling Mortier's corps at Dürnstein on 11 November. Resisting Austrian pressure to defend Vienna, he was intending to fall back on Brünn (Brno) where he hoped to be joined by another 50,000 Russians under Büxhowden. The French, however, were much stronger in numbers and were able to move faster. Kutusov only escaped because Murat, commanding the French advance guard, behaved in a way that foreshadowed the behaviour of General Mark Clark

50 Charles, Archduke of Austria.

51 Marshall Mikhail
Ilarionovich Kutuzov,
Prince of Smolensk.
*Drawing by L. de Saint
Aubin*

in Italy 139 years later. Instead of closing the trap on Kutusov, Murat was
lured away to have the honour of capturing Vienna. Even though he was
Napoleon's brother-in-law, he did not escape an imperial thunderbolt:
'You have lost me two days in order to acquire glory for yourself by being
the first to enter Vienna. Glory can only be won where there is danger; there is none in entering an undefended capital.'

The French entered Brünn on 19 November, and Kutusov, who had
only been joined by the first of Büxhowden's divisions on that day, gave
orders for a further retreat. Unfortunately his headquarters at Olmütz
(Olomouc) were joined two days later by both the Czar and the Emperor of
Austria. From that moment, although the titular command remained with
Kutusov, the effective direction of the armies fell to the Czar, whose
military experience qualified him to drill a battalion on a parade ground.
His ambition was to defeat Napoleon in a great battle and, with the support
of Francis, he insisted that the retreat be halted and preparations made for
an offensive.

Nothing could have suited Napoleon better. Despite the capture of stores at Ulm and Vienna the *Grande Armée* was at the end of its administrative tether. Its position was already dangerously exposed and the morale of the troops was falling fast as they saw themselves marching endlessly eastward into increasingly inhospitable country. Stragglers were counted by the thousand and despair was gaining a hold on those who stayed in the ranks. As Baron Thiébault wrote, 'In ten years of fighting many of our officers had been risking their lives in one battle and another. The thought of making their wills had never occurred to them. Now they started to make them.'

Being anxious to provoke an attack, Napoleon allowed news of this dissatisfaction to reach the allied camp. He replied to peace feelers and did what he could to let the Czar get the impression that one determined push would send the French back in disorder.

Alexander rose to the bait. With the arrival of the Russian Imperial Guard, 10,000 strong, the Austro-Russian army totalled 89,000 men and, on 27 November they started to move westward, despite Kutusov's protests. The French advance units fell back to a position near the village of Austerlitz (Slavkov), thirteen miles east of Brünn, which Napoleon had selected for a defensive battle.

The Austerlitz position had a front of six miles and the French army could deploy 60,000 men. Two thirds of these Napoleon posted on his left which was secured on a fifty-foot mound crowned by a chapel and known to the French as the Santon. The right, which followed the marshy Goldbach stream, was entrusted to Soult's corps of 20,000 men with, on the extreme flank, 7,000 men of Davout's corps which was arriving by divisions from Vienna. The French artillery amounted to 139 guns of which 20, captured Austrian pieces, were placed in earthworks on top of the Santon.

The allies had very little information about Napoleon's position or about the numbers available to him. They did, however, have a plan which had been devised by General Weyrother, an Austrian staff officer, in whom the Czar had complete confidence. The idea was to wheel four columns totalling 50,000 men across the Goldbach so as to emerge on the Brünn–Olmütz road behind the Santon. A fifth column would act as a pivot for this flanking manoeuvre, while the remaining 13,000 men would hold the front to the east of the Santon until their commander, Prince Bagration, saw that the main attack was succeeding. Then they were to storm the Santon. The only reserve, the Russian Guard, was also held on the right.

Provided that the French were obliging enough to keep still, Weyrother's plan might have worked had it been fully understood by the column commanders. In fact he issued it on the evening of 1 December at a conference at which Kutusov was seen to be asleep. The written

instructions, running to several closely written sheets, then had to be translated into Russian and issued to the column commanders. Since the translation was not completed until 3 am, it is not surprising that some Russian generals did not have their written orders when the battle started and their subordinates were in total ignorance of the plan.

As might be expected there was chaos when the allied army started to move at first light on 2 December, the more so as some divisions had to cross the advance of others. With a thick mist over the Goldbach, the French resistance was unexpectedly heavy and soon all the four assaulting columns were irretrievably jammed in the approaches to the stream.

At 7.30 the 'sun of Austerlitz' broke through, clearing the mist and allowing Napoleon to see a wide gap between the two wings of the attacking army. Into this gap—the low heights known as the Pratzen plateau—he advanced two of Soult's divisions. Meanwhile, on the southern flank Davout's men were driving in the flank of the allies who were trying to turn Soult's right on the Goldbach. To the north, Bagration,

52 *Opposite Page* Marshal Nicolas Jean de dieu Soult.

53 Marshal Louis Nicolas Davout.

113

54 *Opposite Page* Marshal Jean-Baptiste Bernadotte, later Prince Royal of Sweden

too impatient to wait for the allied attack to succeed, started making a series of abortive attacks on the Santon.

Once Soult held the Pratzen heights, Napoleon swung his left forward. This mass of men, the corps of Lannes and Bernadotte backed by Murat's cavalry and the Imperial Guard, swept Bagration's corps away and came down on the rear of the confused jumble of 50,000 men trying to cross the Goldbach. A counter attack by the Russian Guard achieved some initial success but was broken after desperate fighting.

Few allied divisions left the field as fighting formations and although the story that 20,000 Russians were drowned when the ice on the Satschan lake gave way under them was an invention of Napoleon's *Bulletin*, their losses were terrible. 24,000 Russians and 3,500 Austrians were casualties, 11,000 being taken prisoner. The French lost 8,000, of whom 1,305 were killed.

The Czar was determined to continue with the war but withdrew his army eastward. The Emperor Francis saw no alternative to seeking a peace. Austria could hardly look for easy terms and in the treaty which was eventually signed at Pressburg (Bratislava) on 27 December 1805 she lost Venezia to the Kingdom of Italy and Dalmatia to France. She also had to hand Tyrol and Vorarlberg to Bavaria as part of a reshuffle of German territory in which the Electors of Bavaria and Württemberg became kings. Both these new sovereigns were promptly bound to the French emperor by marriages. The King of Bavaria had to give a daughter to Eugène Beauharnais, Napoleon's stepson, and a niece to Marshal Berthier who was elevated to the principality of Neufchâtel. The daughter of the King of Württemberg was married off to the raffish and incompetent Jerome Bonaparte, who already had an American wife. Thus Napoleon's brother became the stepson-in-law of the Princess Royal of England. At the same time the Margraves of Baden and Hesse-Darmstadt were promoted to the status of Grand Dukes, and south Germany, hitherto an Austrian sphere of influence, became a French protectorate and was garrisoned by 192,000 French troops who naturally lived at the expense of the inhabitants. Further north Prussia was rewarded for her neutrality by the cession of Hanover although she had to cede Neufchâtel to Berthier, Ansbach to Bavaria and Berg and Cleves to Murat who became a Grand Duke. Further extending the French domination, Marshal Marmont occupied Dalmatia and Marshal Massena took over Naples.

Napoleon made efforts to end the war with Russia and even agreed a peace treaty with a Russian delegation in Paris. The Czar, however, refused to ratify it, preferring to make a secret agreement for mutual aid with Prussia. The terms of this pact, however, became known in London, where war had been declared on Prussia after her occupation of Hanover. They were communicated to Napoleon by the simple expedient of publishing them in the English papers.

*   *   *

William Pitt died on 23 January 1806 and a new government was formed from the Whigs, in opposition since 1783, and the less bellicose of the Tories. Known, not without derision, as the 'Ministry of all the Talents', the new Cabinet contained only one genuine talent in the person of Charles James Fox, a consistent advocate of peace. Although already a sick man he became Foreign Secretary and started negotiations. These were initially carried on through Lord Yarmouth, who had been interned in France since 1803, but he was soon joined by Lord Lauderdale who was sent to Paris for the purpose. Britain was anxious to secure the neutrality of Holland and Naples but Napoleon, while permitting Britain to retain Malta and recover Hanover, insisted that Sicily should be handed over to Naples and that the French occupation of Holland should be recognized. To emphasize the point he created his brothers, Joseph and Louis, Kings of Naples and Holland respectively. Seeing no hope for an acceptable treaty, the two plenipotentiaries asked for their passports on 9 August but not before Lord Yarmouth, in a fit of drunken loquacity, had told the Prussian ambassador of Napoleon's undertaking to restore Hanover to Britain. This setback convinced even Fox that the war must continue but his capacity as a war minister was never tested as he died in September leaving behind him a Cabinet remarkable for its ineptitude.

The continued neutrality of Prussia was far from popular in Berlin and an influential party, headed by the queen, had for some years been pressing for war against France. The news that Napoleon was prepared to rob him of newly-gained Hanover was sufficient to stir even King Frederick William to action. On 9 August he agreed to mobilise his army but then relapsed into his habitual timidity. Napoleon meanwhile was convinced that he had nothing to fear from Berlin. In mid-August he was telling Berthier to make arrangements to reduce the army's strength in Germany: 'Halt all warlike preparations and stop troop movements across the Rhine. Everyone must be ready to return to France.' It was not until 5 September that he began to concern himself with Prussian troop movements southward and ordered some preparatory countermoves.

Frederick William, having spent two months screwing up his courage, despatched an ultimatum on 1 October demanding the withdrawal of all French troops from Germany. He had not concerted this *démarche* with the Czar and, in consequence, no Russian troops were available to support Prussia. His only ally was Saxony who provided 20,000 men towards a combined army of 150,000.

Napoleon received the Prussian demand on 7 October and lost no time in punishing Frederick William's ill-timed temerity. After another splendidly conceived approach march he brought the two parts of the Prussian army to action at the twin battles of Jena and Auerstadt on 14 October. By nightfall the Prussians had lost 25,000 prisoners and 200 guns and the remnants of their army were flying in all directions. Napoleon

entered Berlin in triumph 13 days later and on 28 October 16,000 Prussians surrendered to Murat near Stettin. The French pursuit continued relentlessly, forcing Blücher with 10,000 men to surrender to Soult at Travemünde on 7 November, 24 hours before Kleist and 20,000 men capitulated to Ney at Magdeburg. There remained of the Prussian army, apart from some garrisons, a single division of 6,000 men which was protecting the royal family near Königsberg (Kaliningrad).

Russian help was, however, approaching. Two armies, 91,000 men together, were approaching under the veteran Marshal Kamenski, a 72-year-old who 'affects to imitate Suvarov and plays the antics of a semi-savage: but he has the confidence of officers and men.' What he lacked was confidence in himself and, in January, he 'went, without his shirt, into the streets, and then sent for a surgeon, pointed out all his wounds, groaned as he passed his hand over them, and insisted on a certificate of his incapacity to serve.' The command passed to General Bennigsen, a Hanoverian long settled in Russia, whose capacity for intrigue far surpassed his military talent.

After the Jena campaign and the successful pursuit of the Prussian corps, it was impossible for Napoleon to make immediate moves against the Russians. The army had outrun its supplies and the soldiers were in desperate need of winter clothing, even their summer dress being in rags. Vast requisitions were made on Prussia and in a remarkably short time 280,000 greatcoats, 250,000 pairs of boots and quantities of other supplies, including 6,000 hospital mattresses, were forthcoming. A Polish division was organized from occupied Prussian Poland and 80,000 conscripts were called to the colours. The Elector of Saxony, briskly changing sides, put his army at Napoleon's disposal and was made a king for his pains.

All this activity did not divert Napoleon from his over-riding priority of defeating Britain. He wrote constantly from Berlin and Warsaw urging his Minister of Marine to press on with the building of ships of the line and, on 21 November 1806, issued the Berlin Decrees. These laid down that all British goods found in the territory of France or her 'allies' were to be confiscated and that any ship, neutral or belligerent, trading with Britain or her colonies was to be seized. While this was no more than a repetition of the orders for the blockade of the British Isles which had been in force since 1793, the possible effect was much greater. France now controlled the entire shore of Europe from Stettin to the Dalmation coast with the exception of the coastlines of Denmark and Portugal. Britain replied with the Orders in Council (7 January 1807) declaring that any vessel carrying cargoes to or from French-held ports would be considered as fair prize.

In East Prussia the war resumed in December. On the day after Christmas the French attacked at Pultusk. The Russians defended with desperate courage and though they were eventually forced to retire they inflicted more than 3,000 casualties and the French were too exhausted to pursue them in the thick mud in which the battle was fought. Napoleon decided that further fighting would have to await the spring and retired his troops to winter quarters. There would have been no further fighting until April or May had not Ney decided on his own authority to undertake an ambitious foraging expedition towards the Russian cantonments. He was sharply repulsed but he had set off a chain reaction. Bennigsen believed that Ney's force had been the advance guard of the whole French army and counter-attacked strongly, thus forcing Napoleon to bring up his main strength. After some manoeuvring the two armies met at Preussich-Eylau (Bagrationovsk) on 7 February and in a blinding snowstorm fought each other to a standstill. The French lost 15,000 men, the Russians 18,000. A final attack by the Imperial Guard recovered, for the second time, the village of Eylau, which had been in French hands at the outset and, since Bennigsen took his army back to Königsberg to find food, Napoleon could claim a victory although his army retreated four days later. It was not a battle of which either commander could be proud.

For the four following months the armies rested and tried to feed themselves from the winter landscape. It was not until 14 May, when the French began the siege of Danzig, that any offensive move was made. In this period both sides made efforts to procure troops from their allies. The French, after much persuasion, induced Spain to provide 15,000 men for the garrison of Hanover, thus releasing French troops for service in the east. Russia and Prussia begged Britain to send an expeditionary force to the Baltic. Britain replied that her only disposable military force was a brigade of dragoons which had been promised to the King of Sweden. She sent a military mission and some inadequate subsidies.

The allies believed that Britain was betraying them. She had, they said, 'too great an interest in the protraction of the war', and pointed out that at the end of 1805 she had sent 26,000 men on an abortive expedition to Cuxhaven, withdrawing them two months later without having employed them in any way. Since that time the strength of the British army had increased from 185,000 to 200,000 and it seemed not unreasonable to suppose that a similar force could again be sent to Germany.

It was not British perfidy which prevented the despatch of an expedition. The ineptitude of the Ministry of the Talents had made it impossible. On coming to office they had found a disposable force of 40,000 men ready for any operation that offered, with a fleet of transports capable of carrying 10,000 at a time standing by. This excellent arrangement, the work of Castlereagh as Secretary for War, was immediately dispersed by the Talents on the grounds of economy. The transports were paid off and fresh ones hired to take the troops on a variety of irrelevant missions. The British garrison of Sicily was increased to 19,000 men and 8,000 were sent on an unnecessary expedition to Egypt which started with a shameful defeat by the Turks at Rosetta (31 March 1807) and ended in May with the survivors

56 Plan of the Battle of Friedland

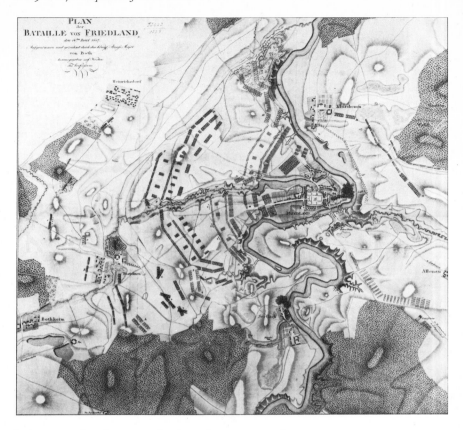

being permitted to re-embark under a convention. 10,000 men were sent to South America in a venture which culminated in Whitelock's disastrously inept attempt to storm Buenos Aires (5 July 1807) and the surrender of the whole force. 4,000 men had to be sent to India where a Whiggishly inclined general had succeeded in stirring up a mutiny by altering the head-dress of the native troops. The only gleam of hope for the British army was an action fought at Maida on 4 July 1806 where a force landed in southern Italy from Sicily had handsomely beaten a slightly larger French force. The consequence was that the British immediately re-embarked and returned to Sicily.

As it happened the presence of 25,000 British troops would have made little difference to the eastern campaign when it was resumed on 4 June. No army, however large, is proof against the incompetence of its general, and Bennigsen made every mistake that was open to him. 14 June 1807, the seventh anniversary of Marengo, found him in position in front of the town of Friedland (Pravdinsk) with little more than half his available troops. There was no need to fight there but as he said, 'false reports, with which every general is beset, had raised in me the erroneous view that Napoleon, with the greater part of his army, had taken the road to Königsberg', 27 miles to the north west. Even if he thought he was faced by only part of the French army, there can be no excuse for the way in which he deployed his own. His 46,000 men were established in a shallow arc. Behind them was a broad river crossed only by a single narrow bridge and their front was bisected by an impassable millstream. It was only after the action had started that his engineers put 'a small plank bridge' across this obstacle.

Although the Russians, 'exhausted with fatigue and unfed for twenty-four hours', put up a magnificently dogged resistance, the battle could have only one end. Napoleon attacked with 86,000 men and Ney's corps blasted its way through to Friedland town, cutting off the Russian right. The Russians lost 10,000 men and 80 guns, and though they had inflicted 12,000 casualties on the French Bennigsen had no alternative to falling back to Tilsit (Sovetsk). Two days later Soult took Königsberg and on 19 June the Czar authorized Bennigsen to ask for an armistice.

On 25 June the Czar of all the Russias and the Emperor of the French met on a flying bridge anchored midstream on the river Niemen. Alexander's first words were 'I hate the English as much as you do and I am ready to assist you in any undertaking against them.' This first meeting lasted four hours during which time the wretched King of Prussia waited on the bank in torrential rain. Eventually the two emperors 'embraced and amicably parted. On gaining the opposite banks, they again took off their hats and waved a salute.'

57 The meeting of Napoleon and Czar Alexander I on a floating bridge moored in the River Niemen at Tilsit. *After a painting by J. B. Debret*

CHAPTER IV

1807–1811

Master of Europe

'Nothing can for long withstand the fulfilment of my wishes.'
NAPOLEON I, 9 DECEMBER 1808

*T*he peace between France and Russia was signed at Tilsit on 7 July
1807 and between France and Prussia two days later. The two treaties were
very different. Prussia barely survived as an independent state and might
not have done so had it not been for the intervention of the Czar who,
nevertheless, took from her the Polish province of Bialystok. She lost all
her territory west of the Elbe and all her Polish acquisitions except for a
corridor linking Brandenburg with East Prussia. Within this corridor
Danzig was declared a free city and given a French garrison. The Prussian
army was limited to 42,000 men, all her ports were closed to British trade,
she was saddled with an indemnity of 200 million *thaler* and forced to
maintain a large army of occupation until she had discharged it. These
terms were so humiliating that a quarter of her officer corps resigned. Many
of them sought service with foreign armies, particularly that of Russia, in
which Scharnhorst and Clausewitz spent several years. Before the end of
1807 Prussia was forced to declare war on Britain.

Most of the Prussian lands west of the Elbe were combined with
Brunswick and parts of Hanover to form a Kingdom of Westphalia for
Jerome Bonaparte. Her Polish provinces, except for Bialystok and the
corridor, became the Grand Duchy of Warsaw, Napoleon's gesture to
Polish nationalism, although the King of Saxony was appointed Grand
Duke. Saxony, Bavaria, Westphalia, Württemberg, Baden, Berg, Hesse
and the greater part of Hanover (which remained in French hands) were
linked together as the Confederation of the Rhine, an agglomeration of
which Napoleon declared himself 'Protector'.

58 *Opposite Page* Privates,
Infantry of the line,
Kingdom of Italy, 1807

The treaty with Russia scarcely reflected her defeat. She ceded to France the Ionian Islands and Cattaro (Kotor), the safest harbour in the Adriatic, but obtained Bialystok. There were no other territorial adjustments but the Czar undertook to offer his mediation between France and Britain on the basis that Britain should restore all France's captured colonies. Failing Britain's agreement to these terms, Russia would join the war against her. In the meantime Russian ports would be closed to British trade. Napoleon undertook to offer his mediation to end the war between Russia and Turkey.

The Franco-Russian alliance against Britain was the most important outcome of the Tilsit settlement and it was cemented by secret clauses by which Sweden, Denmark and Portugal were to be compelled to exclude British trade and to put their fleets at Napoleon's disposal. The coercion of Sweden was to be Russia's responsibility and France would deal with the other two. In this way Britain, already at war with Turkey after her abortive Egyptian expedition, would be denied all European commerce with the trifling exception of the Sicilian trade. The Emperor wrote that he looked forward to the day when England's ships 'laden with useless wealth, wandered round the high seas, which they claim to rule, seeking from the Sound to the Hellespont a port that will receive them.'

Could these measures have been strictly enforced the British economy must eventually be strangled. One third of all her trade was with Europe, and her counter-measures, especially her restrictions on neutral ships, were likely to embroil her in another war with the United States which received 27% of her exports. There was, however, a more urgent threat to Britain. The great alliance against her could mass enough battleships to outnumber the Royal Navy. The French could now send 37 ships of the line to sea, Spain had 24, Holland 6 (apart from 2 in the East Indies) and the Russians had 36 battleships divided between the Baltic and the Black Sea. This gave Napoleon 103 ships of the line, exactly the number which the British had in commission that year. He was realistic enough to realize that the Royal Navy with its unique seagoing experience would be more than a match for any fleet of equal numbers. He believed, however, and the Admiralty in London would not have disagreed, that with a three to two superiority against it the Royal Navy would be overwhelmed. The three neutral navies had between them 45 ships of the line and these he set out to secure for his own purposes. To make up the small deficit, he initiated a huge naval building programme at all the ports he controlled. His orders were '*Tous les efforts doivent se jeter du côté de la marine.*'

Britain was fortunate that at this crisis the Ministry of the Talents had left office in March 1807 and had been succeeded by a Cabinet which, though led by the uninspired and ailing Duke of Portland, contained two active and talented men, Castlereagh as Secretary of State for War and Canning at the Foreign Office. It was less fortunate that they detested each other, but

they did manage to inject some energy into the direction of affairs. On the day after the Treaty of Tilsit was signed 7,000 men of the German Legion were landed at Stralsund to support the Swedish garrison and 18,000 reinforcements were being assembled to follow them when a more urgent objective became aparent. The first warning was a message from the Prince Regent of Portugal that he was under French pressure to surrender his fleet, but this was followed by a remarkable intelligence coup, never satisfactorily explained, whereby London was informed of the secret clauses agreed at Tilsit. It was also learned that Napoleon intended to seize the Danish fleet.

The Cabinet acted with speed and ruthlessness. On 26 July Admiral Lord Gambier sailed for the Skagerrak with 16 of the line. 18,000 troops sailed three days later and orders were hastily despatched to recall the German Legion from Stralsund. Gambier anchored off Elsinore on 3 August and for two weeks endeavoured to persuade the Danes to put their fleet into British safekeeping until the end of the war. Not unnaturally the Danes refused this demand and on 16 August the British troops began to disembark. There was an unimportant skirmish in which the British were commanded by an almost unknown major-general called Sir Arthur Wellesley and Copenhagen was invested. As the Danes still refused to part with their fleet, the capital was bombarded for three days and much of it burnt. On 5 September the Danes accepted the inevitable. 13 of the line and 14 frigates were sailed to English ports and the warships which were not ready for sea were burnt, together with such naval stores as could not be loaded on to British ships. Then the fleet and army sailed for home. Napoleon had been deprived of 20 of the line. Only one Danish capital ship, the *Prinz Christian Frederic* (74), escaped, being away from Copenhagen. She was sunk by two British third-rates off the coast of Jutland in the following year.

Napoleon displayed a characteristically self-righteous indignation over this display of almost Napoleonic ruthlessness on the part of the British. He had been forestalled. As early as 31 July he had told the Danish ambassador that his country must choose between war with England and war with France. On 2 August, before he could possibly know where Gambier's squadron was bound, he appointed Bernadotte to command the army to invade Denmark. It can have been little consolation to the Emperor that Swedish Stralsund surrendered to Marshal Mortier on 20 August. The evidence of British determination was sufficient to make the Swedes resolve not to part with their fleet and although, in 1809, the Russians were to seize Finland, neither France nor Russia could devise a way of inducing Sweden to part with her 12 ships of the line.

While Britain was acting at Copenhagen France was putting pressure on Portugal. On 19 July she required Portugal to close her ports to British goods and ten days later orders were given for the formation at Bayonne of the *Corps d'Observation de la Gironde*. To the command of this ambiguously named body Napoleon appointed General Androche Junot, a former French ambassador to Lisbon. On 12 August an ultimatum was despatched to the Prince Regent of Portugal. He must declare war on Britain or fight France.

Prince Regent John, never a strong character, was in an intolerable dilemma. War with France would mean an army of occupation and a ban on overseas trade. War with Britain would mean blockade. In either case Portugal would be ruined and the populations of Lisbon, Coimbra and Oporto, who were dependent on imported food, would starve. He played for time, making concessions to France, encouraging the British to occupy Madeira and begging London not to impose a blockade. Both sides were inflexible. Napoleon meanwhile was negotiating with Madrid, and since actions against Portugal were always popular in Spain, it was soon agreed that Portugal should be divided between them. On 19 October the *Corps d'Observation de la Gironde* crossed into Spain. 'Our march', wrote their chief of staff, 'was the occasion for a holiday for the Spaniards along the road and a triumph for us.' Next day France declared war on Portugal.

The Prince Regent continued to wriggle. On 5 November the Tagus guns fired ineffectively at a British frigate, and on the 8th orders were given for the confiscation of all British goods and the arrest of all British subjects. The ambassador asked for his passport and on 10 November nine Russian battleships anchored in the Tagus. This was a coincidence. Although Russia had declared war on Britain at the beginning of the month, this squadron, which was sailing from the Mediterranean to the Baltic, had been driven into Lisbon by a gale. Moreover the Russian Navy, which in the days of Catherine the Great had been largely British trained, was strongly anglophile, and the admiral who arrived so inopportunely had actually served in the Royal Navy. He regarded himself as being in a neutral port and announced his intention of staying there. Six British ships of the line soon arrived to blockade the mouth of the Tagus and the British ambassador went on board one of them.

Meanwhile Junot was marching across Spain. He reached Ciudad Rodrigo on the Portuguese border on 19 October and there received an order urging him to hurry but to take the road up the Tagus valley. On the Emperor's map such a road existed but there was no trace of it on the ground. Not for the last time Napoleon had made a serious misjudgment about the topography of the Peninsula. A ragged vanguard, 1,500 out of 25,000, tottered into Lisbon on 30 November, 'without a single gun or a cartridge that would fire . . . fagged out, ghastly objects, no longer even with the strength to march to the beat of the drum.' As they came over the hills leading to the city they saw on the horizon the Portuguese fleet escorting a host of merchantmen. With 24 hours to spare Prince John had decided to go to Brazil with his court until the storm blew over. He was accompanied not only by his own ships but by a British squadron. In the following week the rest of the *Corps d'Observation de la Gironde* straggled into Lisbon, 'some falling dead at the gates of the city.'

Napoleon had failed to obtain possession of the three neutral fleets, but by occupying Denmark and Portugal he had shut every port in Europe to British trade except those of Sweden, which were not closed until 1810. The situation was such that it should have been only a question of time before Britain collapsed from economic atrophy. The actual effects were not as serious as might have been expected. British exports, £41 million in 1806, fell only to £37¼ million by 1808. The export of raw cotton was particularly badly affected, falling from 143,000 sacks to 23,000. There was much suffering in the manufacturing districts and this was accentuated by poor harvests which drove the price of corn up from 66s to 94s a quarter. There was some rioting in Manchester and had this trend continued it is possible that internal dissension might have paralysed the country.

The blockade as conceived by Napoleon, however, was one which differs from those implemented in the twentieth century. His aim was to drain Britain of gold; he was quite ready to trade with her if she paid in cash. In April 1808 he wrote to the King of Holland, 'If you need to sell your country's gin, the English will buy it. Settle the point where the English smugglers are to come to fetch it, and make them pay in money, never in commodities.' When an eccentric Scottish peer offered Jacques Louis David a thousand guineas for a portrait of the Emperor, he was ready to give the painter special sittings provided the portrait was paid for in gold. Nor was Napoleon prepared to exploit the shortage of wheat in Britain as a weapon of war. When the harvest of 1809–10 failed in England, France sold them $1\frac{1}{2}$ million quarters. It is possible that France lost more heavily by the Berlin decrees than Britain. Her custom receipts fell like a plummet. In 1807 they totalled 60 million francs; they were down to 18.6 million in the following year and to 11.6 million in 1809. The trading community in France suffered severely, although not so badly as those of the satellite states.

The fact was that it was impossible to stop British goods reaching Europe. London encouraged smuggling on the largest scale. At one end of Europe Heligoland was seized from the Danes and used as a centre for small boats plying to and from the north German ports. At the other, sugar was landed at Salonika (then Turkish) packed in 2 cwt boxes and taken on muleback over the Balkans and through Serbia before being sold in central Europe, much of it going on to France. Marshal Marmont had to admit that he gave up the attempt to prevent smuggling through Dalmatia.

Nor was trade confined to small boats landing their cargo by night. Although a vast network of custom officers was established at the continental ports, few of these officials were incorruptible and most of them, and their superiors, were very ready to turn a blind eye to the landing of obvious contraband provided that they received a share of the profits. When Napoleon discovered that Massena was selling licences for trade between England and Italy, he confiscated three million francs that the marshal had deposited at Leghorn but Massena still made a profit on the business. The Emperor himself was forced to issue a number of licences, not least because if his army was going to march it needed boots from Northampton.

The chief danger which the Continental System represented to Britain was the threat it posed to the building and repairing of the Royal Navy. Full-grown trees are difficult objects to smuggle, though some were obtained in this way from Dalmatia, where grew the best shipbuilding oak in the world. The official ban on trade with the Baltic would, if continued for long, greatly reduce the strength of the Royal Navy and the equally important merchant fleet. Prussia in 1805 had shipped 11,841 loads of oak timber and planking to Britain. In 1808 only 27 loads were obtained from the same source. Over the same period the supply of masts from Russia fell from 12,748 to 459. Although a substantial quantity of usable timber began to be brought in from New Brunswick, the situation could have become

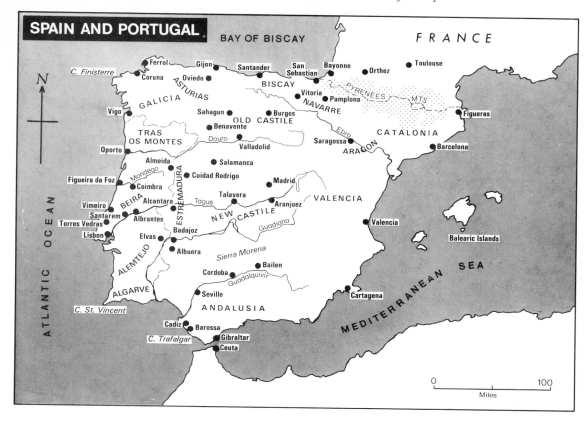

very menacing and the amount of timber used by the merchant fleet had to be cut by half.

Napoleon, however, could not, or would not, wait while economic pressures and the erosion of her fleet brought Britain to surrender. As Wellington remarked, the Emperor 'never in his life had the patience for a defensive war.' In his own words,

> *My power depends on my glory and my glories on the victories I have won. My power will fall if I do not feed it on new glories and new victories. Conquest has made me what I am and only conquest can enable me to hold my position.*

Having pacified the whole continent (except where, to his delight, the Russians were still fighting the Turks), he chose to pick a quarrel with Spain. Though he once said that 'a Bourbon on the throne of Spain is too dangerous a neighbour', it is hard to believe that this was his serious opinion. No country west of the Niemen was more backward than Spain. Her government was corrupt and incompetent and there was little that she could have done to harm France even had she wished to. She was barring British ships from her ports and from the lucrative South American market. She was paying her monthly tribute of £240,000 to France and the battered remnant of her navy was at the Emperor's disposition. Her army was old-fashioned and incapable of reforming itself. 15,000 of her best troops were under French command on garrison duty in Denmark. A large contingent was assisting France in the occupation of Portugal and such of the remainder as were in any way serviceable were languidly prosecuting an interminable siege of Gibraltar.

It is true that Napoleon was misinformed, both by his ambassador and by some Spanish intellectuals, about the kind of reception he was likely to receive in Spain, but his refusal to let Spanish dogs lie suggests that with all western Europe in his power and the Czar as his ally he was in the grip of ambition so overwheening that it bordered on megalomania. As a French historian put it, he was driven on 'by the heroic urge to take risks, the magic lure of the dream, by the irresistible impulse of his flashing temperament.'

Having decided to subdue Spain—the thought of having to conquer the country never entered his head—he set about the task with an arrogant carelessness. Under the pretence of reinforcing Junot's army in Portugal he pushed more and more troops across the Pyrenees and tricked the Spaniards into yielding their frontier fortresses to French garrisons. The troops he sent were mostly drawn from depots and of poor quality, while in supreme command, military and political, he sent his brother-in-law, Joachim Murat, of whom he said, 'He is a brave man on the battlefield, but he has no head. He likes only intrigues and is always deceived by them.' When the marshal reached Madrid and found that Charles IV had been deposed by a popular uprising in favour of his son, he wrote in despair to Napoleon, 'I command your army. I am your representative here. No one in Europe will believe that I am in total ignorance of your plans.'

The fact was that the Emperor had no plan. Although he had earlier offered the Spanish throne to his brothers Joseph and Louis, there is no evidence that he had even considered the means by which this change of dynasties was to be engineered. He was reduced to dealing with events as they occurred and, while he succeeded in decoying both King Charles and King Ferdinand to Bayonne where they were bullied into abdication, he never caught up with the flow of events. The signal for the Spanish uprising was the riot in Madrid on 2 May 1808—*Dos de Mayo*. This was put down by Murat with the loss of 300 Spanish lives and he was able to report that 'the country is tranquil, the state of public opinion in the capital is far happier than could have been expected and the native soldiery is showing an excellent disposition.' If Murat was reporting what he believed to be true he was either grossly misinformed or more stupid than Napoleon supposed, for Spain was in an uproar.

Galicia and Asturias declared war on France. In Valencia the entire French colony, 338 men, women and children, were butchered. At Cadiz and Vigo seven French warships, survivors from Trafalgar, were seized. The *somatenes*, the traditional guerrilla bands, were called out in Catalonia and blockaded a French division in Barcelona. The siege of Gibraltar was raised and the investing army marched for Madrid.

Before it was settled the Spanish imbroglio was to contribute more to Napoleon's defeat than any other single event, not least because it absorbed more than half a million French troops. Its immediate effect was to ensure Britain's survival. Napoleon's naval power, which he was making such efforts to increase, was reduced by 31 ships of the line, 24 Spanish and 7 French, while relieving the pressure on the Royal Navy caused by the need to blockade Ferrol, Vigo, Cadiz and Cartagena. In March 1808 the blockading squadron for Cadiz alone had consisted of 12 of the line, 2 frigates and 4 smaller vessels. Almost more important was the economic effect of opening the Latin American market to British trade. British exports, down to £37¼ million in 1808, rose to £47¼ million in 1809 and £48½ million in 1810. From slump the British economy swung to boom and the industrial unrest died away.

Another immediate effect was to isolate the *Corps de l'Observation de la Gironde* in Portugal. The Spaniards who comprised two thirds of the army of occupation marched back to their own country as soon as the news of the rising reached them, and while Junot managed to detain 5,000 of them they only added to his problems since he had to guard them. He asked Admiral Siniavin to undertake this task but the Russian blandly declared that his country was at peace with both Spain and Portugal so that he could not assist. He continued, nevertheless, to demand rations for his 6,000 seamen.

Junot was left with 26,000 men and the task of holding down a country seething with discontent, and it was not long before his problems became even worse. The British scraped together all the troops fit for service and despatched them to the Peninsula. The government's intention had been to assist the Spaniards but they, mistrusting all foreigners, refused their help. In consequence the expedition went to Portugal and on 1 August a corps of 13,500 men started to land at Figueira da Foz, near Coimbra. Their commander was Lieutenant-General Sir Arthur Wellesley.

While Wellesley's army was sailing towards Portugal, things in Spain had continued to go seriously wrong for the French. Joseph Bonaparte, formerly King of Naples, had been raised to the Spanish throne by a conscripted junta of notables at Bayonne. He entered Spain on 9 July and immediately realized that his brother was making a mistake. 'No one has told your Majesty the truth. Except for a handful of nobles who are travelling with me not a single Spaniard has declared for me . . . 50,000 more men and 50 million francs are needed within the next three months.' Napoleon clung to his illusion. 'I thought that troops would only be needed to maintain public order and to garrison the fortresses.' He assured Joseph that 'the rebels ask nothing better than to be permitted to surrender', and repeatedly urged him to 'Keep fit! Have courage and gaiety and never doubt that we shall be completely successful.'

There were 91,000 French troops in Spain, many of them merely provisional battalions or enlisted foreigners, and these were sufficient to escort the new king to Madrid, breaking through a Spanish force which tried to oppose them at Medina del Rio Seco on 14 July. Thereafter they were dispersed, on Napoleon's orders, all over Spain. One column embarked on an abortive siege of Saragossa, another tried to take Valencia without a siege train and had to march dispiritedly back to Madrid. General Dupont was told to march to Cadiz, 400 miles from Madrid, with 13,000 men including only one regular French battalion. Having taken Cordoba and sacked it, he called for reinforcements which made his strength up to 23,000. Advancing into Andalusia he was surrounded by Spanish armies at Bailen. On 18 July he was defeated and surrendered with 17,635 unwounded men. Joseph's position in Madrid became untenable and he abandoned the city on 1 August, falling back to Vitoria on the Ebro. Three weeks later Junot was heavily defeated by Wellesley at Vimeiro and accepted a convention by which his army should evacuate Portugal by sea.

The news of Bailen, the French empire's first defeat, echoed round Europe. The Spaniards had shown that Napoleon's armies were not invincible. Austria, despite her defeats in 1797, 1801 and 1805, started to rearm. Czar Alexander, concerned at the ruin of his seaborne trade and harassed by a strong anti-French faction among the Russian nobility, reconsidered his alliance. Louis Bonaparte, King of Holland, began issuing licences to trade with England to avert the ruin of the Dutch economy.

It was essential for Napoleon to restore the situation in Spain by a spectacular stroke. He had first to secure his eastern frontiers in case the Austrian army marched in his absence. The Czar was summoned to Erfurt (27 September) but despite expressions of goodwill Napoleon found him 'defiant and unspeakably obstinate. . . . He wanted to treat with me as between equals.' Nevertheless, Alexander agreed to keep Austria in check and made it possible for 100,000 men of the *Grande Armée* to be moved from Germany to the Pyrenees.

On 25 October Napoleon made a farewell address to the Legislative Council in Paris.

> *I leave in a few days to put myself at the head of my army and, with the help of God, I will crown the King of Spain in Madrid and plant my eagles on the ramparts of Lisbon. . . . It is the special blessing that Providence, which has always watched over our armies, should have so blinded the English that they have left the protection of the sea and, at last, exposed their troops on the continent.*

He reached Vitoria in the first week of December. The *Armée de l'Espagne* had 314,612 men on its muster rolls of whom 152,000 were under the Emperor's hand as a striking force.

Opposed to them, spread out on a wide front, were 87,000 Spaniards commanded by five generals who were unable to agree on a plan. The

60 Ceremonial entry of
King Joseph Bonaparte
into Madrid. *Painting by
J. L. Rugendas*

Spanish centre, a sector of 90 miles, was defended by only 12,000 men, since
the Army of Estremadura which should have been holding this front was,
regardless of orders, besieging the French garrison of a Portuguese fortress
which had already surrendered to the British. These regular Spanish
armies, largely composed of recruits, were only the façade of Spanish
resistance. The perfidy with which the French incursion had been managed
had aroused the national pride, and the affront was reinforced by the
requisitions and plunderings by which the invading army supplied itself.
Although in 1808 the guerrilla movement was only in its infancy, it was
already unsafe for Frenchmen to move about the country alone or even in
small detachments. Behind the Spaniards the British were at last preparing
themselves for a considerable incursion on to the Continent. Their
expeditionary force was being raised to 40,000 men and the command had
been entrusted to Sir John Moore. In addition, by an imaginative use of sea
power, the Royal Navy embarked 9,000 of the Spanish troops serving in
the Napoleonic garrison of Denmark and delivered them to Santander.

The first stages of Napoleon's spectacular stroke for the subjugation of
Spain appeared to go splendidly. On 10 November Soult's corps tore
through the Spanish centre and reached Burgos. On either flank the
Spanish armies were defeated and, apparently, dispersed. When the march
was resumed the only opposition encountered between Burgos and Madrid

was a force of 12,000 men holding the Somosierra pass. The Emperor scattered them contemptuously with a single squadron of Polish light horse (30 November) and the capital surrendered on 4 December without firing a shot.

The next step was for the French to push on to Lisbon. Preparations were made to advance by Talavera, Badajoz and Elvas. As Napoleon announced, 'I shall hunt the English out of the Peninsula. Nothing can for long withstand the fulfilment of my wishes.' Certain that the British would not stray far from their transports in Lisbon harbour, he did not trouble to search for them, assuming that they would merely have advanced posts on the Portuguese frontier near Badajoz. In fact, Moore was trying to concentrate a corps of 30,000 men 200 miles from Badajoz at Salamanca. The Spaniards had belatedly invited him to reinforce their centre near Burgos, and when Burgos was lost he was begged to march to Madrid, this plea being sent on the day before the city surrendered. Disheartened, Moore decided to retire to the coast but a French despatch, captured by a guerrilla, showed him that Soult's corps had been left isolated near Valladolid. He decided to attempt to overwhelm it rather than embark on an ignominious retreat. 'I mean to proceed bridle in hand; for if the bubble bursts we shall have a run for it.'

He was at Sahagun on 23 December when he heard that Napoleon had at last discovered where he was and had put in motion a convergent manoeuvre by 70,000 French troops which, if it succeeded, would surround the British. Clearly the bubble had burst and Moore gave orders for a retreat to the north-west corner of Spain. The French pounded after him and Napoleon ordered: 'Put in the newspapers that 36,000 English are surrounded, that I am at Benevente in their rear and that Marshal Soult is in their front. . . . Arrange some ceremonies to celebrate this victory.'

On 2 January Napoleon reached Astorga and realized that there was to be no victory. He handed the pursuit over to Soult and made arrangements to return to France. Moore's army, less a detachment sent to Vigo, reached Coruña on 12 January only to find that their transports had not arrived. Both armies had suffered terribly in their midwinter crossing of the Galician mountains but the British had gained several days' lead. The ships arrived on 14 January and two days later Moore was ready to embark his fighting troops. Soult, however, had now managed to get his divisions forward and, with equal numbers, attacked to prevent the embarkation. He was decisively repulsed and had Moore not been mortally wounded might have suffered a serious defeat. Next day, 17 January, the British took to their ships and sailed for home.

The immediate reaction in England was that the Coruña campaign had been an unrelieved disaster which had cost them 6,000 men. Napoleon assumed that they had been taught a lesson which would prevent them meddling further in the Peninsula. In this he was to be proved disastrously

61 Lieutenant-General Sir John Moore. *Painting by Thomas Lawrence*

wrong, but he also deceived himself on two other important points. The first was that the Spanish armies had been broken and that the Spanish people would passively accept French rule as the Italians and Germans had done. The second was, in the long run, even more misleading. His short stay in Spain had convinced him that the country was well supplied with food. 'I have never seen an army better fed or one so lavishly supplied.' Once again he under-rated the Spanish problem and wrote to his brother Jerome, 'The Spanish business is finished.'

*   *   *

Reports of renewed belligerency in Austria had reached Napoleon in Spain and when he returned to Paris on 23 January he devoted his energies to building up his army in Germany which had been reduced to 90,000 men by the withdrawal of corps for Spain. Before the end of March he had more than doubled its strength by adding to it the 3rd and 4th battalions of French regiments and by raising large contingents from the German satellites and the Grand Duchy of Warsaw. From Spain he withdrew only the Imperial Guard (22,000 men) and a few dragoons. Being convinced that the Austrians would not move before the end of April, he stayed in Paris and left the German command to Marshal Berthier, an admirable chief of staff but no field commander.

Opinion in Austria was divided on the wisdom of renewing the war, but fortified by a subsidy of £2 million and £400,000 a month and the promise of diversionary attacks by Britain, she moved sooner than Napoleon had anticipated. On 9 April the Archduke Charles invaded Bavaria with 140,000 men, and three days later the Archduke John with 50,000 advanced into Italy, and on 15 April defeated the French viceroy, Eugène Beauharnais, at Sacile. Simultaneously the peasants of the Tyrol rose against their Bavarian masters and demanded to be returned to Hapsburg rule.

Charles's attack caught the French unprepared and dispersed. The three corps available to resist him were scattered over the triangle formed by Munich, Augsburg and Ratisbon (Regensburg), and Berthier gave orders for them to concentrate at Ratisbon, a scheme which would have left their main strength, under Davout, isolated from France and liable to encirclement. Reaching the front on 17 April, Napoleon found a very dangerous situation, in which he was saved by the fact that even the Archduke, an excellent but epileptic commander, could not make the Austrian army move fast. There was just time for Napoleon, in one of his most inspired manoeuvres, to bring up Masséna with two reserve corps to Augsburg and Landshut, thus threatening the Austrian flank. Davout nevertheless had to abandon Ratisbon, but by 20 April he started to conduct a desperate defence of Eckmühl (Eggmühl) 16 miles to the south. By the 22nd his ammunition was almost exhausted and his men dropping with fatigue, when Napoleon crashed into the open Austrian flank. 50,000 prisoners were taken and the Archduke retreated towards Bohemia in some confusion. The road to Vienna was open and the French marched into the city on 13 May. In Italy Archduke John retreated to bring his men to the defence of Austria.

Eckmühl, however, was no Austerlitz. Charles soon brought his army, 100,000 strong, back into action and faced the French across the Danube near Vienna. The only practicable way to attack him across the wide river was by way of the islands of Lobau which split the Danube into three channels, respectively 500, 250 and 125 yards wide. The islands were taken without difficulty and on 20 May, the last, narrowest, channel was brilliantly bridged with improvised pontoons. By dawn on 21 May Massena with four infantry and two cavalry divisions was established on

i   Nelson's fleet lying at anchor in the Bay of Naples. *Painting by Giacomo Guardi*

ii   The Battle of Trafalgar, as seen from the VICTORY by J. M. W. Turner

iii   *Above left* French horse grenadier, 1805
iv   *Above* French *chasseur à cheval*, 1812
v   *Left* French infantry of the line, 1793-1806

vi French carabinier, 1812

vii Grenadiers of (left to right) France, Belgium, the United Kingdom, Bavaria, Austria, Prussia, Russia, in 1815

viii The Battle of Borodino; the death of General Gualaincourt, brother of Napoleon's ambassador to Russia and Foreign Minister. *Painting by F. von Habermann*

ix   The occupation of Paris, 1814, Cossacks marching through the city. *Watercolour by*
Georg Opitz.

x   The Battle of Leipzig

xi Napoleon at the Battle of Waterloo. *Painting by Sir William Allan*

xii The Duke of Wellington raising his hat as the signal for the British line to advance at the end of the Battle of Waterloo

the far bank, holding the villages of Essling and Aspern, each some two miles from the river.

This was the moment, with the French astride the river, for which Charles had been waiting. He attacked and captured Aspern, and while the French were endeavouring to mount a counter-attack, the river, already in flood, rose and washed away the bridge. Massena managed to cling on until the bridge was repaired at midnight when Napoleon sent reinforcements, Lannes' corps and the Guard. Scarcely were these all across when the bridge was again broken, this time by the Austrians who floated barges loaded with stones down the river. The villages of Aspern and Essling changed hands repeatedly. So desperate was the fighting that Napoleon felt himself obliged to encourage his men by exposing himself so much to the fire that the Old Guard threatened to ground their arms if he would not retire to a safer position. Massena's men were exhausted after 48 hours of continuous fighting and the reinforcements were also tired, while all were short of ammunition. On the afternoon of 22 May Napoleon gave up the attempt and ordered a retreat to Lobau island which was covered to the last by the indomitable Massena. Marshal Lannes was killed during the withdrawal and in all the French suffered 44,000 casualties, a number reduced to 4,100 in Napoleon's *bulletin*. The Austrian casualties were

62 The Battle of Aspern – Essling, where the Archduke Charles prevented Napoleon's army from crossing the Danube. This was the first serious setback that Napoleon suffered

137

PRISE DE
CASTEL GENEST   BREC ET FIGARETO
DEFAITE DES AUSTRO SARDES A PONTE DI NAVE
SUR TANARO
PRISE DU FORT D'ORMEA . ENLEVEMENT DE
LA FAMEUSE REDOUTE DE FELT ET COL ARDENTE
PRISE DE SAORGIO ET COL DE TENDE
BATAILLE DU 2 FRIMAIRE ANNO 4 .

23,000 and they had every reason for pride for they had inflicted on Napoleon his first undoubted defeat.

64 *Above* Napoleon at the Battle of Wagram

After a pause of six weeks the French attacked again somewhat further downstream. By a remarkable feat of organization and discipline 150,000 men were passed across three bridges in a single night and on 5-6 July the Archduke was defeated in a closely contested battle at Wagram. The Austrians lost 26,000 killed and wounded but were able to retreat northward in good order, taking with them 7,000 prisoners and 21 captured guns. Napoleon had incurred 30,000 casualties, largely because Wagram saw the culmination of the attack in column, when Macdonald broke through the Austrian centre with a mass of 21 battalions, a formation made necessary by the inexperience of many of the French troops. This column consisted of 8,000 men and despite an intense artillery preparation, 6,500 of them became casualties.

Five days later the Emperor Francis asked for an armistice which was made permanent by the Treaty of Schönbrunn in October. It was inevitably a harsh peace. Austria ceded her last outlets to the sea, Trieste and Fiume (Rijeka) with Friuli (Venezia Giulia) and Carniola (Slovenia) to France, while part of Galicia went to Russia and the remainder to the Grand Duchy of Warsaw. Salzburg was given to Bavaria. In all she lost three and a half

63 *Opposite Page* André Massena as General de Division in 1797. *Painter unknown*

million subjects and had to pay an indemnity of £3.4 million.

The Austrian war of 1809 started with Napoleon at his most brilliant when he recovered from the effects of Berthier's blunders, but the subsequent fighting showed that the writing was on the wall. France had lost 74,000 men in two battles and had secured no decisive victory. After Wagram the Archduke had withdrawn with an 'army-in-being' and one which, in contrast to the survivors of Austerlitz and Jena, could have fought again. The armistice on this occasion was a political decision, not a military necessity. The Archduke Charles could not match Napoleon's strategic flair but he demonstrated to Europe that the Emperor's blows could be ridden and that the French armies could be subjected to attrition at such a rate that, if only the powers of Europe could combine, even Napoleon's victories must lead to his downfall.

* * *

The French forces which marched to Vienna did not have to detach a single man to deal with the promised British diversionary operations. An expedition from Sicily captured the island of Ischia, off Naples, in June and abandoned it in July. Another failed to take Scilla on the toe of Italy. Tiny forces took three of the Ionian Islands but this scarcely inconvenienced the French who retained Corfu. A British alliance with the Pasha of Albania proved, despite initial promise, wholly worthless.

In northern Europe British operations were more imposing but no more fruitful. Orders were given at the end of May 1809 for a force of 40,000 men to attack the estuary of the Scheldt. The Royal Navy was very anxious for this operation since there were in this area ten French battleships ready for sea and eight more in various stages of construction. It was not, however, until 28 July, three weeks after the Austrian campaign had been settled at Wagram, that the expedition sailed, and two days later they started to land on Walcheren Island. There were few French troops in the vicinity but Napoleon took a detached view of the danger. 'The defences of Walcheren are the fever and the bad air which have always prevented me from keeping troops there. Flushing, moreover, is impregnable because of the inundations.' He was wrong on the second point since Flushing, with a garrison of 7,000 men, surrendered on 16 August. A frigate and a brig were destroyed on their slipways and the *Fidèle* (38), a brand new frigate, was captured. The only other British trophy was the timbers of a third-rate which were eventually assembled at Woolwich and put into commission as H.M.S. CHATHAM (74).

Antwerp was discovered to be unassailable and as Napoleon had foreseen, fever broke out among the invaders. Most of the troops were re-embarked in September but one division did not return to England until December. The cost to the army in dead was 67 officers and 3,999 other ranks. Of these only 7 officers and 99 other ranks died in action. 11,000 of the surviving participants were still on the sick list with 'Walcheren fever' in the following February.

Although the expedition failed to come up to the navy's expectations, 1809 was a good year for Britain at sea. France lost six of the line, one 50-gun ship and 16 frigates, while Britain lost only one ship of the line, a 64 wrecked in the Rio de la Plata, and four frigates, only one of which, the recently captured JUNON (38), was lost to the enemy. A French attempt to supply Barcelona by sea ended with two of the line driven on to Spanish rocks while 19 out of 20 transports were wrecked or captured. Even more spectacular was the attack on a French fleet, ten of the line and four frigates, bound for Martinique, in the Aix roads on 12 April. It ended with the *Varsovie* (80), *Aquilon* (74), *Tonnerre* (74) and *Indienne* (40) destroyed as well as the *Calcutta* (50), a converted Indiaman which had been captured by the French four years earlier.

This success was marred by the trouble it caused within the Royal Navy. Admiral Lord Gambier had asked London for fireships with which to carry out the raid and the Admiralty had insisted on sending Captain Lord Cochrane to command them. This affronted every captain in the fleet and led to Rear-Admiral Harvey being sentenced by a court martial for using 'grossly insubordinate language' when he was told that he could not command the fireships. To make matters worse Cochrane, though an able and dashing commander, was an intolerable subordinate. He was determined to force Gambier to take the battle fleet into the dangerous waters of the roads to complete the destruction of the French. To achieve this he did not scruple to signal, untruthfully, that his own frigate IMPÉRIEUSE (38) was in distress and in need of immediate assistance. His complaints of lack of support later became so strident that Gambier sought a court martial on his own conduct. At this he was exonerated despite the number of lies and half-truths told in evidence by Cochrane (and later repeated with embellishments in his autobiography). The action so divided the navy between the supporters of Gambier, not a sympathetic character, and those of Cochrane, that it must be doubted whether the loss to France of four ships of the line was worth the resulting ill-feeling.

1809 also saw the reduction of Martinique, Guadaloupe and all the remaining French, Dutch and Danish islands in the West Indies, so that by the end of the year there were no longer any enemy naval bases in the Caribbean.

*   *   *

When Napoleon returned to Paris in January 1809 he left a set of instructions for the complete subjugation of the Peninsula. Unfortunately these instructions reflected his illusion that the Spanish business was over, and bore no relation to reality. The main operation was entrusted to Soult who was ordered to march from Coruña by way of Vigo and Oporto so as to reach Lisbon on 10 February, four weeks after the Battle of Coruña. He

was then to detach troops to join Marshal Victor who was instructed to seize Seville, Cadiz and Gibraltar. This operation, wrote the Emperor to King Joseph, 'will settle the Spanish business. I leave the glory of it to you.'

This was moonshine. Even if Soult had had the 44,000 men shown on his muster-rolls it would have been physically impossible for him to have reached Lisbon on 10 February. As it was the pursuit of Moore and the Battle of Coruña had reduced his marching strength to 23,000 and although he was opposed only by an armed peasantry, he did not reach Oporto until 29 March. There he had to halt in a vain attempt to re-establish his communications with Galicia and Leon. By that time Britain had taken the decision which was irrevocably to frustrate all Napoleon's plans for the Peninsula and elsewhere.

65 *Opposite Page* Captain the Honourable Thomas Cochrane. *Paining by P. E. Stroehling*

66 *Below* Captain Cochrane's frigate IMPÉRIEUSE among the French fleet at Aix Roads

The decision was not reached easily. Public opinion had been shocked by the wretched state in which Moore's men had returned to England and the Cabinet, under Portland's failing leadership, was bitterly divided on the next course the country ought to adopt. Canning was for basing a British force on Cadiz; Castlereagh preferred Lisbon; while the Admiralty, usually in favour of securing Lisbon at all costs, allowed itself to be diverted by the desirability of destroying the French naval base at Antwerp, the scheme which led to the Walcheren expedition. When the Spaniards refused to sanction the landing of British troops at Cadiz, a compromise was reached. The main effort was to be made in the Scheldt while 30,000 men, mostly second-line troops, were to be sent to reinforce the 10,000 men still at Lisbon. The commander was to be Sir Arthur Wellesley, and another British officer of exceptional talent, William Carr Beresford, was sent to Lisbon to rebuild the Portuguese army.

The decline of Napoleon's empire can best be dated from the moment when Britain decided to reinforce her small force in Portugal, using the manpower of Portugal and Spain to make up for the numbers which she herself could never deploy in the field. Henceforward the French were to be committed to a struggle which cost her armies an average of 50,000 lives a year and which she could never win. The presence of the British army, with their Portuguese auxiliaries, meant, even when they were confined to the Lisbon peninsula, that Spain and Portugal still had hope. Thus the operations of the ever-growing guerrilla force made possible the operations of the Anglo-Portuguese army, which in their turn made it impossible for the French ever to deal with the guerrillas.

Wellesley landed at Lisbon in mid-April and lost no time in ejecting Soult. He advanced to the Douro with 16,000 men, crossed the river in broad daylight under the noses of the French sentries (16 May) and bundled Soult's corps out of Portugal with the loss of 4,000 men and all his guns. Next, hoping to benefit from France's preoccupation with the war in Austria, he concerted an operation with the Spaniards which was intended to take Madrid. Here he was too optimistic. The French reaction was sharper than he had anticipated and the cooperation of his Spanish allies left everything to be desired. Despite a costly victory at Talavera de la Reina (27-28 July), which earned Wellesley the title of Lord Wellington, the British had to retreat hastily on Portugal and Wellington had to recast his plans. Refusing all cooperation with the Spaniards, whose schemes he described as 'rank nonsense', he decided that he must concentrate on one essential point, the security of Lisbon. If he could make himself strong enough there the French would exhaust themselves in trying to break through. On 20 October 1809 he gave orders for a system of defensive works across the Lisbon peninsula—the Lines of Torres Vedras.

Once Austria's defeat had been sealed for the fourth time by the Treaty of Schönbrunn, Napoleon was able to devote France's full strength to settling 'the Spanish business'. He ordered 138,000 reinforcements into Spain but one soldier he did not send—himself. Devoting his own energies to the task of securing an heir to his throne, he nominated Marshal Massena, Duke of Rivoli, Prince of Essling, '*L'enfant chéri de la victoire*', to command the *Armée du Portugal* and promised him 138,000 men with whom to take Lisbon. If a substitute for the Emperor had to be found, Massena was the obvious choice, but at 52 the hero of Switzerland, Genoa and Essling was, by his own admission, past his best. To make matters worse, he found that of his 138,000 men only 65,000 were available on the ground for the invasion of Portugal. 10,000 more were sick, 16,500 were still in France when the campaign began, and the balance of his theoretical strength was needed to guard the communications between France and the Portuguese frontier. Nevertheless, 65,000 seemed a sufficient number with which to drive back to their ships a British army estimated by the Emperor at 23,000. Napoleon, indeed, was so confident of Massena's success that he gave no orders to Marshal Soult, who commanded in southern Spain, to cooperate with him.

Massena did everything that a gallant, talented and obstinate general could do but his task was impossible. He penetrated deep into Portugal, suffering only one check when Wellington stood for battle on the dominating ridge of Busaco (27 September 1810), a battle in which the British general deployed not only 27,000 British but 25,000 Portuguese troops. As Wellington retired, the advancing French found the country stripped of supplies and inhabitants, while an invisible net of Portuguese militia and irregulars closed round their rear. On 14 October 1810 the French outposts were within 20 miles of Lisbon and the Marshal rode forward to reconnoitre the Lines of Torres Vedras. One look was sufficient. 'I should', he reported, 'compromise the army of his Majesty if I attacked lines so formidable.'

For almost four months the *Armée du Portugal* managed to subsist near Lisbon while Massena hoped that either Soult would come to his assistance or Wellington would emerge to fight. He was disappointed on both counts although Soult, who was belatedly ordered to invade Estremadura, took the frontier fortress of Badajoz on 10 March. By that time even Massena's iron determination had cracked. On 6 March he had started to retreat and by 5 April the only Frenchmen in Portugal were the beleaguered garrison of Almeida. The third French invasion of Portugal had cost them 25,000 men (of whom only 1,500 had fallen in battle) and 6,000 horses.

It was Britain's first unflawed success on the Continent since the war began but to set against it was the most serious naval defeat she suffered in the whole war. Having secured all the enemy colonies in the Caribbean, the navy and army turned their attention to the east. Île de France (Mauritius) and Île Bourbon (Réunion) had long menaced the East India trade. Bourbon was taken without difficulty in July 1810 and, as a preliminary to the capture of Île de France, the Île de la Passe, which blocked the entrance to Port Bourbon, was seized by the Royal Navy. Port Bourbon was the main harbour of Mauritius and inside it were moored the bulk of the French naval strength in the Indian Ocean. All that had to be done was to wait until 10,000 British and Indian troops arrived to do the land fighting. Unfortunately, the captain commanding the blockade was a renowned fire-eater and, like too many of his colleagues, found the lure of prize money irresistible. He decided to sail into Port Bourbon and capture the French squadron. Since he was pitting four 36-gun ships against five 40-gun frigates backed by shore batteries, the enterprise was as unwise as it was unnecessary.

In five days' fighting (23-28 August 1811) the frigates NEREIDE and IPHIGENIA were forced to surrender while the MAGICIENNE and SIRIUS, which had gone aground, were burned to save them from capture. The small garrison of Île de la Passe also had to surrender. This gave the French temporary naval command of the area and in September two more British frigates were taken, one of them carrying the commander-in-chief of the expeditionary force. Fortunately both ships were recaptured and the arrival of a ship of the line and another frigate squadron enabled Île de France to be taken without serious loss at the beginning of December. The authorities in India were then able to make ships and men available to begin the subjugation of the Dutch East Indies and by September 1811 the conquest of Java was complete.

Imperial zenith

On 9 June 1811 a magnificent ceremony was held at Notre-Dame de Paris. Prince François Charles Joseph Napoleon, King of Rome, was christened, his godparents being his grandfather, the Emperor Francis of Austria (who was represented by the Grand Duke of Wurzburg) and his uncle, King Joseph of Spain (who, very much to his imperial brother's displeasure, attended in person). After seven years on the throne Napoleon had settled the vexed question of his successor.

It had not been an easy question to solve. Napoleon had been genuinely devoted to Josephine Beauharnais, his first Empress, and despite her inability to bear him a child he had postponed divorcing her in the hope that the succession might be entrusted to one of his brothers or their children. Unfortunately, as he said, 'My family give me no help. They are all insanely ambitious, ruinously extravagant and devoid of talent.' Only one brother, Lucien, had any political ability, but when the Emperor refused to sanction his second marriage he embarked for America, was captured by the British and spent the rest of the war as a country gentleman in Worcestershire writing an epic poem. The eldest brother, Joseph, would also have made a country gentleman but, by Napoleon's standards, he was a failure as King of Spain. He took his coronation oath seriously and tried to do his best for his unwilling subjects. To make matters worse, he constantly importuned Paris for money while, according to the imperial system, Spain should have been contributing to the wealth and glory of France. Jérome, the youngest brother, was King of Westphalia. He caused little overt trouble but, said Napoleon, cared for 'nothing but pageantry, women, plays and fêtes.' Louis, who was also the son-in-law of the Empress Josephine, not only failed as King of Holland but advertised the fact. When his attempt to revive trade by opening the Dutch ports was forbidden he abdicated and fled to Austria. Louis, however, was the only one of the brothers who managed to have a legitimate son, and the little prince was nominated as the imperial heir. Inconveniently, he died in 1807 and by the

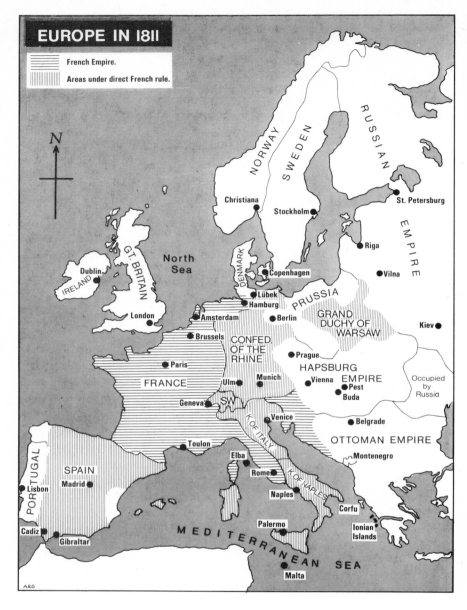

EUROPE IN 1811

French Empire.

Areas under direct French rule.

N

NORWAY

SWEDEN

RUSSIAN

EMPIRE

Christiana

St. Petersburg

Stockholm

Riga

North
Sea

DENMARK

Copenhagen

Vilna

G.T. BRITAIN

Lübek

Hamburg

PRUSSIA

Dublin

IRELAND

Amsterdam

Berlin

GRAND
DUCHY OF
WARSAW

Kiev

London

Brussels

CONFED.
OF THE
RHINE

Prague

Paris

HAPSBURG

Occupied
by
Russia

FRANCE

Ulm

Munich

Vienna

EMPIRE

Geneva

SW.

Pest
Buda

Venice

Belgrade

K. OF ITALY

OTTOMAN EMPIRE

Toulon

Montenegro

PORTUGAL

SPAIN

Elba

Rome

K. OF NAPLES

Lisbon

Madrid

Naples

Corfu

Cadiz

Palermo

Ionian
Islands

Gibraltar

MEDITERRANEAN SEA

Malta

ARG

time another son was born to Queen Hortense (for King Louis denied
paternity), the Emperor was disgusted with all his brothers and the boy had
to wait until 1852 before he became Emperor of the French.

Having proved, with the assistance of the Countess Walewska, that he
could father a son, Napoleon decided on a dynastic marriage, and after
attempting to obtain a Russian princess, secured the hand of the Austrian
Archduchess Maria Louisa (2 April 1810), it being noticed that the
marriage contract was copied, clause for clause, from the contract between

Louis XVI and Marie Antoinette. It was for the sake of the new Empress that he delegated the conquest of Portugal to Massena, but the Emperor had his reward. On 20 March 1811 the King of Rome was born.

The alliance represented by the Austrian marriage appeared to establish Napoleon as indisputably supreme in Europe. The two great eastern empires were his allies, while Prussia was under French occupation and crushed by her enormous indemnity. The rest of Germany was a confederation of French puppets. Western Poland was a subordinate satrapy. Denmark, with its appendage of Norway, was a loyal ally and in 1810 even Sweden, so long an enemy, was forced by Franco–Russian pressure to declare war on Britain. Switzerland was under Napoleon's 'protection', all mainland Italy was, in one form or another, under French control, Dalmatia was French and the Adriatic a French lake. Joseph Bonaparte ruled in Madrid, although Cadiz and Valencia were unconquered, Galicia had liberated itself and, in the rest of King Joseph's realm, authority was in constant dispute between the royal officials, the French commanders and the ever-growing guerrilla forces. Although Turkey, an ally in 1807, was sinking into a sullen neutrality, Napoleon's only enemies were Britain, Portugal and Sicily, the last two being wholly dependent on British garrisons and British subsidies.

France herself was larger and more prosperous than she had ever been. Her boundaries extended northward through Belgium, Holland (annexed after King Louis's defection) and Friesland until they reached the Baltic at Lübeck. To the south they enclosed Piedmont and Genoa and stretched south to the point at which the *département* of Rome met the Kingdom of Naples, ruled by Napoleon's brother-in-law, Joachim Murat. In the absence of British competition French industries were flourishing and internal trade was facilitated by the construction of excellent roads, notably those over the Simplon and Mont Cenis passes and that along the Corniche on the Riviera. These roads had been built primarily for military purposes but their commercial value was undoubted, although some of them, notably the Corniche, were more costly and less efficient to use than the old coastal shipping which the British blockade made difficult and, at times, impossible.

While the imperial edifice was grandiose and imposing, there were serious flaws. French prosperity was founded on the impoverishment of the satellite states. Those parts—Holland, Genoa, Venice and the Hanse towns—where prosperity depended on maritime trade faced ruin as grass grew on their quays. When, as an alternative, they traded with France they found themselves faced with custom barriers for the protection of French goods. Elsewhere the Napoleonic overlordship had undoubted advantages in the sweeping away of the anachronisms and injustices of a jumble of temporal and ecclesiastical states, but although the peasant no longer had to pay tithes to the priest and taxes to the princeling, he must not only pay

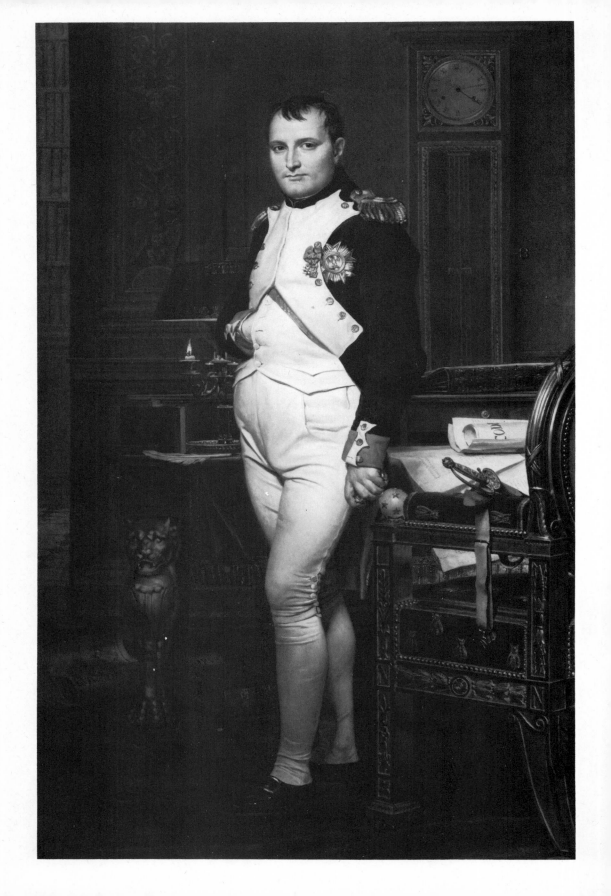

higher taxes for the benefit of France but suffer the requisitions of an occupying army and, worst of all, give his sons to the unprecedented conscription.

The greatest flaw in the imperial structure was at the top, in the Emperor himself. In 1805 he had remarked, 'One has only a certain time for war. I will be good for six more years; after that I must stop.' When the King of Rome was born the six years were up and the war continued. Napoleon was putting on weight and becoming subject to fits of lethargy. On occasions he misunderstood what was said to him and although his mind was to remain an immensely powerful and precise instrument until 1815 and later, it was no longer the almost infallible calculating machine that had won him power. The 1809 campaign against Austria had started with a defeat, due to over-optimism, and ended with a victory that was far from overwhelming and terribly costly. It was a collapse of political will rather than of military strength that made Austria sue for peace after Wagram. Spain was turning out to be an expensive and insoluble problem. Once he had set Massena's army in motion towards Lisbon Napoleon lost interest in the Peninsula. He refused to appoint a supreme commander and let his marshals flout the authority of King Joseph and quarrel with each other. Meanwhile he bombarded them with instructions which were always out of date and frequently contradicted each other, thus making any form of concerted operation impossible.

In 1811 he announced to the *Corps Législatif* that, 'A clap of thunder will put an end to the Peninsular business, will destroy the English army and will avenge Europe and Asia by ending this second Punic war.' However, he put forward no suggestion as to how this thunderbolt was to be procured. He poured reinforcements into Spain (the army there was 353,000 strong in 1811) but developed the habit of putting into his pocket unread any despatch from Spain which he suspected of containing unwelcome news. In June 1811 he reverted to planning the invasion of England. '80,000 men can be made available to threaten England across the Channel; these, together with the steps I am taking to raise a party in Ireland, should bring satisfactory results.' Ten days later he was working on a more realistic scheme, soon to be abandoned, for seizing the Channel Islands. His fleet was growing month by month. 15 ships of the line were building in the Scheldt where work was in hand to construct a safe anchorage for 90 battleships. More capital ships were on the slips at Cherbourg, Lorient, Rochefort, Toulon, Genoa, Naples and Venice. Meanwhile the French squadrons seldom ventured out of their harbours. They were being hoarded against the day when they could drive the Royal Navy from the seas. 'We shall be able to make peace with safety when we have 150 ships of the line and, in spite of the obstacles of war, such is the state of the empire that we shall shortly have that number.'

Having made himself master of Europe, Napoleon had allowed himself to be impressed by his own prestige. He was drifting into a dream world where he believed himself capable of imposing his will everywhere. This state of mind was intensified when he dismissed first Talleyrand, his Minister for Foreign Affairs, and then Fouché, the Minister of Police. Both men were amoral and much given to intrigue but they both had acute minds and they were the only men prepared to tell their master unpalatable truths. Henceforward his entourage was to consist of officials and sycophants.

Like its great leader the French army was past its best. 19 years of almost continuous fighting, however victorious, would sap the strength of any army and by 1811 veterans were becoming rare and experienced regimental officers were hard to find. Of the 148,000 men of the *Armée de l' Allemagne*, exclusive of the Guard, in 1809 47,119 were conscripts of the class of 1810, boys who, in theory, were too young to be called up. Of the infantry which had fought at Austerlitz, 28 regiments out of 41 had been transferred to Spain, which had also absorbed every one of the Austerlitz dragoon regiments and more than half the light horse. In the line regiments the scarcity of experienced men was accentuated by the constant drain of veterans to the Middle and Old Guards. The Household Troops became an incomparable body of fighting men but they became so at the expense of the quality of less favoured units. Nevertheless, although service in Spain was intensely unpopular, there remained in the ranks much of the fervour which had made the armies of the Revolution so formidable. It was among the higher officers that, increasingly, enthusiasm was lacking. The marshals and the generals longed for peace and leisure in which to enjoy the riches and titles which, to retain their loyalty and their services, Napoleon had heaped upon them.

Nor was the French army keeping ahead of its competitors in *matériel*. The French musket had always been slightly inferior to the British and in the Prussian army the new model introduced after the *débâcle* at Jena was also more serviceable than the French. Not the least of the disadvantages under which the French laboured in the Peninsula was the Emperor's decision, taken in 1807, to discontinue the issue of rifles on the ground that they were too slow to load. As a consequence the *tirailleurs*, hitherto one of the French army's most effective arms, were always at a disadvantage when faced with the British Riflemen and the Portuguese *caçadores*, who could shoot accurately at 200 or even 300 yards against the 80 to 100 yards of the musket. Even in artillery, the arm of the service in which Napoleon might be expected to be most interested, the French were being overtaken. The family of guns designed by Gribauval before the Revolution continued to be the staple weapons of the French artillery although they were beginning to be outclassed, especially in the 6- and 9-pounder calibres, by the new models coming from the British and Russian arsenals. The only major advances in artillery technology which emerged during the wars, the shrapnel shell and the rocket, were both British, and the French showed little eagerness to copy either of them.

As the French army began to deteriorate, the other European armies improved, frequently by adopting French techniques. Austria, Prussia and Russia all made their armies more flexible and widened the basis of officer selection, although none of them ever achieved the standard of staffwork which made Napoleon's army so formidable. While the eastern armies adopted the columnar tactics and the mass formations which the French had demonstrated so effectively, the British went in the other direction. Since alone of the great powers Britain did not adopt conscription, her small army could not afford heavy losses and reverted to the best of the tactics of the *ancien régime*. The French admitted that they never encountered anything so lethal as the musketry of the British infantry in their two-deep line. As one French officer remarked, 'The British infantry are the best in the world. Fortunately there are not many of them.' Moreover the British had found in Wellington a general and an organizer who was more than equal to any of Napoleon's subordinates. It was not until 1815 that the Emperor himself was to admit that 'Lord Wellington at the head of an army is the equal of myself—with the advantage of possessing more prudence.'

In 1811, however, Wellington as a commander of the first class was still unproved and the French considered him only as a lucky general with a talent for choosing defensive positions. Nor was his reputation much higher in Britain. After his victory at Talavera he was attacked in the House of Commons as a rash and ambitious adventurer and the Corporation of the City of London passed a resolution deploring everything about him except his courage. Britain was deeply divided about the wisdom of continuing the war in Portugal, and although there was no longer an effective peace party a very powerful lobby believed that financial considerations must force the country to fight a purely defensive war. As the Secretary of War wrote in 1810, 'If the House of Commons had been left to act upon their own feelings they would, in the month of February, have decided for withdrawing the army from Portugal.'

The government was fortunate that they were able to keep Parliament in check, for in 1809 the two most talented members of Portland's Cabinet met with pistols on Putney Heath and the government collapsed. A new ministry, headed by 'this honest little fellow', Spencer Perceval, took a long time to form. Perceval, competent but uninspiring, needed to be plucky. The economic problems were daunting. Although exports had reached a record £61 million in 1810 (£35.2 million in 1808), the boom was beginning to collapse. The newly opened market in Latin America was glutted with British goods and the closing of the Swedish ports seriously hampered, though it did not stop, the lucrative Baltic trade. Five great Manchester firms became bankrupt in August 1810 and a wave of smaller

failures followed. In September a great gale caused 240 British merchant ships to be wrecked or driven into hostile ports where they were confiscated.

The slump intensified in 1811. Exports fell to £39.5 million. Cotton mills were reduced to a three-day week and a wave of machine-smashing by unemployed weavers meant that 12,000 regular troops were required to keep the peace. The subsidies to Spain, Portugal and Sicily with the cost of the army in the Peninsula drained gold out of the country. The outflow of gold, which had averaged £3 million in 1805–7, rose to £14 million in 1810 and the value of the pound at Hamburg fell from 35 to 28 schillings, intensifying the nagging suspicion of the worthlessness of paper money. A committee of the House of Commons demanded a return to gold but Perceval, declaring to the full house that 'I am bound to regard the proposed measure as a declaration by Parliament that we must submit to no matter what conditions of peace rather than continue the war,' secured its rejection, thus making it possible for Britain to continue fighting overseas.

The Berlin Decrees (with the subsequent Milan Decrees) and the British Orders in Council were harming both Britain and France almost equally and both governments soon recognized the fact. By tacit agreement Franco-British trade began to be restored under licence from April 1811. Cotton, sugar, cinchona, dyestuffs and coffee became tolerated imports in France while silk, brandy and corn were exported to England. The economies of both countries benefited and Britain began to earn the gold that, over the next three years, she was to be called upon to supply in ever increasing quantities.

68 *Opposite Page* Field Marshal the Duke of Wellington. *Painting by P. E. Stroehling*

CHAPTER V
1811 – 1812

Overlord of the World?

'My manoeuvres have disconcerted the Russians; before a month has passed they will be on their knees to me.'

NAPOLEON I, 28 JUNE 1812

*B*etween 1803 and 1811 the French navy lost 33 ships of the line (of which three were lost to the perils of the sea, seven to the Spaniards and the remainder to the Royal Navy), while the Dutch fleet lost four and the Danes 18. Nevertheless, Napoleon, who had 45 battleships in 1803, could call upon 60 by January 1811. Although the Toulon squadron occasionally made a cautious training cruise, the French fleet seldom appeared on the open sea and the only major naval action in 1811 was fought between squadrons of frigates.

In the Adriatic where the whole coastline was under French control the British reaped a rich harvest among the ships carrying on the coastwise traffic and supplying the garrison of Corfu. One frigate alone, AMPHION (32), captured or destroyed 218 vessels within 18 months. Her captain, William Hoste, established a shore base on the island of Lissa (Vis) and in 1811 was the senior officer of the force in the area, consisting of three 32-gun frigates and a 20-gun ship. The French were unwilling to suffer the presence of this force at Lissa and in the spring of 1811 sent out six frigates, four of them of 40 guns, which sailed from Ancona escorting some smaller vessels carrying 500 soldiers who were to occupy the island. This squadron approached the north end of Lissa on 13 March, whereupon Hoste formed his ships into line and hoisted the signal 'Remember Nelson'. After an action lasting five and a half hours two French frigates were captured and a third was on the rocks. A fourth frigate had struck her colours but, finding that AMPHION had no sound boat with which to put a prize crew aboard, rehoisted the *tricolore* and limped after her consorts to their home port.

69 *Opposite Page* Admiral Sir William Hoste. *Painting attributed to S. Lane*

156

Hoste was wounded, one of 190 British casualties, but the French lost 500 killed and wounded apart from the survivors of the two captured ships who became prisoners.

Misfortune struck the Royal Navy later in the year when a violent gale in northern Europe caused ST GEORGE (98) and HERO (74) to founder in the Baltic, while DEFENCE (74) went down off Texel Island. This Christmas Eve disaster, which cost the Royal Navy 2,000 seamen, meant that at the beginning of 1812 Britain had only 102 ships of the line in commission, several of them in far-distant waters. At that time the French fleet had 80 battleships.

After Massena had withdrawn the *Armée du Portugal* to Spain in April 1811 there was deadlock in the Peninsula. Wellington could not invade Spain until he had secured all the four fortresses which commanded the two practicable roads across the frontier. On the northern road Massena held Almeida on the Portuguese and Ciudad Rodrigo on the Spanish side of the frontier. In the south Soult held Badajoz and Wellington had Portuguese Elvas. In May the allies tried to take both Almeida and Badajoz. Massena came forward to relieve Almeida but was repulsed at Fuentes de Oñoro (3-5 May) while Soult's attempt to relieve Badajoz was bloodily defeated by Beresford at Albuera (16 May). Almeida was evacuated by its garrison but Badajoz resisted two sieges and was still defiant at the end of the year. Nor could a serious attempt be made against Ciudad Rodrigo.

The Anglo-Portuguese army was 60,000 strong but the combined French armies in Spain outnumbered them by six to one. Napoleon constantly urged commanders to combine against the British but it was not a practicable operation. The duties entailed in holding down a rugged country with a murderously hostile population allowed the French no respite. Napoleon described the Spanish regular armies as 'a rabble who cannot stand against us in the field' but he under-rated their stamina. Although they were repeatedly defeated between 1808 and 1813 they were never destroyed. As often as the French scattered them they reassembled. Their ranks were constantly filled with recruits, their generals were uniformly incompetent but Spanish ardour matched that of the French and they always had new British muskets and an infinite supply of courage. The guerrillas were even more formidable, since their numbers grew every time the French requisitioned or plundered food. By 1811 there was scarcely an area in Spain where a courier could ride without an escort of 1,000 men or where a straggler could lie down to rest with the hope of remaining alive. Wellington was the first to admit that the eventual defeat of the French

is to be ascribed to the enmity of the people of Spain. I have known not less than 380,000 men of the French army in Spain at one moment and yet with no authority beyond the spot where they stood and their time passed and their force exhausted by the mere effort of obtaining subsistence.

It was Napoleon who broke the deadlock on the border between Portugal and Spain. Unable to stop meddling in a war he imperfectly understood, he gave orders for the conquest of Valencia. This was an irrelevant operation which could only result in his army, already overstretched, being further dispersed. To undertake it troops had to be detached from many areas of Spain, and the *Armée du Portugal*, now commanded by Marmont, was ordered to send to Valencia 10,000 men including all the light cavalry. Simultaneously the Emperor withdrew 27,000 men from Spain for use in the east.

Not least of the benefits Wellington derived from the guerrillas was excellent information about what was happening in French-held Spain. By the middle of December 1811 he knew that both the *Armée du Portugal* and the *Armée du Nord*, whose task was to support Marmont, had been fatally weakened. Moving with a speed that astonished the French, the Anglo-Portuguese army invested Ciudad Rodrigo in the first week of the new year and stormed it on 19 January, long before Marmont could move to its relief. Wellington immediately ordered his siege train, which moved with

70 William Hoste with three British frigates defeating six French frigates off the island of Lissa on 13 March 1811. *Anonymous*

agonizing slowness, to be transported to Badajoz and here again Napoleon stepped in to ensure allied success. Badajoz was the responsibility of Soult and his *Armée du Midi*, based in Andalusia, and if Marmont and Soult brought their available forces towards the threatened fortress Wellington could not take it. Marmont realized this and started to march his troops southward. Napoleon intervened to prevent this move in terms that bordered on insult: 'You must be mad if you believe that the English are capable of marching on Badajoz while you remain at Salamanca and could reach Lisbon before they could.' Marmont was not mad nor could he march on Lisbon, since he had neither transport nor supplies of food. Soult was helpless without assistance and Badajoz was stormed on the night of 5-6 April among scenes of slaughter and brutality which made Wellington write,

> *The capture of Badajoz affords as strong an instance of the gallantry of our troops as has ever been displayed, but I anxiously hope that I shall never again be the instrument of putting them to such a test as that to which they were put last night.*

Badajoz cost 4,670 allied casualties of whom 1,800 fell within two hours in a space less than a hundred yards square. Its capture gave Wellington the fourth of the keys to Spain. Once it was taken, he held the initiative and could strike when and where he chose. Napoleon's lack of interest in Spain became total.

*   *   *

The peace between France and Russia in 1807 lasted for five years but it was satisfactory to neither side. Napoleon regarded the Tilsit settlement as no more than a convenient truce. He had been in no position to invade Russia in 1807 but he could not indefinitely tolerate another great power on the continent of Europe. As has been seen, he was shocked in 1808 when the Czar presumed to treat with him as an equal, but until he could be confident of mounting a campaign which would crush Russia he was content to accept whatever advantage could immediately be extracted from the situation, notably the closing of Russian ports and the elimination of Sweden as an enemy.

It was never easy to know what Czar Alexander was feeling but even if his admiration for Napoleon was not always simulated, his disenchantment with the French alliance was not long in growing. The establishment of a French puppet, the Grand Duchy of Warsaw, on Russia's frontier was regarded as an affront which was magnified when Austrian Galicia was added to the Duchy. Although all-powerful in theory, no Czar could afford to neglect the opinion of the Russian nobility. Too many of his predecessors had lost their thrones and their lives by doing so and Alexander had always before his eyes the example of his father who had been murdered in a palace revolution with General Bennigsen as one of the leading conspirators. Now most of the aristocracy saw the Tilsit settlement as a national humiliation, necessary perhaps in the aftermath of defeat but not to be endured for long.

The trading community was even less happy than the nobility. Russia's economic situation had never been strong and the closing of her ports made it desperate. The value of the rouble fell from 2.90 francs to 1.50. To avert disaster Alexander, in a ukase of 31 December 1810, laid down a new scale of custom charges, lower for goods imported by sea than for those of, for example, French origin, which came overland. At the same time Russian ports were reopened to neutral shipping. The majority of the goods brought by these vessels were of British origin and had certainly sailed under British licence, so that this move was clearly a breach of the Continental System, although as Alexander pointed out it was no more so than Napoleon's issue of trading licences.

Friction between Russia and France might have been lessened if Napoleon had been prepared to treat the Czar with some consideration. Instead he annexed the Grand Duchy of Oldenburg in 1810 without prior notice to St Petersburg. Oldenburg, lying to the west of Hamburg, was the domain of Alexander's brother-in-law and had been guaranteed to him at Tilsit. Even the Austrian marriage could be construed as an insult to Russia, since the match was announced before Napoleon's negotiations for the hand of a Russian princess had been broken off.

A reform of the Russian army had been in progress since Friedland and this the Czar had entrusted to General Barclay de Tolly, a Livonian of Scottish ancestry. He formed corps of all arms on the French model and breaking away from the parade ground niceties obsessively favoured by Paul I, emphasized musketry training. At the same time, he followed Suvarov's belief that the bayonet was the Russian soldier's natural weapon and advocated the use of mass formations, again on the French model, so that the bayonet could be used to its greatest effect. Much was done to improve the lot of the soldier in the ranks. The disciplinary code was made less severe, rations were improved, a more practical uniform was introduced and the basis for officer selection was widened although it remained rare for an officer not from the nobility to reach field or general rank. Barclay himself, it should be noticed, had spent 14 years in the ranks of the cavalry before receiving his first commission. Traditionally Russia had always had a sound military engineering service and the artillery was, after Tilsit, enlarged and improved so that it was at least a match for that of France.

Five years were too short a time to cure all the Russian army's defects. Medical and supply services remained rudimentary and staff work was poor. Few Russians of any social class were sufficiently educated to make competent staff officers, most of the officers preferring a good stand-up fight to the minutiae of paperwork. As a result most of the administration of the army fell to foreigners, many of them Prussians, and since most

71 General Mikhail
Bogdanovic Barclay de
Tolly. *Painting by George
Dawe*

Russians have a strong streak of xenophobia, foreigners tended to be blamed for anything that went wrong, especially anything that prevented the fighting of a full-scale battle. Another serious shortcoming was the lack of standardization in small arms. In 1812 the army had muskets of 28 different calibres and rifled carbines of 11 types.

Notwithstanding these flaws the Russian army was a very formidable machine. If the men in the ranks were not very intelligent they were tougher than any other soldiers in the world. They were almost indestructible in defence and could outmarch even the French. In 1812 the Russian strength was 400,000 but only half of these were available for the Polish front, the remainder being required on the Persian frontier, in Finland, in garrisons, or in the war with Turkey, that had been in progress since 1806.

By 1811 there was no doubt that war between Russia and France was inevitable and both sides did their best to gain what diplomatic advantages were available. Alexander failed in his attempts to secure the support of Austria and Prussia but he was more successful elsewhere. A peace, albeit an unsatisfactory one, was concluded with Turkey on 28 May 1812 and this allowed 35,000 experienced men from the Danube to be available in Poland before the winter set in. Equally important was the understanding reached with Sweden. The two countries had been enemies for a century and Swedish enmity had mounted when Russia seized Finland in 1809. In the following year the Swedes, who had a mad king and a disputed succession, elected the French Marshal Bernadotte, Prince of Ponte Corvo, to be Prince Royal and effective ruler of their country. The Czar was much affronted, believing that Napoleon had insinuated Bernadotte, the brother-in-law of Joseph Bonaparte, into Stockholm as a threat to Russia. As it happened Napoleon had mistrusted Bernadotte for years and was most reluctant to agree to his move to Sweden. The Czar had no need for alarm since the new Prince Royal was only concerned with being on the winning side and picking up whatever was to be gained from any set of circumstances. Knowing that France must fight Russia, he offered Napoleon 50,000 Swedish troops on condition that Norway be ceded to Sweden but with more delicacy than he usually showed the Emperor refused, on the ground that Norway belonged to his Danish ally. Bernadotte thereupon offered Swedish neutrality to Russia on the same terms. Alexander, who had no special concern with the status of Norway, immediately agreed. He was much relieved by Bernadotte's assurance that Sweden would not try to regain Finland since its boundaries were uncomfortably close to St Petersburg, and he relied on this assurance to remove the majority of his garrison in Finland for use against the French. A strong body of Swedish opinion favoured a Finnish campaign but this was disarmed by Napoleon's tactless seizure of Pomerania (which was ruthlessly plundered by Marshal Davout) in January 1812, whereupon Sweden resumed trade with Britain.

Napoleon believed that a war with Russia was necessary 'for crushing England by crushing the only continental power still strong enough to give him any trouble by joining her.' He made preparations on a gigantic scale. He secured the support of Austria and Prussia since neither was in any position to refuse. The Emperor Francis undertook to provide 34,000 men to cover the right flank of the French but he sent secret messages to St Petersburg assuring Alexander that Austrian hostilities would be kept to a minimum. Prussia was less fortunately placed. With Berlin occupied by the French and most of their 1807 indemnity still to pay, she had no alternative to providing a corps of 25,000 men and to supplying the *Grande Armée* with quarters and rations while they were assembling for the campaign. In fact, even the most anti-French among the Prussian leaders were not wholly averse to this cooperation with their enemies. It would give an opportunity for expanding their army, limited to 42,000 men since Tilsit, and it would enable them to test under battle conditions the reforms that had been carried out in the army since Jena.

The rest of the *Grande Armée*, save for two regiments of Portuguese who had been drafted eastward in 1807, came from countries under Napoleon's direct control. The Kingdom of Italy sent a corps of 45,000 men, the Grand Duchy of Warsaw 35,000. The Kingdoms of Bavaria, Saxony and Westphalia each sent 15-20,000 men and there were contingents from Anhalt, Baden, Berg, Croatia, Dalmatia, Denmark, Hesse-Darmstadt, Illyria, Lippe, Mecklenberg, Naples, Spain, Switzerland and Württemberg. In all the army totalled 600,000 men but of these only 270,000 were native Frenchmen, even including the Belgians, Dutch, Frieslanders and western Italians whose countries had been anexed to France. From Spain Napoleon had only dared withdraw two divisions of the Young Guard and the Polish troops—about 27,000 men. There remained in Spain as many native French troops as were about to march into Russia.

While this vast horde—40 divisions of infantry, 25 of cavalry with 1,500 guns—outnumbered the Russian forces facing them by three to one, they posed an enormous logistic problem. Though Napoleon announced that 'on the plains of Russia nature produces fodder beneath the hooves of the horses', he made unprecedented preparations for supplying the troops. A chain of huge depots was established at Königsberg (Kaliningrad), Danzig, Thorn (Torun), Marienburg (Malbork), Marienwerder (Tczew), Kolberg (Kolobrzeg), Modlin and Warsaw, the depot at Danzig alone holding rations for 400,000 men for 50 days. To bring the provisions forward a supply train was organized consisting of 3,024 four-horse waggons each capable of carrying $1\frac{1}{2}$ tons, 2,400 one-horse waggons (12 cwt) and 2,400 ox waggons (1 ton), while elaborate arrangements were made to bring supplies forward by water whenever this was possible.

These preparations, vast as they were, were not intended to provide all that the troops would need as they fought their way to Moscow. Napoleon

10th Reg.t Portuguese Cavalry.

envisaged a short campaign ending in a decisive victory. In his proclamation to the troops on 22 June he announced that 'The second Polish war has opened', for it was in Poland that he expected to decide the campaign. At about the same time he remarked that 'In less than two months time the Russians will be suing for peace.' While he looked forward to occupying both Moscow and St Petersburg he envisaged this being done by a triumphal march after the fighting was over.

His main striking force consisted of 235,000 men. Two smaller forces, each of 70,000 men and commanded respectively by Eugène Beauharnais and Jérome Bonaparte, were echeloned back on his right, and the wings were covered by the Prussian and Austrian corps each supported by French-controlled troops. The attacking force alone consisted of 375,000 men with more than 100,000 horses and these would be advancing on a comparatively narrow front, where after the first wave of men and horses had passed there would be not a blade of grass left to feed those who followed. While French armies were accustomed to living off the countryside through which they passed, it cannot be supposed that Napoleon, who was well-informed about conditions on the road ahead, believed it possible to subsist on the vast plains between the Niemen and Moscow during anything but a steady, orderly, unopposed march giving the waggons and the barges plenty of time to ply between the depots and the army. Some thought of this kind must have crossed his mind when he was dining with Murat, Berthier and his ADC, Colonel Rapp, just before the campaign began.

He was silent for a time; then suddenly he asked Rapp how far it was from Danzig to Cadiz?

'Too far, Sire.'

'It will be much further in a few months.'

'So much the worse.'

*   *   *

In the space between the Baltic at Memel (Klaipeda) and the Pripet marshes lay two Russian armies. Barclay de Tolly's First Army of the West, 110,000 strong, was around Vilna (Vilnyus) and on their left was the Second Army, 60,000, under Prince Bagration. The Third Army under Tormasov, consisting of 45,000 men, mostly recruits, was stationed to the south of the marshes, and had the unexacting task of keeping the Austrians under observation. Further Russian armies were being formed and large bodies of men were marching towards the Polish front from Finland and Romania, but in the high summer of 1812 only the three Armies of the West, 215,000 men, were available to resist the half million and more of the *Grande Armée*. Napoleon's plan was to separate Barclay's army from Bagration and annihilate the former while Eugène and Jérome held Bagration at bay. He was fortunate that the Russian plan also called for the First and Second

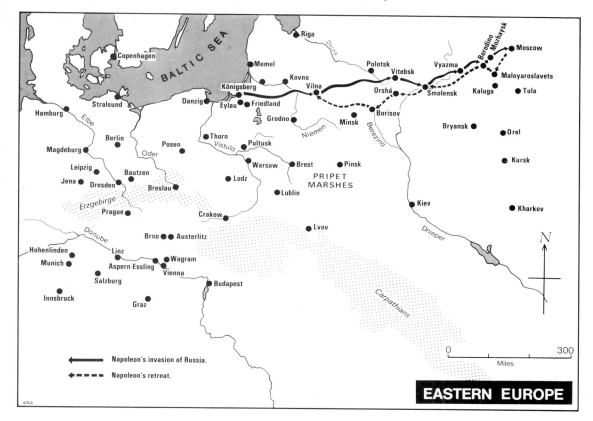

Armies to separate. The Czar, always susceptible to charlatans, had adopted a plan put forward by a Prussian colonel, Ernst von Phull, a man who believed that war could be conducted in much the same way as a quiet game of chess. Phull planned that Barclay should fall back 150 miles to the town of Drissa on the east bank of the Dvina river. There the First Army would take up a position in an entrenched camp on which much labour had been expended. While Napoleon was puzzling over the obstacle thus presented, his army would be surrounded by Bagration's 60,000 men and forced to surrender. How the disparity in numbers was to be overcome was not explained, although it is fair to add that the Russians were under the impression that Napoleon had only 300,000 men.

The Russians had no commander-in-chief. The Czar gave Barclay the task of coordinating the movements of the First and Second Armies but Bagration was his senior, disliked him, and did not feel obliged to comply with his requests. Accompanying the army was Bennigsen, the discredited general of Eylau and Friedland, who was also senior to Barclay. The Czar, who had imposed the Phull strategy without consulting Barclay, Bagration or Bennigsen, also started the campaign at headquarters but was induced to return to Moscow to organize the home front.

On 24 June the French began to cross the Niemen into Russian territory and found themselves unopposed. Napoleon reached Vilna four days later and although disappointed that no battle had been fought, declared, 'My manoeuvres have disconcerted the Russians; before a month has passed they will be on their knees to me.' There was still no sign of the Russian army and the Lithuanian population was apathetic when not actively hostile. Already there was a shortage of forage, and 5,000 horses died from being fed on green rye. 100 guns and 500 ammunition waggons had to be abandoned. Dysentery began to appear among the troops.

Barclay fell back as instructed but when he reached Drissa he found that the entrenched camp was too small and tactically indefensible. Napoleon meanwhile, had found the gap between the two Russian armies and was driving on Vitebsk. For a time there was a possibility that Bagration might be surrounded, but he was saved by Jérome's lethargic handling of his army. The Russians scrambled back to Smolensk and Jérome, superseded by Davout, retired to accumulate more debts in Westphalia.

At Vitebsk Napoleon was 280 miles from his base and there seemed to be no prospect of fighting the decisive battle on which he had grounded his plan. Already he was beyond the range of his supply train. His Master of the Horse wrote:

Our waggons, built for metalled roads, were in no way suitable for the country we had to traverse. The first sand we came to overwhelmed the horses.... The Emperor was always anxious to obtain everything with the least possible expense and the result was that, to move large depots, everything had been loaded on waggons in the hope of being able to commandeer horses from the countryside. This had always been done in previous campaigns, both for draught horses and to replace casualties, but in Russia there were no means of doing this. Horses, cattle, inhabitants had all fled and we found ourselves in the middle of a desert. Every branch of the service abandoned its equipment beside the road.... Here we were at Vitebsk without even fighting a battle and already there was no surgical lint.... All the enormous quantity of supplies which had been amassed at such expense vanished either by theft or because there was no way of bringing it forward.

The fighting troops were in no better condition than the supply train. Murat sent his Chief of Staff to the Emperor to tell him that the cavalry were disintegrating.

The horses were not shod, the harness was in a deplorable state, the forges, like all the rest of the stores, had been left in the rear. There were no nails, no iron suitable for making them and no smiths. Nothing had been foreseen and the most indispensable things were lacking.

It was calculated that already half the horses with which the army had started were no longer serviceable. Nor were the infantry in good condition.

*The roads were covered in stragglers who destroyed and wasted everything. . . .
Disorder reigned everywhere, everyone was in want. The Guard was in no better
plight than the other corps, and thence arose indiscipline and all its attendant evils.*

73 Platov and his Cossacks
in 1812. *From a coloured
aquatint by G. Schadow*

Two options were open to Napoleon. He could wait at Vitebsk and hope
to be attacked or he could press on to seek a battle. His own preference was
for the second course, but so many of his officers, led by Berthier, advised
him to wait that he might have adopted the more prudent course had not a
Russian officer prisoner told him that the Russians were preparing to stand
at Smolensk. This was partly true. Barclay was under such pressure from
Bagration and other senior officers to stop retreating that he had agreed
that both armies should counter-attack from Smolensk. On 8 August some
French cavalry was successfully attacked at Inkovo by Cossacks led by their
hetman, Platov, but this was the total of the counter-attack. Barclay believed
that his right was threatened and halted the advance but Inkovo was
enough to convince Napoleon that the Russians had decided to fight. He
decided to continue his advance.

He almost succeeded in forcing a great battle at Smolensk, for Barclay

74 *Opposite Page* Matvei
Ivanovic Platov, Hetman
of the Cossacks.

and Bagration were scarcely on speaking terms and coordination between
their armies was for a time non-existent. Moreover, while Barclay was
anxiously guarding his right, Napoleon swung round the Russian left,
crossed the Dnieper and attacked Smolensk from the south. Only a gallant
rearguard action by 9,500 Russians under General Neverovsky gained
enough time for the two armies to unite in the city and for Barclay to
impose a momentary single command. Bagration and most of the generals
were determined to make a stand but Barclay over-rode them. He
recognized that his outnumbered army would be destroyed in a battle and
insisted on a retreat (17 August), holding Smolensk for 24 hours with a
rearguard. For the Russian fire-eaters this was the last straw. They
despatched a British officer, Sir Robert Wilson, to St Petersburg with a
thinly veiled ultimatum to the Czar calling for the supersession of Barclay
and, for good measure, demanding the dismissal of the Foreign Minister
who was suspected of pro-French sympathies. As it happened, Alexander
had already decided to appoint the 67-year-old Kutusov to the supreme
command. He disliked and distrusted him but knew him to be greatly
admired by the Russian generals and the army.

The French found quantities of supplies, including standing corn, in the
Smolensk area and Napoleon decided to halt.

> *I will fortify my positions. We will rest the troops and from this base we will
> organize the country. . . . My army will then be more formidable and my position
> more threatening than if I had won two battles. I will set up headquarters at
> Vitebsk, raise Poland in arms, and if later on it is necessary I will choose between
> marching on Moscow or St Petersburg.*

This wise decision did not stand for long. Murat, commanding the advance
guard, reported, with very little evidence, that the Russians were making a
stand. Once more the delusive hope of a decisive victory drew Napoleon
forward. As Caulaincourt wrote, 'The Emperor always hoped to have on
the morrow what had escaped him that day.'

On 29 August the Russian army was still retreating when Kutusov
joined them west of Gzhatsk. He found only 100,000 exhausted men being
pursued by Napoleon with 133,000. He continued Barclay's policy of
retreating until 3 September, when he reached a passable defensive position
near Borodino. Having been joined by sufficient reinforcements to give
him a rough equality in numbers with his enemies, he decided that he could
no longer postpone allowing the army to fight the battle they had been
demanding ever since the French crossed the frontier.

Napoleon attacked the Borodino position on 7 September. The Battle of
the Moskva, as the French call it, was one of the bloodiest fought before the
twentieth century and on neither side did the high command show to great
advantage. Kutusov stationed himself well to the rear and left the tactical

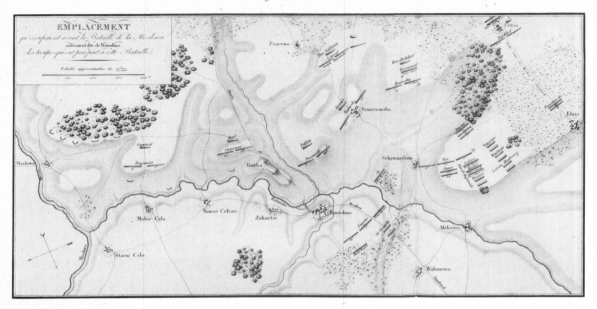

75 Plan of the positions of the armies before the Battle of Borodino

control to Barclay and Bagration, who cooperated no better than might be expected of two generals who were not speaking to each other. Napoleon rejected a scheme put forward by Davout for an enveloping movement and launched instead a series of costly frontal attacks. Then he relapsed into lethargy until most of Kutusov's positions had been stormed, when he refused to commit the Imperial Guard to a final thrust which might have turned a costly tactical advantage into the overwhelming victory he needed so badly. Desperate bravery was shown by the troops on both sides but the clumsiness with which they were handled was reflected in the casualty lists. The French lost 30,000 men, the Russians 44,000, including Prince Bagration who died of his wounds.

The Russians were more able to afford their great loss. There were limitless reserves of manpower behind them while Napoleon was 500 miles from his base and 1,500 from his capital. He still had 100,000 men in hand but he had failed to crush the Russian army. His front was a monstrous salient pointing at Moscow. His flanks were appallingly vulnerable but still he was driven forward by the belief that the capture of one of Russia's capital cities would end the war. 'Peace lies in Moscow. When the great Russian nobles see us masters of their capital they will think twice before continuing the war.'

Kutusov was changing his view on this point. In his despatch from the battlefield he claimed, falsely, that 'the enemy has in no part gained an inch of ground' and added, 'Tomorrow I shall place myself at the head of the army and drive the enemy, without further ado, from the soil of Holy Russia.' Wiser counsels prevailed in the morning. Only Bennigsen, bold now that he had no responsibility, opposed the decision to continue the

retreat when Kutusov declared, 'I see my first duty as the preservation of the army. The loss of Moscow does not mean the loss of Russia.'

The French entered a deserted Moscow on 14 September without further fighting. That evening, for reasons which have never been explained, the city caught fire and burned until heavy rains extinguished the flames six days later. About a sixth of the buildings were destroyed.

A month before Napoleon captured Moscow he had lost Madrid. On 13 June Wellington had marched into Spain at the head of 50,000 men, of whom 18,000 were Portuguese and 3,500 Spanish. There were five weeks of manoeuvre between Salamanca and the Douro before Marmont, at the head of the *Armée du Portugal*, over-reached himself near the village of Arapiles, a few miles south of Salamanca. Wellington proved that he was not, as the French had believed, a defensively-minded commander by seizing the fleeting opportunity which he was offered and rolling up the over-extended left wing of the French army. Marmont was seriously wounded and on the following day his successor reported that he had only 20,000 men with the eagles. Wellington entered Madrid on 12 August.

76 Russian cavalry and infantry at the Battle of Borodino. *Painting by Denis Dighton*

173

It was a success which Britain badly needed for it had been a depressing summer. In May Spencer Perceval, the Prime Minister, had been assassinated in the lobby of the House of Commons, and the formation of a new ministry under Lord Liverpool had been a long and difficult business. On 18 June the United States, determined to filch Canada while British attention was engaged elsewhere, declared war. There were only four British battalions in Canada but the American attacks were so ill-managed that those four were enough. More serious was the naval threat. The US Navy was very small, only eight frigates and eight smaller ships, but three of the frigates were 44-gun ships, magnificently designed. They could outshoot any British frigate and outsail any ship of the line. In 1812 three British 38-gun frigates were captured and with a swarm of privateers also at large, the Royal Navy was put under greater strain than at any time since the French Revolution. The war with America might also have crippled Wellington's campaign in the Peninsula since much of the corn which fed both the British army and the Portuguese population was imported from the United States. Fortunately the maritime states disapproved of President Madison's war and continued to ship grain to Lisbon on the grounds that they were not at war with Portugal.

The capture of Madrid brought about the concentration of French armies that Wellington had always foreseen. Soult evacuated Andalusia and by October Wellington, who had undertaken a somewhat half-hearted siege of Burgos, found himself in 'the worst military situation I was ever in.' With 78,000 men, of whom one third were Spaniards of dubious reliability, he was in danger of being surrounded and defeated in detail by 114,000 Frenchmen. He made a masterly retreat and by 19 November his army was back in Portugal. This retreat was a great disappointment to public opinion in Britain but the gains for the year had been very great. Spain south of the Sierra Morena, 3,000 guns and 20,000 prisoners had been taken, Ciudad Rodrigo and Badajoz were in allied hands, and Wellington himself had established a moral superiority over his French opponents as great as that which Napoleon had held over the eastern European generals.

*   *   *

From Moscow Napoleon sent peace proposals to the Czar. Throughout his life he clung to the idea that the occupation of an enemy capital should mean the end of the war. He received no reply from Alexander who promised his army, 'I will abide by the worst. I am ready to remove my family into the interior and undergo every sacrifice. If necessary I will let my beard grow to my waist and eat potatoes in Siberia.' Napoleon was thus faced with three possible courses of action. First, he could stay where he was and hope that the army, which had no winter clothing, could find enough food to last through the Russian winter. Although considerable stocks of food had been found in Moscow it soon became clear that these would not last until the snows melted. Secondly, he could retreat to Poland or some centre within Russia where he would be in closer touch with his depots. Such a retreat would, he feared, diminish his prestige and tempt Austria and Prussia to desert him. The third course was to break out to the south and head for the fertile Ukraine. If he did this he would not escape the menace of an ever-growing Russian army while his own force must shrink still further. If he was to make a successful move southward he must first defeat Kutusov, and his experience told him that Kutusov would not accept a major battle.

Faced with these unattractive options and with winter approaching, the Emperor decided to defer a decision, hoping for a conciliatory reply from the Czar. Already his communications with Poland were becoming difficult. Cossacks and irregulars were taking a heavy toll of stragglers and small bodies of men around Moscow itself, and soon after his arrival Napoleon was forced to issue an order that no force of less than 1,500 men should move on the Moscow–Smolensk road. An observer on the Russian side wrote,

Every day prisoners in parties of fifty, and even of a hundred, have been brought in, chiefly wounded. In five days 1,342 were delivered to headquarters. Of course, many more are killed; for such is the inveteracy of the peasants that they buy prisoners of the Cossacks and put them to death.

Immediately after the French reached Moscow they lost track of the Russian army. Murat insisted that they had marched eastward on the Kazan road and it was not until 26 September, 12 days after the entry into the capital, that it was discovered that they were only 25 miles from the city on the river Pakra to the south. Two corps were sent against them but Kutusov, determined to avoid unnecessary fighting, withdrew 25 miles to Tarutino. This further retreat made Kutusov as unpopular among the Russian generals as Barclay had been at Smolensk. He was accused of cowardice and of being in league with the French. The fact was that he had appreciated that, sooner or later, Napoleon must retreat to Poland and the later he started to do so the more damage would be done to the French army. His tactics were those Wellington had employed against Masséna except that he was using Russia's vast distances to serve the purpose of Wellington's impenetrable Lines. He was, nevertheless, persuaded to mount a limited attack against Murat's advanced cavalry which was encamped, with culpable carelessness, at Vinkovo. As Kutusov had foreseen, the Russian night-move before the attack was chaotic, but those forces which did manage to get within striking distance achieved complete surprise and Murat lost 2,500 men and 38 guns. Three days earlier, on 15 October, Napoleon had given orders for the evacuation of Moscow on 20 October.

77 Russian cuirassiers, 1812

His intention was to put the army into winter quarters in the area Smolensk–Vitebsk–Minsk where there were huge stores of supplies guarded by the corps of Marshal Victor. His orders called for the move to be made on the Kaluga road so as to avoid the direct road to Smolensk which had long before been gleaned bare of provisions. Murat's defeat induced him to put the evacuation forward by 24 hours and it was on 19 October that the advance guard, Prince Eugène's Italian corps, left the city. Behind them came some 90,000 fighting men with a crowd of followers, sutlers, actresses, commissaries, women, children and sick soldiers travelling in every kind of carriage, waggon and cart which 'poured through the fields in three great columns. Inexhaustibly they seemed to pour out from the ruins of Moscow, and the heads of the columns vanished far away on the horizon.'

At first the Russians assumed that Eugène's move was no more than an unusually strong foraging expedition but after a day of desperate fighting they succeeded in checking its advance at Maloyaroslavets on 24 October. Napoleon rode up to the head of his column and weighed the chances of breaking through by a set-piece attack. Here was the opportunity of fighting the decisive battle which he had sought for six months. Now that it seemed to be offered to him, he could not afford the risk. Another Borodino would destroy the army. He gave orders to make for the main Smolensk road and the prospect of starvation. Had he known it, Kutusov, to the fury of his generals, had decided not to fight it out at Maloyaroslavets.

At this stage the strategic direction of the Russian armies reverted from Kutusov to the Czar. From St Petersburg Alexander laid down a plan to surround and destroy the *Grande Armée*. From the north General Wittgenstein, with the corps that had been guarding St Petersburg and the troops withdrawn from Finland, was to block the gap between the Dvina and Beresina rivers. From the south Admiral Tchitchagov, with the Third Army of the West reinforced by 35,000 men withdrawn from the Danube, was to drive the Austrians back towards Warsaw and, leaving a corps to keep them in check, wheel round the west of the Pripet marshes and seize the line of the Beresina, thus blocking the French retreat. To Kutusov's army was allocated the rôle of following the French so as to give them no

78 The French retreat from Russia

79 Napoleon's guard at the Beresina. *From an original drawing by Peter Hess*

rest until they were blocked by the barrier formed by the armies of Wittgenstein and Tchitchagov.

Thanks to the impetuosity of General Miloradovitch, commanding Kutusov's advanced guard, the rear of Napoleon's column was repeatedly harassed. On 4 November, the day the first snow fell, Miloradovitch succeeded in causing a panic in Davout's corps and the French lost 8,000 men. Two days later, with the *Grande Armée* reduced to living on partially cooked horseflesh, the winter set in in earnest and the French morale began to collapse. When they reached Smolensk on 8 November they found that Victor's corps had marched north to hold Wittgenstein back and had taken most of the store of provisions with him. The distribution of what remained was grossly mismanaged, the corps of the rearguard getting nothing. By this time the army was down to 49,000 men. Even the Imperial Guard, who had entered Russia 47,000 strong and had not fired a shot, could only put 16,000 men into the field. The Polish corps was reduced to 800 men, the Westphalians to 700. The retreat continued.

The rearguard left Smolensk on 15 November, the day on which Miloradovitch tried without success to block the march of the Guard at Krasnoye. Next day he ambushed the Italian corps at the same place.

Eugène fought his way out with 900 from the 5,000 men who had left Smolensk. On 18 November Kutusov was induced to try to cut off the French rearguard of 15,000 men under Davout and Ney who were accompanied by a mass of unarmed stragglers. Napoleon and Eugène turned back to rescue the two marshals but Ney with 6,000 men was trapped. The Russians, however, could not hold *le brave des braves* and making a wide circuit Ney rejoined the Emperor at Orsha on 21 November with 900 men. In a week the French army, through battle and hardship, had lost 25,000 men.

Meanwhile Tchitchagov had taken Minsk, the huge supply depot on which Napoleon was depending for the army's rations. On 16 November the admiral reached Borisov just in time to destroy the bridge, 600 yards long, before Marshal Oudinot arrived to secure the crossing, while to the north Victor was barely able to hold Wittgenstein back on the Ulla river. The Czar's trap had almost shut but it was not proof against Napoleon and his chief engineer, General Eblé. Tchitchagov could not be driven from the west bank of the Beresina but his reserves were lured away to the south by a demonstration. Eight miles north Eblé went to work at Studianka to make two bridges from the timber torn from demolished houses. Between 26 and

80 The remains of the French army crossing the two bridges built by General Eblé across the Beresina at Studianka. *Painting by Albrecht Adam*

179

29 November 25,000 men of the *Grande Armée* struggled across and marched through the snow towards Vilna. A rather larger number were killed or captured on the east bank. By mid-December Russia was clear of French troops except for prisoners.

The central thrust of Napoleon's advance had, with its reinforcements, consisted of 400,000 men. It left Russia with a formed strength of 1,000, large numbers of stragglers coming in later. The Russians suffered as much from the weather and, since Kutusov's army had to march on a road already picked bare by the enemy, they suffered even more than the French from the lack of food. They lost 90,000 men between Moscow and the frontier.

*   *   *

On 5 December French headquarters were at Smorgon, east of Vilna, and Napoleon decided that he must leave his army, entrusting the command to Murat.

> *I must go. I can only keep my grip on Europe from the Tuileries. I must watch what Austria does and keep Prussia loyal.... When they know I am in Paris, leading the nation and at the head of the 200,000 men I shall raise, they will think twice before they make war against me.*

As he travelled westward in his sleigh, accompanied only by Caulaincourt, his Master of the Horse, he talked of the campaign that was ending and of the future:

> *It is the winter that has been our undoing. We are the victims of the climate. The fine weather tricked me.... Everything turned out badly because I stayed too long in Moscow. If I had left four days after I had occupied it, as I thought of doing when I saw it in flames, the Russians would have been lost. The Czar would gladly have accepted the terms I would have offered from Vitebsk.... If the King of Naples does not make any foolish mistakes things will soon be all right.*

He seemed not to realize the magnitude of the disaster that had overtaken his army. He clung to the illusion that he still had 150,000 men on the eastern front and that they could keep a bridgehead in Russia by holding Vilna:

> *Vilna is well stocked with food, and will put everything to rights. There is more material there than they will need to withstand the enemy. The Russians will be at least as tired as we are, and they are suffering just as much from the cold; they are sure to go into winter quarters. Nothing will be seen of them except for Cossacks.*

He took an optimistic view of his other problems. According to the last news he had received, Wellington was still in Madrid, but he asserted:

> *As for the war in Spain, it is now little more than a matter of guerrilla contests. On the day that the English are driven out of the Peninsula there will be nothing left to do but to round up isolated bodies of rebels....*

He recurred continually to the subject of England, which occupied his mind above everything else.

> *. . . The only way to harm England is to undermine her credit, and that requires time. They still have, it is true, great resources but in England everything depends on confidence and the least thing may paralyse them and ruin their whole monetary system.*

He reached Paris on 18 December, the day after the 29me *Bulletin* (written on 3 December) had been published in the capital. This gave a reasonably truthful account of the army's misfortunes but attributed all of them to the weather. It stressed the harm done to the cavalry but omitted to mention that the loss had fallen even more heavily on the infantry. It ended 'His Majesty's health has never been better.'

The *Grande Armée* could not hold Vilna. There were not enough men and the will to fight left the army with the Emperor. Berthier wrote, 'Every human effort is useless. One can only resign oneself to the inevitable.' Only Ney was indomitable. He organized a rearguard but with the rivers frozen there was no place to make a stand. On 13 December he burned the bridge over the Niemen at Kovno (Kaunas) and marched his remaining troops, 400 infantry and 600 dismounted cavalry, into East Prussia. He was 'wearing a brown coat and had a long beard. His face was black and seemed to be burned, and his eyes were glistening and red.' When all the stragglers had been collected there were 20,000 men available to guard the eastern front.

There was worse to come. Murat, who even before the snow had set in had been heard to remark '*Ce n'est pas un climat pour un roi de Naples*', slunk off to his sunny kingdom and left the command to Prince Eugène. The King of Prussia, cowed as always, declared his continued loyalty to Napoleon but his generals felt otherwise. The Prussian corps of the *Grande Armée* had spent the campaign besieging Riga. When the retreat from Moscow forced them to fall back their commander, General Yorck von Wartenberg, decided that the time had come to call a halt. On 30 December he signed the Convention of Tauroggen (Taurage) by which the Russians agreed that his troops should be considered as neutral. Schwarzenberg was not long in following his example on behalf of the Austrian corps.

CHAPTER VI

1813–1814

'Majestic though in Ruin'

'I grew up on a battlefield and when one has done that one cares little for the lives of a million men.'

NAPOLEON I, 26 JUNE 1813

When he reached Paris Napoleon announced to his ministers, 'I have made a great error but I have the means of repairing it.' Although the *Grande Armée* had been destroyed, his resources were still vast. Europe was still under his control from Jutland to Calabria, from the Vistula to the Sierra Morena. He calculated that he could raise an army of 650,000 men and he knew that his prestige was still immense. His presence on a battlefield could paralyse the will of his opponents.

What he needed was time and, even allowing that the Russian troops were as tired as the French, time would only be available if Eugène with 20,000 exhausted men could hold his ground in the east. Yorck's defection at Tauroggen allowed the Russian right to swing forward into East Prussia and by the end of January Eugène was back behind the Elbe despite Napoleon's urgent order:

Stay in Berlin as long as you can. Maintain discipline by making examples. Burn down any Prussian town or village which shows signs of revolt. Burn Berlin if need be. In any case you must not retreat further than the Elbe. . . . By May I shall have assembled the three corps of the Armée du Main*, with my Guard and plenty of artillery and cavalry; then I shall drive the Russians back to the Niemen.*

The Russians were not in good order and could not put more than 110,000 men in the field, while most of their generals were opposed to continuing the pursuit once Russia was free from the invader. Kutusov was strongly opposed to invading Germany, saying,

81 Czar Alexander I in Germany, 1813. *From an original watercolour by L. M. Hess*

I am by no means sure that the total destruction of the French emperor and his army would be a benefit to the world; his succession would not fall to Russia or to any other continental power, but to that power which already commands the sea, and whose domination would be intolerable.

It was Czar Alexander, in his favoured rôle as Deliverer of Europe, who insisted that the war must continue and who gave orders for the raising of new armies.

If Russia was to succeed outside her own boundaries she must have allies. Austria had relapsed into a sullen neutrality so that Russian success or failure hinged on the King of Prussia. That flawed sovereign was anxious to be on the winning side and concerned only to decide which that would be. He connived at Yorck's Convention but dismissed him for signing it. He left Berlin for Breslau because the capital was full of French troops and wrote to Napoleon assuring him that he would never side with the Russians. On the same day he wrote to Alexander enclosing a draft treaty of alliance. This was an impertinent document in which he put the price of Prussia's support as the return of all the territory she had held before Jena with the addition of Austrian Galicia and augmentations in north Germany. The Czar dealt firmly with these suggestions and persuaded the wretched Frederick William to sign a secret treaty (26 February) on the understanding that he was to be compensated at the expense of Saxony. A month later Prussia declared war on France. Meanwhile a raid on Hamburg by 200 Cossacks had so terrified the French General Lauriston that he evacuated the city on 12 March. Davout was ordered to recapture it but to collect the necessary troops felt obliged to abandon Dresden.

By the end of April Napoleon had created a new *Grande Armée* of 145,000 men (exclusive of garrison troops) and 400 guns. It could not compare in quality with the army that had marched into Russia since it was short of cavalry and had a high proportion of very young recruits. Nevertheless it was a formidable force and its improvisation and equipment was a striking example of the Emperor's administrative genius. Less than 17,000 of these new troops for Germany were drawn from the *Armée de l'Espagne* which was left with a nominal strength of 240,000 of whom 195,000 were *présents sous les armes*. Marshal Soult was also withdrawn from Spain where he had made himself obnoxious to King Joseph. He was badly needed in Germany where capable corps commanders were scarce. Of the marshals, Lannes had been killed at Aspern-Essling, Berthier was on the verge of a nervous breakdown, Massena was in ill-merited disgrace, Bernadotte was Prince Royal of Sweden and Murat, who was negotiating with the Austrians for a guarantee of his kingdom, had only left Naples in response to a peremptory order from the Emperor. The situation rapidly became worse because Davout, having taken Hamburg, was ordered to stay there and never rejoined the main army, while Bessières was killed in a skirmish on 1 May.

The allies also lost an outstanding general when Kutusov, created Prince of Smolensk, died on 24 April. His successor, Wittgenstein, did not have the old man's caution. His field force was only 68,000 strong but, realizing that Napoleon would march on Leipzig, tried to attack the French right as they crossed the Saale. The two armies met at Lützen on 2 May and although the French were superior by two men to one, they had to fight hard to win a narrow victory which cost each side 10,000 men.

Shortage of cavalry prevented Napoleon from pursuing but he re-entered Dresden and continued eastward until, 35 miles beyond the Saxon capital, he came up with Wittgenstein, who had been reinforced by a newly arrived Russian corps, at Bautzen on 20 May. In a two-day battle the French again won a narrow tactical victory inflicting 20,000 casualties while suffering 13,000 themselves.

The allied armies, though mauled, were still intact but their high command was deeply divided. The Russians insisted on falling back into Poland while the Prussians were determined to defend Berlin. If Napoleon could have won one more victory the alliance against him would have disintegrated but he had his own problems, not least the raids made by Cossacks and German partisans on his communications, in one of which, on 30 May, a convoy of artillery escorted by 1,600 men was captured. When the allies proposed an armistice he agreed, explaining,

This armistice interrupts the course of my victories. I decided on it for two reasons: the shortage of cavalry, which prevents me from striking decisive blows, and the hostile attitude of Austria. . . . The armistice will, I expect, last through June and July. I hope to wait until September when, by a decisive blow, I shall be able to crush my enemies.

The armistice was signed at Pleischwitz on 4 June. It was to prove one of the Emperor's most serious errors. The allies had more to gain by delay than the French.

*   *   *

Despite the American war Lord Liverpool's government was resolute in reinforcing success in the Peninsula. Counting on the continued incompetence of the United States army they sent only five battalions to strengthen Canada while six regiments of cavalry and five battalions of infantry went to reinforce Wellington. By May 1813 the Anglo-Portuguese army could advance into Spain with a strength of 80,000 men to whom could be added a fluctuating number of Spaniards in various states of training and equipment.

King Joseph should have been able to oppose them with 95,000 French troops apart from those in eastern Spain and on the lines of communication, but since his return from Russia, Napoleon had resumed his practice of attempting to control events in Spain from Paris or Germany. He insisted that priority must be given to keeping open the road between Bayonne and Madrid which had been dominated by guerrillas since the French armies had concentrated to drive Wellington back to Portugal in the previous year. He ordered six infantry divisions to be moved from the Portuguese frontier, redeployed on the north bank of the Ebro and employed in hunting 'rebels'. This left Joseph with 33,000 infantry, 9,000 cavalry and 100 guns on Wellington's front but from Paris he was told:

Bearing in mind the circumstances in which the enemy finds himself, there is no reason to suppose that he will take the offensive. His remoteness, his shortage of transport, his constant and timid caution in any operation out of the ordinary, all demonstrate to us that we can act as seems most suitable without worry or inconvenience.

Joseph's 'timid' opponent was, meanwhile, writing, 'I cannot have a better opportunity for trying the fate of a battle which, if the enemy should be unsuccessful, must oblige him to withdraw altogether.' In May 1813 Wellington put himself 'in fortune's way' and embarked on a strategic manoeuvre as ambitious and farsighted as anything Napoleon ever attempted. Keeping a convincing screen on the line by which the French expected him to advance, the Ciudad Rodrigo–Salamanca road, he passed 50,000 men through the supposedly impassable mountains of Tras os Montes and swept round the French right. He continued to use this manoeuvre for the next four weeks and was across the Ebro after no more than a few minor skirmishes which cost his army only 201 casualties.

On 21 June he found King Joseph's army, 60,000 men with 138 guns, in the plain of Vitoria and expecting to be outflanked once more. Wellington had advanced so fast that, although he was driving the enemy back on their reserves, less than half their detached troops had managed to rejoin them. The Battle of Vitoria was a small affair compared with Borodino—the French lost 8,000 men, the allies 5,000 (of whom 3,675 were British)—but it was decisive. By 24 June King Joseph's army was making its best speed for the Pyrenees accompanied by a single howitzer, the only cannon left to it. There were still garrisons in Pamplona, San Sebastian and Santoña but the Bonaparte kingdom of Spain was at an end. All that remained was Catalonia which had been incorporated into France as four *départements* and was held by Marshal Louis Gabriel Suchet.

Wellington's victory resounded throughout Europe. The Russo-Prussian alliance was in danger of dissolution. Only the adherence of Austria could save it and Austria, as was to be expected after four humiliating defeats in 17 years, was havering. Few of her leaders did not wish to see France defeated but many doubted the wisdom of fighting her again until victory was certain. Sweden had undertaken to join the allies but no one trusted Bernadotte to produce actual help. All looked to Britain for support but apart from a subsidy of £2 million shared between Prussia and Russia and the promise of £$\frac{1}{2}$ million to Austria should she take part, Britain could only provide six under-strength battalions to garrison Stralsund and a troop of the new-fangled Congreve rockets to serve in the field. The allies felt that she was not doing her share. On 6 June the British Commissioner at allied headquarters wrote to London, 'We are not considered here (from all I see going on). Wellington must send you a victory to bruit forth.' On 30 June the news of Vitoria arrived and Count Stadion burst into Metternich's bedroom, waking him with the cry '*Le roi Joseph est f——— en Espagne.*'

Four days earlier Metternich had called on Napoleon at the Marcolini Palace near Dresden. He went to offer Austria's mediation between France and the eastern allies but he had met with a brusque reception:

So you want war? Well, you shall have it. I have annihilated the Prussian army at Lützen; I smashed the Russians at Bautzen; now you want to have your turn. Very well—we shall meet at Vienna.

Metternich quietly said what he had come to say. Europe could have peace if France would agree to the dissolution of the Duchy of Warsaw, the liberation of Hamburg, the restoration of Prussia's former territory and the return of Dalmatia to Austria. These were very moderate terms but they drove Napoleon to renewed anger:

Never! I know how to die; but never shall I agree to cede an inch of territory. Your sovereigns, who were born to thrones, can be beaten twenty times and still return to their capitals. I cannot do that. I am a self-made soldier.

Austria, said Metternich, was prepared to back her mediation with an army of a quarter of a million men while the new French conscripts were 'no more than children. What will be left to you when these infants are wiped out?' Hurling his hat into the corner, the Emperor screamed,

You are not a soldier! You know nothing of what goes on in a soldier's mind. I grew up on a battlefield and when one has done that one cares little for the lives of a million men.

Soon the imperial temper cooled and, after an interview lasting nine hours, it was agreed that the armistice should be extended until 17 August while a peace conference under Austrian chairmanship met at Prague.

The conference failed because Napoleon refused to make any meaningful concessions. According to his own account,

I could not afford to risk my hegemony in Europe while the balance of power between myself and England was still unsettled.... I thought the coming campaign would settle everything. There was more than a fair chance of driving the Russians and the Prussians back and of frightening the Austrians, whose resolution I underestimated. I believed that a single crashing victory would bring England to the conference table in order to save her allies from total destruction.

His calculations were wrong. Austria declared war on 12 August and when the armistice lapsed the allies gave the supreme command to Prince Schwarzenberg, an Austrian who was two years younger than Napoleon. His military talents were modest but he had a real genius for keeping the allies together, a nineteenth-century Eisenhower.

On a front that stretched from Hamburg to Prague, Schwarzenberg commanded 435,000 men against Napoleon's 375,000. On the right of the allied line was the Army of the North, 110,000 men under the nominal command of Bernadotte, Prince Royal of Sweden. Their main task was to protect Berlin but their orders were to threaten Hamburg if possible. In the centre Blücher was instructed to take Görlitz (Zgorzelec) and Torgau with

83 Marshal Prince Karl
Schwarzenberg

the 95,000 men of the Army of Silesia. The main striking force, 230,000 men under Schwarzenberg himself, assembled round Prague and was known as the Army of Bohemia. Their aim was to invade Saxony from the south.

Faced with an enemy so widely dispersed General Buonaparte would have defeated them in detail by a series of lightning blows but the Emperor Napoleon wrote, 'My intention is to leave the initiative to the enemy.' He stationed himself with the reserve near Görlitz and gave Macdonald 100,000 men with whom to check Blücher. His only offensive move was to send Oudinot with 72,000 to take Berlin, a task the marshal would have fulfilled had Bernadotte had his way. The Prince Royal gave orders to abandon the city but his Prussian subordinate, Bülow, turned to him and said,

> 'Is it possible that your Royal Highness would surrender Berlin without a fight?'
> 'What is Berlin? It is only a town.'
> 'Permit me to remind you that for us Prussians Berlin is the capital of the kingdom and I and my men prefer to die, sword in hand, in front of the place.'

Without Swedish help, Bülow attacked Oudinot at Gross-Beeren, 12 miles from the city, on 23 August. He drove the French back, inflicting 3,000 casualties and taking 23 guns. Then he turned on an isolated French division which lost a further 6,000 men. Blücher dealt even more harshly with Macdonald. He surprised him on the Katzbach river (26 August) and routed him with the loss of 20,000 men and 103 guns.

Napoleon was more fortunate. Schwarzenberg crossed the Bohemian mountains and tried to storm Dresden. The city had been turned into a fortified camp and the 20,000 men of its garrison were able to beat off the poorly coordinated allied attacks until, on 26 August, Napoleon arrived with the Guard and Mortier's corps. By the following morning two more French corps had arrived and Schwarzenberg, who had lost 38,000 men, ordered a retreat to Bohemia.

As the allies straggled back through the defiles of the Erzgebirge there was another chance for a grand Napoleonic stroke, but the Emperor busied himself with administrative concerns and merely told three corps commanders to follow the enemy. Only Vandamme pressed his pursuit and he allowed himself to be trapped by Kleist's Prussians at Kulm (Chumlec) on 28 August. Only 10,000 of Vandamme's 30,000 men managed to escape and their commander was not among them. Worse was to follow. Oudinot was superseded by Ney who again marched for Berlin. Bernadotte ordered another retreat and Bülow made another attack. Ney, for all his courage, was no tactician and at Dennewitz, 40 miles south of the capital, he was routed, losing 24,000 men (of whom 15,000 were taken prisoner) and 80 guns (6 September). In two disastrous weeks the new *Grande Armée* had lost 78,000 men and 298 guns. At 55,000 men and 26 guns the allied

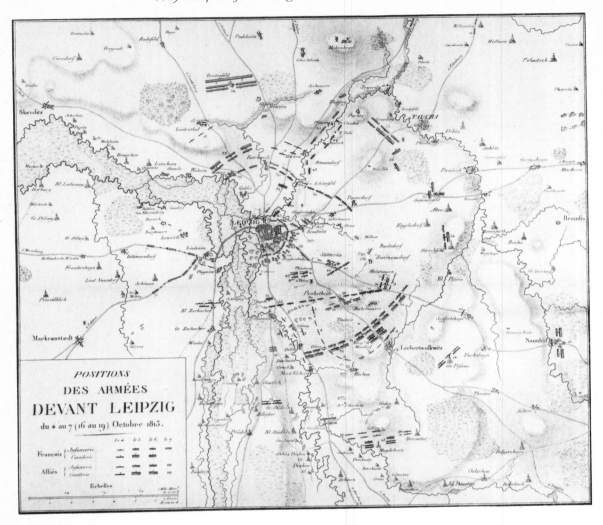

85 Plan of the positions of the armies before the Battle of Leipzig

casualties were sufficiently serious but reinforcements were constantly reaching them while the French had no reserves and their German auxiliaries were beginning to desert.

Again Schwarzenberg ordered a convergent offensive in three columns aiming at Leipzig but this time his orders were that any column counter-attacked by Napoleon in person should retreat while no effort should be spared to hammer his subordinates. After days of fruitless marching, the Emperor was forced to change his tactics. He fell back on Leipzig and invited a battle. By 14 October he had concentrated 177,000 men in his chosen position although he had left a useless garrison of 26,000 men in Dresden.

On 16 October Leipzig was attacked from north and south. Napoleon had intended to strike the first blow but he was anticipated by

Schwarzenberg who attacked from the south with 203,000 men. On this front the battle swayed backwards and forwards throughout the day and when night fell the allies were still four miles from the city. Blücher with his 54,000 men had a more successful day on the northern front, taking the village of Möckern, two miles from Leipzig. He would have made more progress had not Bernadotte with the third allied column decided to dally on his march until he received some indication of how the day was likely to go. 16 October could be considered a bloody draw with each side losing 20,000 men without gaining any clear advantage.

The following day was quieter while both armies prepared to renew the struggle. Believing that he needed to gain time, Napoleon sent a flag of truce proposing a peace conference. This gave the allies the impression that the invincible Emperor was hard pressed and the time gained benefited them rather than the French. During 17 October Napoleon was joined by a corps of 18,000 men while Schwarzenberg was reinforced by 40,000 Russians and Bernadotte decided that the odds were sufficiently favourable for him to join the battle. He reached the field with 60,000 men including 2nd Rocket Troop, Royal Horse Artillery. This, however, was not Britain's only contribution. She had also provided 124,119 muskets (with 18½ million cartridges), 218 artillery pieces, 34,433 swords, 175,596 pairs of boots, 150,000 suits of uniforms and 187,000 yards of uniform cloth.

On 18 October the battle went to the big battalions. The allies were employing 335,000 against 175,000 and, staunchly though the French fought, they were inexorably forced back into the city.

Some of their Saxon and Württemberger auxiliaries deserted to the allies. Even the Old Guard had to be thrown in to hold the line. By evening Napoleon saw that his only hope was a phased withdrawal. At 2 am on 19 October he began to thin out the fighting troops and, since the allies were reprehensibly incurious about the inevitable noise made by the withdrawal, it seemed as if the French were going to break cleanly away.

Unfortunately the Leipzig position had a lethal drawback. To the west of the city runs the river Elster which was crossed by a single narrow stone bridge. This could be approached only by a causeway, two miles long. To defile an army still 150,000 strong through this bottleneck would be a considerable feat at any time. To do it under enemy pressure would be a triumph but despite some crowding and isolated outbreaks of panic, the operation was well on the way to success when, at 1 pm an engineer corporal of the Imperial Guard lost his nerve and blew up the bridge. 33,000 men, 260 guns and huge quantities of waggons and material fell into the hands of the allies. A few, including Marshals Oudinot and Macdonald, managed to swim the river, but Prince Poniatowski, who had been promoted marshal on the previous evening and was four times wounded during the battle, was swept away and drowned.

The French loss at Leipzig, from death, wounds, capture and desertion, was 70,000 men, half as many again as their opponents. The march back to the Rhine, during which the French had to brush away an Austro-Bavarian corps which tried to block their road near Hanau, was also extremely costly. Straggling lost the army thousands of men, 10,000 fell into allied hands in the last three days of October alone, and many of the German conscripts took the opportunity to make their way home. When the west bank of the Rhine was reached there were not more than 60,000 with the eagles and while 40,000 straggled in later, deaths from typhus cost as many as 30,000. 100,000 men had been left in useless garrisons in Germany. The 26,000 in Dresden surrendered on 11 November but Davout with 30,000 held Hamburg until the end of the war.

As the Austrians, Prussians, Russians and Swedes closed up to the Rhine, another allied army was already on French soil. Wellington had established his front on the western Pyrenees after Vitoria and set about besieging San Sebastian and Pamplona which sat squarely on the roads leading from Spain to France. The delay caused by these sieges was not unwelcome as he was reluctant to invade France until he heard the result of the armistice of Pleischwitz. If it had led to peace on the eastern front Napoleon would have been able to send enough reinforcements to the Spanish frontier to make the allied position untenable.

On the French side, Soult was sent to supersede King Joseph and to command the *Armée de l'Espagne*. He lost no time in taking the offensive and on 25 July sent 60,000 men through the Maya and Roncesvalles passes in an attempt to relieve Pamplona. Aided by irresolution among some subordinate British commanders he got within five miles of his goal when he was first stopped and then driven headlong back into France at the two battles of Sorauren (28 and 30 July), having lost 13,000 men. He made an abortive attempt to relieve San Sebastian on 31 August, the day on which the town fell, and then set about fortifying the frontier. Pamplona was starved into surrender at the end of October but before then Wellington had slipped his left across the Bidassoa and entered France by crossing a stretch of the estuary which the French believed impassable (7 October). A month later, he struck with his right in the battle of the Nivelle (10 November) which carried the army clear of the Pyrenean barrier but brought them face to face with the fortress of Bayonne.

News of the battle of Leipzig reached Wellington on 9 November and one of the prisoners taken at the Nivelle was a French colonel who dined that evening at Wellington's table. In the course of conversation the field-marshal asked him where the emperor's *quartier-général* was according to the last information.

> 'Monseigneur,' *said our man with a tragic grimace,* 'Il n'y a plus de quartier-général.' *He alluded to the rout of Leipzig, and then I saw my way clearly to Bordeaux and Paris.*

*   *   *

Once again Napoleon was faced with the task of reconstructing the *Grande Armée*. The difficulties were even greater than those a year earlier, for France was weary of unending war, the *Corps Legislatif* was uncooperative, the treasury was empty and the senior officers were longing for peace. More than a million conscripts of the classes of 1814 and 1815 were called to the colours but evasion was on a gigantic scale. Customs officers, *gardes forestiers* and others hitherto exempt from military service were now called up and many units of the National Guard were embodied into the regulars. The army of 1814 was creditably enthusiastic but it was very young, there were many in the ranks who were no more than sixteen and some were even younger. They were, however, almost wholly French. The German states,

86 Cossacks stripping a corpse after the Battle of Leipzig

195

so long a recruiting ground for Napoleon, now sent their contingents to the allied armies and all the Italian soldiers who could be raised were needed on the line of the Adige where Prince Eugène, with 50,000 men, was trying to hold the lethargic attacks of 75,000 Austrians under Marshal Bellegarde, while in Naples Murat was making an alliance with the Austrians. In November 1813 Cossacks crossed into north Holland and the population rose and declared for the House of Orange.

Soon after the new year of 1814 Napoleon had 100,000 men to defend the eastern frontiers of France but his enemies could deploy 350,000 on that front. Unless he could conjure up a military miracle, the best chance of saving his throne was by diplomacy. His first attempt to buy off an enemy was naïve to the point of self-delusion. He signed a treaty with King Ferdinand of Spain by which that monarch was to be restored to his throne and, in return, was to see that both French and British troops left his realm. In 1808 Napoleon had said of Ferdinand, 'I could not entrust myself to his bad faith', but in 1814 he was prepared to accept his word. Writing that 'I have come to an agreement with the Spaniards which leaves me free to make use of my troops in Aragon, Catalonia and Bayonne', he withdrew 24,000 men from his armies in Spain (10 January) and told Soult and Suchet that they would no longer have Spaniards fighting against them. Ferdinand, as was to be expected, repudiated his agreement as soon as he was sent back to Spain and his troops continued to fight until the end of the war.

A more profitable field for French diplomacy could be found in exploiting the dissensions of the allies. Three great coalitions had been raised against France since the Revolution and each one had collapsed through disunity. There was every chance that the Fourth Coalition would go the same way if only the internal stresses could be exploited. The basis of the Russo-Prussian alliance was the secret Treaty of Kalisch signed on 28 February 1813. This proposed that France should be reduced to her 'natural frontiers'—the Pyrenees, the Alps and the Rhine—and that Poland should be re-created by adding the Grand Duchy of Warsaw to the Polish provinces of the Russian empire. Although theoretically independent the new Poland would have as her king the Czar of Russia. Since this arrangement would deprive Prussia of her Polish provinces, she was to be compensated by acquiring Saxony on the pretext that the king of that country had been Napoleon's ally, an interesting exercise in hypocrisy by both Alexander and Frederick William. Britain had not been consulted about these arrangements, although she had agreed that Sweden should have Norway, but it was tacitly assumed at Kalisch that she would be content if she was allowed to make what arrangements she saw fit about Spain, Portugal, Sicily and the French colonies.

The advent of Austria to the coalition upset this tidy and unscrupulous arrangement. Her main aim was to recover her Italian duchies and add the

Venetian provinces to them but she had no intention of agreeing to a revived Poland, including her own Polish acquisition of Galicia. In particular she was not prepared to tolerate Poland as a Russian satellite stretching as far west as the river Oder. She was no happier about Prussia's acquisition of Saxony. Austria and Prussia had been disputing for supremacy in Germany since the middle of the eighteenth century and a Prussia which had engulfed Saxony would almost certainly become predominant.

Since the Emperor Francis preferred making toffee to conducting diplomatic business, the burden of contesting the Russian and Prussian claims, as put forward by the Czar in person, fell to the Austrian chancellor, Metternich. Metternich was not an Austrian, having been born in Coblenz, and despite being a count with 16 quarterings and having been created a prince in 1813 was something of an outsider in Vienna. In fact he was a European who believed that the supreme task of a statesman was to keep a balance between extremes. He feared Russian dominance in Europe as much as French, and, having seen the Belgian Revolution of 1789–90, he loathed violence. He believed that it was more important to maintain a general peace than to stir up unnecessary conflicts by attempting to remedy every minor injustice. Alone of the statesmen of the eastern allies he was well informed about Britain. He had visited the country, met many of the leading figures, and attended the trial of Warren Hastings. He also realized the power of the Royal Navy, for he had visited Lord Howe's fleet before it sailed to the Glorious First of June and had with difficulty been dissuaded from sailing with the admiral. Metternich saw that only an Anglo-Austrian understanding could frustrate the plans of Russia and Prussia.

At the end of 1813 there were three British representatives at allied headquarters who were accredited respectively to the Russian and Prussian armies and to the Austrian court. It was difficult to judge British policy from their pronouncements since they disagreed with each other on most points. Metternich, very properly, made his approaches to the British ambassador to Austria and was so successful that he nearly frustrated his own ends. The ambassador was the Earl of Aberdeen, a young man of antiquarian interests and no diplomatic experience, who was so susceptible to Metternich's flattery that he ignored the most important points in his own brief from London.

Not only did Aberdeen agree to Metternich's proposal that Murat should retain his Neapolitan throne, a concession diametrically opposed to Britain's treaty obligations to King Ferdinand of Naples and Sicily, he also agreed to Napoleon being offered peace on the basis of a French withdrawal within her 'natural frontiers'. Fortunately for the alliance, Napoleon rejected out of hand this peace proposal which was made to him from Frankfurt on 6 November 1813.

In associating Britain with the Frankfurt Proposals, Aberdeen had

overlooked the one unchanging factor in British foreign policy, her insistence that Antwerp should not be held by the French. Antwerp was a great naval base which could not be attacked from the sea and it was very close to the British coast. 'To leave it in the hands of France is little short of imposing on Great Britain the charge of a perpetual war establishment.' Antwerp is on the south side of the Rhine and thus within the 'natural frontiers' and the thought that peace might be made on such a basis brought the Foreign Secretary hurrying out to allied headquarters in red breeches, jockey boots and complete with 'a fur cap with a gold band'.

Castlereagh, who had been an outstanding Secretary for War before moving to the Foreign Office, was the ideal ally for Metternich. Both men thought in terms of Europe as a whole, and believed that a lasting peace could only be achieved if no single power was allowed to become predominant. Since the first task of the allies was to guard against French expansion in the future, Castlereagh proposed that the states on her north-eastern and south-eastern frontiers should be strengthened into effective powers. At one end of the line Holland should be expanded to include Belgium, Liège and Luxemburg, thus ensuring the safety of Antwerp. At the other end, Sardinia should be consolidated by recovering Savoy, Nice and Piedmont and by acquiring the territory of the former republic of Genoa. Metternich, the representative of the former rulers of Belgium, was happy to fall in with this plan, but pressed, on grounds of immediate expediency, that Murat should be allowed to retain Naples. Reluctantly Castlereagh agreed. The British were heartily sick of King Ferdinand and even more so of Queen Caroline who was, moreover, an Austrian princess. If the Austrians were prepared to sacrifice her Britain could scarcely cavil. In other parts of Europe there was no difficulty in reaching an understanding. Spain and Portugal were to be guaranteed by all the powers and it was agreed that Britain would oppose the Prussian acquisition of Saxony though it was thought that she might be allowed to take some territory on the right bank of the Rhine as a further security against France.

Britain was prepared to make considerable concessions to achieve European stability. She had at her sole disposal all the colonies of France and her allies and she was ready to use these as bargaining counters in the interests of securing a balance in Europe. The only prizes she intended to retain on strategic grounds were Malta, Mauritius, Heligoland and the Cape of Good Hope, although for the last she was ready to pay compensation to Holland. She was ready to forgo the rest of her captures in the general interest, saving only Guadaloupe which, inscrutably, she had promised to Sweden. On the Austrian side, Metternich was prepared to support Britain in her idiosyncratic interpretation of the Freedom of the Seas, a subject in which the Hapsburg Empire had very little interest.

The resulting Anglo-Austrian understanding was at least as firm as the Kalisch agreement and was, in the long run, to form the basis of a joint

87 *Opposite Page* Prince Clements Lothar Wenzel Metternich. *Painting by Thomas Lawrence*

allied policy but, in the winter of 1813–4, it did little for allied unity. On one point Britain and Austria could reach no agreement. Britain was most unwilling to see Bonaparte left on the French throne, but the Emperor Francis was reluctant to see his son-in-law dispossessed. The other allies were undecided on the future government of France. No one had any enthusiasm for a Bourbon restoration and the Czar swung between a wish to keep Napoleon, under severe limitations, and a desire to replace him with Bernadotte. This aberration, unacceptable even to the King of Prussia, had the fortunate effect of keeping a token presence of Swedish troops with the allied army. Bernadotte would have preferred to keep them for coercing the Danes, but, unable to resist the dream of reigning at the Tuileries he kept a contingent on the Rhine.

The armies were on the march even before Castlereagh joined allied headquarters on 18 January 1814. The Rhine had been crossed and an Austrian corps had moved into Switzerland. The allies were still in three columns. In the centre Blücher's Army of Silesia, 100,000 men, was ordered to march from Lorraine to Paris while Schwarzenberg's Army of Bohemia, 200,000, was to turn the French right through Switzerland and act against the flank of the troops opposing Blücher. They were also to detach a force to march across southern France and join hands with Wellington. Bernadotte's Army of the North was divided. Part carried on the siege of Hamburg and, until they surrendered on 14 January, engaged the Danes, while a Prussian corps, supported by a small and improvised British force, moved into Holland.

When Wellington heard of this plan he remarked acidly that he would not march a corporal's guard on such a system and it did reek of having been designed by a committee. Nevertheless, it achieved some early success since the French forces on the frontier were small, under-trained, under-equipped and over-extended. Blücher advanced 75 miles in nine days and had his advance guard across the Marne at Joinville on 23 January. Schwarzenberg could not move so fast but on the same day had troops at Bar-sur-Aube and the gap between the inward flanks of the two armies had been reduced to 25 miles. Contrary to Napoleon's exhortations, the French were not rising against the invaders as the populations of Spain, Russia and, latterly, Germany had done.

All might have gone well if Schwarzenberg had not ordered a halt so that a new diplomatic offensive might be launched. At that moment, 26 January, Napoleon arrived at the front and immediately attacked. He struck first at Blücher near St Dizier but the Prussian pulled back. A partial encounter near Brienne (29 January) could be represented as a French victory but Blücher counter-attacked at La Rothière three days later and drove Napoleon back with the loss of 73 guns. Instead of allowing the Army of Silesia to follow up this advantage Schwarzenberg ordered the two armies to separate. Blücher marched north west towards Paris while the Army of Bohemia aimed for the Seine valley intending to reach the capital by way of Fontainebleau. It was unfortunate that Wellington was not present to say, as he did at Waterloo, 'Gentlemen, we are in the presence of the greatest general in Europe.'

Napoleon was quick to take advantage of the division of his opponents. His only hope lay in defeating the allies in detail and his attempt to do so showed him in better military form than at any time since the Italian campaign of 1796. He turned first on Blücher who was advancing on Montmirail against the corps of Macdonald and Marmont. Leaving Victor and Oudinot to watch Schwarzenberg, Napoleon marched north with the Guard, 27,000, and the cavalry, 12,000. On 10 February he cut into the centre of Blücher's line of march when he destroyed a Russian division at Champaubert. He then swung west and, on the 11th, routed Sacken's 18,000 men near Montmirail. Next day he defeated Yorck's Prussian division at Château-Thierry. With their advance and flank guards destroyed, the Army of Silesia fell back to the Aisne at Soissons, burning the bridge at Château-Thierry and thus making the Marne a barrier to both sides.

Blücher, undeterred by these reverses, struck at Montmirail, now in Napoleon's rear, with 20,000 men. On 14 February he was driving in Marmont's corps at Vauchamps when he was taken in the flank by the Imperial Guard while Grouchy and the French cavalry swept round his rear. It cost the indomitable Prussian 7,000 men and 16 guns to fight his way out. The Army of Silesia had lost more than 20,000 men in five days but these losses were more than made good by the arrival of 30,000 Russians from the Army of the North. Napoleon had given a dazzling display of military skill but he was fighting not only against overwhelming numbers but, for the first time, against a general who could not be disheartened by defeats.

He now had to deal with Schwarzenberg who had driven Victor back to Nagis and had a clear road to Paris up the Seine valley. Taking the Guard and Macdonald's corps, Napoleon made forced marches southward and drove the Austrian advance guard back from Montereau (18 February) and across the Seine. Schwarzenberg was so disheartened that he proposed an armistice and, when it was refused, fell back first to Troyes and then to Bar-sur-Aube.

The diplomats were at work throughout these busy days. The allies had proposed peace on the basis that France should retire to her 'ancient limits', the frontiers of 1792, and that all other European questions should be deferred until a great conference, to be held at Vienna. Simultaneously Caulaincourt, now Napoleon's Foreign Minister, suggested a conference on the basis of the Frankfurt Proposals. It was agreed that plenipotentiaries should meet at Châtillon-sur-Seine on 5 February.

The conference of Châtillon opened with the allies apparently triumphant after their victory at La Rothière. Caulaincourt, intensely loyal

88 Napoleon at
Montereau. *Original wash
attributed to E. Lami*

to his Emperor but urgent for peace, accepted the offer of the 'ancient
limits' but was over-ruled by Napoleon. 'The idea of cutting France back to
her former frontiers means her downfall and disgrace. Without the
Rhineland, Belgium, Ostend and Antwerp, France would be nothing.' He
was adamant that France should retain Antwerp and raised the question of
the freedom of the seas, thereby trying to show the eastern allies that it was
only British insistence on her narrow interests that kept Europe at war. It
was, however, the Czar who insisted on breaking off the conference on 10
January.

The week that followed contained the French victories at Champaubert,
Montmirail, Château-Thierry and Vauchamps and brought the allies back
to the conference table while Schwarzenberg was retiring to Bar-sur-Aube.
They were nevertheless not to be deflected from their insistence on the

'ancient limits' and Napoleon turned his attention to detaching Austria from the coalition. He wrote to his father-in-law, 'since I can approach neither the English, whose policy centres on the destruction of my fleet, nor the Czar, because he thinks only in terms of passion and revenge.' He offered peace in return for France's natural frontiers but was tactless enough to offend Francis by remarking adversely on the performance of the Austrian troops at Montereau. Stiffened by Metternich, the Emperor refused to disrupt the alliance and the Châtillon conference wrangled on until the end of the month.

* * *

The final act of the long tragedy began on 1 March 1814 when, 21 years late, the allies by the Treaty of Chaumont defined their war aims and pledged themselves to fight on until they were achieved. This was Castlereagh's triumph and he was able to cement the alliance by providing a further £5 million in subsidies. Britain's economic position was now secure. The liberation of much of Holland and the opening of the Baltic trade had, with the assistance of an excellent harvest, produced another boom, with exports soaring to a record £70 million in 1814. To provide her eastern allies with the money they needed the government was even ready to starve the Peninsula army of coin and, when he broke into France, Wellington was reduced to assembling 40 experienced coiners from the ranks to remint Spanish coins into gold Napoleons.

The Treaty of Chaumont defined the allied war aims as the reduction of France to her ancient limits, the re-establishment and augmentation of Holland and Sardinia, the restoration of the Bourbon monarchy in Spain, of several Italian duchies and of an independent and neutral Switzerland. Germany was to be confederated. A conference at a later date was to decide the future of Poland and Saxony. No decision was reached about the future government of France beyond a pious resolution that the feelings of the French people should be consulted.

Schwarzenberg meanwhile had called Blücher's army down to join his own at Bar-sur-Aube, but once the Army of Silesia was on the move he recovered his nerve and ordered them to resume their march on Paris. This counter-order was to have important effects as Napoleon momentarily lost track of Blücher and did not rediscover his whereabouts until he attacked Marmont at Sézanne and drove the marshal back to Meaux. By the time the Emperor had raced north with 30,000 men Blücher had retired across the Marne at Ferté, destroying the bridge. It was 36 hours before the French could cross and by that time Blücher was beyond the Aisne. Determined to crush his most dangerous enemy once and for all, Napoleon followed and on 7 March attacked Blücher's rearguard in position on the Chemin des Dames. It was dislodged after heavy fighting (Battle of Craonne) but next day he attacked the main body of the Army of Silesia, strongly reinforced from the Army of the North, in a good defensive position near Laon. Like his troops the Emperor was now very tired and he mismanaged the battle. Attacking in two uncoordinated columns he was heavily repulsed in a two-day battle (8-9 March) and had to fall back to Soissons. There he learned that Schwarzenberg was advancing again and had driven the French under Macdonald back across the Seine to Provins. At last he had to admit that Paris was in serious danger and on 11 March wrote to his brother Joseph, now governor of the capital, that 'Orders must be given for redoubts to be built on the heights of Montmartre.'

Still refusing to contemplate the Chaumont terms he moved to turn the right of the Army of Bohemia and, on 13 March, routed a Russian division isolated near Reims. 'I am', he declared, 'still the man I was at Wagram and Austerlitz'. He wrote to the allies demanding that they evacuate France and offering in return to evacuate all his conquests 'beyond France's borders', which he did not define, and to establish an independent Belgium under a prince of the house of Bonaparte.

This offer went unanswered. The victory at Laon had greatly heartened the allies and good news had arrived from the south.

> *A very brilliant affair has taken place between Orthez and St Sever with the whole of Soult's army, about 32,000 strong—four generals were killed and 40 guns taken. The affair was decided by a charge of cavalry, led by Lord Wellington accompanied by the Duc d'Angoulême.*

These details, which came from an Austrian source, were picturesque rather than accurate but the victory at Orthez (27 February) was a fact and showed that Wellington had broken loose from the Bayonne position and that Soult could no longer face the allies in the field. The Duc d'Angoulême, nephew to Louis XVIII, had not taken part in a cavalry charge (the charge itself was a romantic figment) but his presence with Wellington's army had called forth such demonstrations of enthusiasm in south-western France that first Britain and soon the other allies began to regard a Bourbon restoration as a practical proposition.

On 20 March Napoleon was repulsed by the Austrians at Arcis-sur-Aube and thereafter his genius deserted him. Having given an eight-week display of brilliant generalship, he made an irreparable mistake. It may be that he was exhausted by his own virtuosity or that 'he never in his life had the patience for a defensive war' but, whatever the reason, he decided to stake everything on a single decisive throw. Leaving Mortier and Marmont to cover Paris with quite inadequate forces, he marched eastward with 40,000 men. His aim was to augment his army with fresh troops from the garrisons of Metz and Pont-à-Moussons and with this refreshed army force Schwarzenberg and Blücher to withdraw by cutting their communications with Germany. Under any circumstances it would have been a desperate gamble but any chance of success it might have had was destroyed by the

Emperor's own act. He outlined his plan in a letter to Marie-Louise which he did not trouble to send in cypher. The letter fell into the hands of a Cossack patrol.

The allies saw their chance and seized it. Only a screen of cavalry stood between Blücher and Paris. Schwarzenberg, after detaching 8,000 to shadow Napoleon, marched with 100,000 men to Fère-Champenois where Mortier and Marmont tried to bar his way with 17,000. In the last battle of the campaign (25 March) the two marshals lost 9,000 men and 50 guns. Both allied armies marched relentlessly on the capital and, in accordance with Napoleon's instructions, the Empress and Joseph Bonaparte left the city on 29 March. Marmont, having no alternative, surrendered the shattered remnant of his corps thus giving the Napoleonic legend the scapegoat it needed to explain the Emperor's defeat. Next day Austrian, Prussian and Russian troops marched into Paris.

> *The Emperor of Russia with all his staff, his generals and their suites were joined by the King of Prussia with a similar cortège. These sovereigns, surrounded by all the princes in the army, together with Prince Field-Marshal Schwarzenberg and the Austrian* État-Major, *passed through the Faubourg St Martin and entered the barrier of Paris about 11 o'clock, the Cossacks of the Guard forming the advance of the march. Already was the crowd so enormous, as well as the acclamations so great, that it was difficult to move forward. . . . All Paris seemed to be assembled and concentrated upon one spot. They thronged in such masses round the emperor and the king that with all their condescending and gracious familiarity, extending their hands on all sides, it was vain to attempt to satisfy the populace; they were positively eaten up amidst the cries of* 'Vive l'empereur Alexandre! Vive le roi de Prusse! Vive nos libérateurs!' *Nor did the air alone resound with these peals for, with louder acclamations, if possible, they were mingled with those of* 'Vive le roi! Vive Louis XVIII! Vive les Bourbons! Bas le tyran!'

Napoleon was 120 miles from Paris at St Dizier when he heard, on 27 March, of the Battle of Fère-Champenois. Realizing his mistake, he set out by forced marches to save the capital. Inevitably he was too late. With a handful of staff officers he was almost within sight of Paris, at Essonnes, near the present site of Orly airport, when he heard that the city had surrendered. He turned back to Fontainebleau to enable his remaining troops to catch up with him. Soon he had 36,000, including the Guard, and gave orders for a march on Paris. The remaining marshals had had enough. Macdonald said, 'We have determined to make an end.' Napoleon repeated his order but Ney, Prince of the Moskva and the bravest man in the Emperor's service, interrupted:

'The army will not march.'

'The army will obey me.'

'The army will obey its generals.'

Napoleon offered to abdicate in favour of his three-year-old son but the allies would not accept Napoleonic rule by proxy. On 6 April he recognized the inevitable and renounced 'for himself and his heirs, the thrones of France and Italy.' That day the rump of the Senate, manipulated by Talleyrand and the Czar, voted that 'The French people freely call to the throne of France, Louis Stanislav Xavier, brother to the late King.'

News travelled slowly, no faster than a horseman could ride, and it did not reach the south of France in time to prevent one last battle. On 10 April Soult with his remaining 42,000 men was holed up in the city of Toulouse and Wellington set out to extrude him with 48,000 British, Portuguese and Spaniards. By nightfall the allies held the ridge which dominated the city at a cost of 4,500 casualties. The French slipped out of the city under cover of darkness before the heavy guns could be brought up to compel them to leave. While they were marching, news arrived from Paris. The messenger

'found Wellington pulling on his boots, in his shirt.'
'I have extraordinary news for you.'
'Ay, I thought so. I knew we should have peace; I've long expected it.'
'No, Napoleon has abdicated.'
'How, abdicated? Ay, 'tis time indeed. You don't say so upon my honour. Hurrah!' said Wellington, turning round on his heel and snapping his fingers.

Vienna and Waterloo

With Louis XVIII restored to the throne of his ancestors, the allies had two immediate problems before they could set about redrawing the map of Europe, which had been altered out of all recognition since Rochambeau's revolutionary rabble had surged over the Belgian frontier 22 years earlier. They had to dispose of Napoleon and his family and they had to make peace with France. Despite a half-hearted attempt to commit suicide with stale poison, Napoleon agreed to the Treaty of Fontainebleau (13 April) by which he was awarded the sovereignty of Elba with a revenue of £2 million from French funds. He was allowed to retain the title of Emperor and to maintain a bodyguard of 400 French and Polish soldiers (a number which soon expanded itself to 1,100) and a navy consisting of the brig *Inconstant*. He renounced all claims to rule over France and Italy but successfully strove to get an Italian territory for the Empress, who was granted the duchies of Parma, Piacenza and Guastalla, since 'I am not willing for Louise to shut herself up on this island of Elba. It must be possible for her to live in fair Italy for a part of the year.'

Having bidden an emotional farewell to the Old Guard on 16 April, he set off for Elba escorted by officers from Austria, Britain and Russia. He met violent hostility on the road and, to escape the anger of his former subjects, was reduced to leaving his coach and riding a horse dressed as a postillion. On 28 April he embarked on the frigate UNDAUNTED at Fréjus. A French warship was available but knowing his unpopularity with his own navy he refused to board her. He landed on Elba on 4 May.

At the end of the month the allies signed the Treaty of Paris with France. It was an astonishingly mild document. Not only did France retain her 'ancient limits' she gained some small territories, notably Chambéry, Annecy and the papal enclave at Avignon. No indemnity was imposed on her and she was permitted to keep the works of art she had looted from all over the Continent. She lost only Tobago, Santa Lucia and Mauritius.

In granting this lenient peace the allies hoped to readmit France as a cooperating member of the community of nations. The hard bargaining was still to follow for the allies were deeply divided on the eastern question, the chief bone of contention being Prussia's claim to the whole of Saxony in exchange for her Polish provinces with the exception of the fortress of Thorn. Austria and Britain were determined that Saxony should survive and the Czar was unwilling to lose Thorn from his projected Polish kingdom.

A meeting of sovereigns (except for the Emperor Francis who was represented by Metternich) in London failed to make progress on this point. It was a difficult meeting and was made more difficult by the behaviour of the Czar and his sister, the Grand Duchess Catherine. The former was pointedly rude to the Prince Regent and hobnobbed ostentatiously with the leaders of the Whig opposition, who thought him 'a vain silly fellow'. The Grand Duchess offended almost everyone, most particularly when she forced her way into an all-male banquet at Guildhall where she insisted on having the band stopped, since she said music always made her sick. It was with difficulty that she could be persuaded to allow 'God Save the King' to be played for the loyal toast.

Although most European questions had to be deferred to the projected Vienna conference, one positive agreement was reached during the London meeting. The Anglo-Austrian understanding on the Low Countries was generally approved, Belgium was attached to Holland and the Prince of Orange (whose heir was, temporarily, engaged to marry the Prince Regent's daughter) was recognized as King of the Netherlands. Thus Britain succeeded in fulfilling her original war aim—a strong state on France's north-eastern border which could guarantee the security of Antwerp. In gratitude the Dutch ceded Ceylon to Britain and sold the Cape of Good Hope to her for £2 million which they undertook to spend on fortifications on the French frontier.

The Congress of Vienna was the greatest diplomatic extravaganza ever mounted. The Emperor of Austria, who cared very little for social occasions, found himself as host to the Czar and Czarina of Russia, the Kings of Prussia, Württemberg, Bavaria and Denmark, two Crown Princes and a crowd of grand dukes and princes of various bloods royal, to say nothing of his daughter, formerly Empress of the French, her son, the *ci-devant* King of Rome, and her step-son by marriage, Eugène de Beauharnais, formerly Viceroy of Italy. Also present were the heads of 215 princely houses although, unlike the royalty these were not entitled to dine and sleep at the Hofburg palace. There were diplomatic missions from every European state, including a pasha to represent the Sublime Porte and a cardinal to watch over the interests of the Pope. Naples had two mutually antipathetic delegations, one accredited by King Ferdinand Bourbon and one by King Joachim Murat. Switzerland had 19 delegations, one for each of the cantons which were unable to agree among themselves.

The Congress had been due to open on 1 October 1814 but circumstances prevented the formal inauguration. The representatives of

the four victorious great powers, Austria, Britain, Prussia and Russia, had met in advance to arrange how the business was to be dealt with but, although they devised a workable basis for proceedings, they had reckoned without the formidable talents of Talleyrand. This ex-bishop, who had served as a Minister under the Revolution, the Directory, the Consulate and the Empire, had emerged as Foreign Minister for the restored Bourbons and was determined to have France included among the great powers. When shown the protocol prepared by the plenipotentiaries he pounced on the word 'allies'. Who, he asked, was allied against whom? He recognized that there had been an alliance against the Emperor Napoleon but were the powers still allied against Louis XVIII, his master? If that was the case why had France been invited to send a delegation? Lamely they explained that the term 'allies' had been used for the sake of brevity. 'Brevity', he replied, 'is not to be purchased at the expense of accuracy.'

From that moment France took her seat as a great power and Talleyrand

89 Victory banquet at Guildhall, London, attended by the Prince Regent, the Czar of Russia and the King of Prussia, 18 June 1814. *Painting by George Clint*

90 Meeting of heads of delegations at the Congress of Vienna. From left to right: Prince Hardenberg of Prussia (seated), the Duke of Wellington (standing), the Comte de Lobo, Portugal, the Comte Saldanha, Sweden, the Comte de Noailles, France, Metternich, Austria, the Comte de la Tour du Pin, France, the Comte de Nesselrode, Russia, the Comte de Palmela, Portugal, Lord Castlereagh, the United

harassed his colleagues to such an extent that the plenary sessions of the Congress were delayed until on 30 October they were postponed indefinitely. The business was deputed to specialist committees. The Foreign Ministers of the five great powers met constantly in private and the horde of minor delegations and royal entourages found themselves with months of idleness on their hands. The Austrian Emperor and his officials racked their brains to devise entertainments for their multitudinous and apparently permanent guests while the Austrian secret police, over-stretched and inexperienced in dealing with eminent foreigners, churned out reports of astonishing fatuity. One agent complained that the Czar's delegation always spoke Russian, a language he did not understand, when talking among themselves.

Naturally it was Poland and Saxony that caused most of the trouble. Russia had set her heart on the former and Prussia on the latter. Austria opposed both arrangements, but since there was little that could be done to prevent the Czar seizing most of Poland, efforts were concentrated on keeping Prussia out of Saxony, a move in which Metternich could count on the support of Castlereagh and Talleyrand. When the latter asked why among the sovereigns of mainland Europe only the King of Saxony had not been invited, the Russians replied that he had been Napoleon's ally to the last. That, replied Talleyrand, 'is only a question of dates', thereby gravely offending both the Czar and the King of Prussia. Before the end of the year tempers were frayed on both sides and when the Russians handed over the administration of Saxony to the Prussians, Austria mobilized and France augmented her army. Talleyrand organized the minor states to make a formal protest against Prussia's annexation of Saxony and Castlereagh reported that the Prussians were 'organizing their field army and fortifying Dresden'.

On 29 December the Prussians over-reached themselves. Their delegate, Hardenberg, announced that he would regard it as a matter for war if all the powers did not immediately recognize his country's right to Saxony. The Czar supported him, adding that in his view France should no longer take part in the councils of the great powers. That evening Castlereagh, Metternich and Talleyrand met and agreed to an alliance drafted by Castlereagh. Rather than submit to Russo-Prussian dictation they would fight. Austria and France would each put 150,000 men into the field while Britain would subsidize as many more. News of this treaty was carefully leaked to the Czar who, for a moment, thought it was a bluff. He knew that Britain's Peninsular army had, for the most part, been sent to take part in the American war and that opinion in London was running strongly against continental entanglements. Castlereagh was, indeed, acting directly contrary to his instructions but on 2 January when the news arrived that peace between Britain and the United States had been signed at Ghent, he said, 'We have become more European and by spring can have a very nice army on the continent.'

The effect was immediate. Russia was not prepared to go to war over Saxony and on the evening the news of the peace arrived, it was possible to report to London:

> *The American peace has made an immense sensation. The Emperor of Russia, in congratulating Lord Castlereagh at court, said meanly, he thought it would be expedient that France should be admitted to the conference. The Prussians very low, and begin to talk of modification.*

Following up this advantage, Castlereagh spoke firmly to Hardenberg, telling him that 'Great Britain would resist such menaces with her whole power and resources.' Prussia backed down. She settled for a strip of Saxony, leaving the kingdom independent, and instead pressed for a share of Poland, succeeding in prising the province of Posen (Poznan) loose from

Kingdom, Prince Razumovski, Russia, the Duke de Dalberg, France, Lord Stewart, the United Kingdom, Lord Clancarty, the United Kingdom, Baron de Vissenberg, Austria, Don Pedro Gomez Labrador, Spain, Baron de Wacken, Austria, Talleyrand, France (seated), le Chevalier de Gentz, Austria (standing), Comte de Stackelberg, Russia (seated), Baron de Humboldt, Prussia (standing), Lord Cathcart, the United Kingdom. *Sketch by J. B. Isabey* the Czar's grip. There had never, in fact, been any chance of stopping Alexander from obtaining most of Poland but, as things fell out, he had to be content with a Polish kingdom smaller than Napoleon's Grand Duchy while Austria regained Galicia.

From the second week in January 1815 the business of the Congress went smoothly. Europe was redistributed in such a way as to give the greatest chance of peace for the longest possible time. Austria regained Milan and took the Venetian lands, except for the Dodecanese Islands which went to Britain rather than to Russia. France was insulated by the Kingdom of the Netherlands, the augmented Kingdom of Sardinia, and a Prussian presence on the Rhine, while the Bourbons of Spain were guaranteed by the powers. The Bourbons of Sicily lost Naples, for a short time, to Murat.

Historians have pilloried the Vienna settlement for ignoring all the best liberal principles, but the statesmen who formed it were not concerned with ideals. What they wanted was peace. As Castlereagh explained to the House of Commons, 'The Congress of Vienna was not assembled for the discussion of moral principles, but for great practical purposes, to establish effectual provisions for the general security.' Undoubtedly some of the minutiae of theoretical justice were overlooked but peace was secured until another Napoleon arose, and there was no general European war for a century. The same cannot be said for the high-minded posturings at Versailles in 1919.

Detailed arguments went on into the spring and on the night of 6 March, five months after the Congress had been due to open, the representatives of the great powers had to sit until 3 am. When Metternich finally went to bed he told his valet:

> I was not to be disturbed under any circumstances. Nevertheless, at six in the morning, he brought me a despatch marked 'Urgent'. On the envelope I read From the Imperial and Royal Consulate, Genoa. Having had only two hours sleep, I did not open it and put it on the table beside my bed and lay down again. Having once been roused, I could not sleep, and, having lain awake until half past seven, I opened the despatch. It contained only six lines.
>
> 'The English Commissioner on Elba has just entered the harbour asking whether there has been any sign here of Napoleon as he has disappeared from Elba. We have seen no sign of him and the English frigate immediately put to sea again.'
>
> I dressed at once and reported the news to my Emperor. He ordered our army to march against France.

Hearing that France was disenchanted with the restored Bourbons and that the army was longing for his return, Napoleon embarked on the *Inconstant* on 26 February and sailed for France. He was accompanied by three generals and 1,050 soldiers. He landed near Antibes on 1 March and re-entered the Tuileries on the 20 March to start the reconstruction of his army and his empire. At Vienna, the powers declared him *hors la loi* and mobilized their armies to crush him. On 9 June the plenary session of the Congress was at last called and met for long enough to sign the treaty which had been worked out so laboriously behind closed doors in the previous eight months.

Nine days later the last scene was played out in Belgium where the great tragedy had begun. Napoleon had realized that the vast but slow-moving armies of Austria and Russia must take time before they could threaten France, and that a single brilliant victory would wipe away the army's humiliation of 1814 and consolidate the half-hearted civilian support which he was receiving. 'All Frenchmen', he believed, 'would go to war for the sake of acquiring Belgium or the Rhineland.'

Leaving covering forces on the other frontiers, he assembled his last army in the north east of France. His aim was to capture Belgium and to destroy the armies of the two generals who had shown themselves to be the most formidable among the allied commanders. These were Blücher, at the head of 120,000 Prussians, and Wellington, who had 88,000 men of assorted nationalities of whom only 23,000 were British. Napoleon's *Armée du Nord* had a marching strength of 124,000 but the purely numerical comparison was more than usually misleading. The French army was more highly trained than any he had led since the Treaty of Tilsit. There was a very high proportion of veterans, many of them released from prisoner-of-war camps, and, except for a few Poles, some Swiss and a regiment of Dutch lancers, it was entirely French. Half the strength of Blücher's army was made up by untrained *Landwehr* and also included 14,000 Saxons who, before the campaign opened, mutinied against their newly acquired Prussian masters. Similarly, Wellington's army had a large contingent of Belgians, whose political reliability was doubtful, and 13,000 Hanoverians who, though staunch, were no better trained than Blücher's *Landwehr*. Even his British troops and the 6,000 men of the King's German Legion contained too high a proportion of recruits. He was desperately short of the infantry who had fought in the Peninsula, and both he and Blücher had to leave a substantial number of their men as garrisons for fortresses.

Napoleon's plan was to divide his two enemies and defeat them singly, believing, wrongly as it happened, that if things went badly the Prussians would retreat to the east while the British would make for their ships at Ostend. He struck his first blow on 15 June, driving back the Prussians and crossing the Sambre at Charleroi. Next day he defeated them at Ligny, almost on the site of Jourdan's victory of Fleurus in 1794. Meanwhile his left wing had fought an inconclusive battle with Wellington's advanced troops at Quatre Bras. So far his plan was developing satisfactorily but next morning his preconceived idea took control of his strategy. He assumed that Blücher had been routed and that he was retreating eastward. All that remained was to drive away the English and march into Brussels.

By the evening of 17 June Wellington had concentrated 60,000 men and 154 guns on the ridge of Mont St Jean, near the village of Waterloo. That night the French army, 67,000 men with 258 guns, massed on the heights of La Belle Alliance, 1,400 yards south of the allies. When, the following morning, the redcoats were still to be seen to the north, the Emperor rubbed his hands and said, 'Wellington has gambled and lost. He has made his defeat certain.'

What Napoleon did not know was that Blücher had not fled eastward but had gone north to Wavre and that, soon after 6 am on the morning of 18 June, Wellington had received a long-delayed message from his ally promising that at least two Prussian corps would support him during the day. The Emperor had also overlooked the steadiness of the British infantry in defence which he had seen briefly at Toulon. He had forgotten the unknown Irishman who had wounded him with a bayonet at Fort Mulgrave. Of Wellington he affected to have no opinion, describing him as fit only to defeat Indians. When Soult pointed out the difficulty of driving the British from their ridge by frontal attacks, the emperor replied,

Just because Wellington has defeated you, you think he is a great general. I tell you that Wellington is a bad general, that the English are bad troops and that this is going to be a picnic.

92 *Above* Russian artillery, 1815. *Drawing by J. Adam Klein*

91 *Opposite Page* Austrian Jagers, 1815. *Painting by J. A. Langendyk*

93 Lord Anglesey leading the Life Guards against French lancers the day before the Battle of Waterloo

At almost the same moment, Wellington was remarking to his Prussian liaison officer, 'Now Buonaparte will see how a Sepoy general can defend a position.'

Allowing for the fact that Napoleon was tired and suffering the agonies of piles, his tactics at Waterloo can only be attributed to overweening pride and contempt for his opponent. As Wellington wrote, 'He did not manoeuvre at all. He just moved forward in the old style, and was driven off in the old style.' The first great French attack was delivered by four massive columns each a division strong. They were fought to a standstill by half their number standing steadily in their two-deep line and firing their devastating volleys. Had the Prussians been able to get forward as fast as Blücher wished the battle would have been over by mid-afternoon. Everything, however, conspired to delay them and by early evening Wellington's centre seemed ready to disintegrate. When the strongpoint of La Haye Sainte fell Napoleon had his last chance of attaining the break-through he had been trying to achieve all day. He hesitated. The Imperial Guard was ready but it was more than an hour before he could bring himself to commit it to battle.

Finally, at seven o'clock, he ordered the *Moyenne Garde* forward and led them in person to the bottom of the valley. It must therefore be assumed that he approved, if he did not actually direct, the formation in which they attacked. Of the five battalions that ascended the ridge four marched in column and one in square. It was a fatal error. They came on

216

94 The attack on Hougoumont, the Battle of Waterloo

in as correct order as at a review. As they rose step by step before us, and crossed the ridge, their red epaulettes and cross-belts put over their blue greatcoats gave them a gigantic appearance, which was increased by their high hairy caps and long red feathers, which waved with the nod of their heads as they kept time to a drum in the centre of their column.

The sight of the Guard's advance might have frightened away a rabble of Spanish recruits but to attack steady troops in such a formation was suicidal. Six years earlier Napoleon had written to Marshal Victor, 'When one attacks good troops, like the English, in good positions without reconnaissance and without the certainty of success one condemns men to death to no purpose.' The main strength of the attack of the Guard was directed at the sector held by the British Guards, who were lying down behind the shelter of a bank.

95 The Scots Greys capturing an eagle at the Battle of Waterloo. *Painting by Denis Dighton*

Suddenly the artillery ceased and as the smoke cleared away a most superb sight opened on us. A close column of La Moyenne Garde *were seen ascending the rise* au pas de charge, *shouting 'Vive l'Empereur'. They continued to advance till within 50 or 60 paces from our front, when the brigade was ordered to stand up. Whether it was from the sudden and unexpected appearance of a corps so near them, which must have seemed as if starting out of the ground, or the tremendously heavy fire we threw into them,* La Garde, *who had never before failed in an attack,* suddenly *stopped. Those who from a distance and more on a flank could see the affair, tell us that the effect of our fire seemed to force the head of the column bodily back.*

218

In less than a minute more than 300 were down. They now wavered, and several of the rear divisions began to draw out as if to deploy, whilst some of the men in their rear beginning to fire over the heads of those in front was so evident a proof of their confusion, that [Lieutenant Colonel] Lord Saltoun holloaed out, 'Now's the time, my boys!' Immediately the brigade sprang forward. La Garde turned and gave us little opportunity of trying the steel.

Napoleon's last army disintegrated when the *Moyenne Garde* broke. The last chance of victory had gone and the Prussians were pressing in on their right rear. The flight was covered by three magnificent battalions of *Ancienne Garde* and Napoleon was able to make his way to Paris. His army was defeated and civilian opinion had swung firmly against him. 'Alas', he said, 'I have accustomed them to such great victories; they cannot endure one day of misfortune.'

He made for the west coast, hoping to escape to America. As always, the Royal Navy thwarted him. 'Whenever', he said, 'there is water to float a

96 British artillery at Waterloo

The Artillery Officers had the range so accurately that every shot & shell fell into the very Centre of their Masses 15.43. Vol. 2

Published by J. Booth Feb 29 1816

97 Napoleon leaving the
field of Waterloo covered
by two squares of the Old
Guard

ship, we are to find you in our way.' At 6 am on 15 July he went aboard H.M.S. BELLEROPHON (74) and surrendered himself to Captain Frederick Maitland, R.N., who wrote:

> *He was received without any of the honours generally paid to persons of high rank; the guard was drawn up on the poop, but did not present arms. His Majesty's Government had merely given directions, in the event of his being captured, for his being removed into any of his Majesty's ships that might fall in with him; but no instructions had been given as to the light in which he was to be viewed. As it is not customary on board a British ship of war to pay any such honours before the colours are hoisted at eight, I made the early hour an excuse for withholding them upon this occasion.*

It was to Captain Maitland that Napoleon handed his last official letter which he had dictated two days earlier and addressed to the Prince Regent.

Rochefort, 13 July 1815

Altesse Royale,
> *Exposed to the factions which divide my people, and to the enmity of the greatest powers of Europe, I have terminated my political career; and I come, like Themistocles, to seat myself at the hearth of the people of Britain. I place myself under their laws, seeking this protection from your Royal Highness as the most powerful, the most constant and the most generous of my enemies.*

SELECT BIBLIOGRAPHY

ALBION, R. G., *Forests and Sea Power: the timber problem of the Royal Navy, 1652–1862*, Oxford University Press, 1927.

BERTRAND, H. G., *Napoleon at St Helena: memoirs of General Bertrand, from January to May of 1821*, ed. P. F. de Langle, trs. Frances Hume, Cassell; Doubleday, 1952.

BONAPARTE, Joseph, *Mémoires et correspondance politiques et militaire du roi Joseph*, ed. P. E. A. Du Casse, Paris, 1853.

BONAPARTE, Napoleon, *Correspondance de Napoleon Ier*, 32 vols, Paris, 1858–69.

BRETT-JAMES, A., ed. and trs., *1812: eyewitness accounts of Napoleon's defeat in Russia*, Macmillan; St Martin's Press, 1966.

ed. and trs., *Europe against Napoleon: the Leipzig campaign, 1813*, Macmillan; St Martin's Press, 1970.

de CAULAINCOURT, A. A. L., *Memoirs of General de Caulaincourt, Duke of Vicenza, 1812–14*, 2 vols., ed. J. Hanoteau, trs. H. Miles and G. Libaire, Cassell; William Morrow, 1935.

CHANDLER, D. G., *The Campaigns of Napoleon*, Macmillan, New York, 1966; Weidenfeld & Nicolson, 1967.

COOPER, A. D. *Talleyrand*, Cape; Harper, 1932.

CRAWLEY, C. W., ed., *War and Peace in an Age of Upheaval, 1793–1830*, vol. 9, New Cambridge Modern History, Cambridge University Press, 1965.

DUFFY, C., *Borodino and the War of 1812*, Seeley Service; Scribners, 1973.

Austerlitz 1805, Seeley Service, 1977.

FORTESCUE, J. W., *A History of the British Army*, (13 vols.), vols. 4–10, Macmillan, London and New York, 1915–20.

GIROD DE L'AIN, M., *Vie militaire du Général Foy*, Paris, 1900.

GLOVER, M., *Wellington as Military Commander*, Batsford; Van Nostrand, 1968.

Legacy of Glory: the Bonaparte kingdom of Spain, Scribners, 1971; Leo Cooper, London, 1972.

The Peninsular War, 1807–14: a concise history, David & Charles, Newton Abbot; Archon Books, New York, 1974.

GLOVER, R. *Peninsular Preparation: the reform of the British Army, 1795–1809*, Cambridge University Press, 1963.

Britain at Bay: defence against Bonaparte, Allen & Unwin; Barnes & Noble, 1973.

HECKSCHER, ELI F., *The Continental System: an economic interpretation*, ed., H. Westergaard, trs. from Swedish C. S. Fearenside, Oxford University Press, 1922.

HENDERSON, J., *The Frigates*, Coles, 1970.

HERIOT, A., *The French in Italy, 1796–9*, Chatto & Windus, 1957.

HOUSSAYE, H., *1815*, (42nd ed.), Paris, 1903.

JAMES, W., *The Naval History of Great Britain from the Declaration of War by France in 1793 down to the Accession of George IV*, 6 vols., new ed., London, 1837.

JOURDAN, J. B., *Mémoires militaires du Maréchal Jourdan—guerre d'Espagne*, ed. Vicomte de Grouchy, Paris 1899.

LEFEBVRE, G., *Napoleon: from 18 Brumaire to Tilsit, 1799–1807*, trs. H. F. Stockhold, Routledge; Columbia University Press, 1969.

LEWIS, M., *A Social History of the Navy, 1793–1815*, Allen & Unwin, 1960.

MACKESEY, P., *The War in the Mediterranean, 1803–10*, Longmans; Harvard University Press, 1957.

MAHAN, A. T., *The Influence of Sea Power in the French Revolution and Empire, 1793–1812*, 2 vols., Sampson Low, 1892.

MARSHALL-CORNWALL, J., *Marshal Massena*, Oxford University Press, 1965.
Napoleon as Military Commander, Batsford; Van Nostrand, 1967.

METTERNICH, C. W. N. L., *Memoirs of Metternich*, 5 vols., ed. Prince R. Metternich, trs. Mrs Alexander Napier, Bentley, 1880–2.

NICOLSON, H. G., *The Congress of Vienna: a study in allied unity, 1812–22*, Constable; Harcourt Brace, 1946.

PALMER, A., *Metternich: Councillor of Europe*, Weidenfeld & Nicolson, 1972.

PARET, P., *Yorck and the era of Prussian reform, 1807–15*, Princeton University Press, 1966.

PERICOLI, U., and GLOVER, M., *1815: the armies at Waterloo*, Seeley Service; Scribners, 1973.

PETRE, F. L., *Napoleon's campaign in Poland, 1806–7: a military history of Napoleon's first war with Russia verified from unpublished official documents*, Sampson Low, 1901.
Napoleon and the Archduke Charles: a history of the Franco-Austrian campaign in the valley of the Danube in 1809, John Lane, 1908.

PHIPPS, R. W., *The Armies of the First French Republic and the rise of the Marshals of Napoleon I*, Methuen, 1926.

QUIMBY, R. S., *The Background of Napoleonic Warfare: the theory of military tactics in eighteenth-century France*, Oxford University Press; Columbia University Press, 1958.

RODGER, A. B., *The War of the Second Coalition, 1798–1801: a strategic commentary*, ed. C. Duffy, Oxford University Press, 1964.

ROSE, J. H., *Napoleonic Studies*, Bell, 1904.

STEWART, C. W., *Narrative of the War in Germany and France in 1813 and 1814*, London, 1830.

STEWART, R., *Correspondence, Despatches and other Papers of Viscount Castlereagh, 2nd Marquess of Londonderry*, 12 vols., ed. 3rd Marquess, London, 1848–53.

WARNER, O., *A Portrait of Lord Nelson*, Chatto & Windus, 1958; published as *Victory: the life of Lord Nelson*, Little Brown, Boston, 1958.
Trafalgar, Batsford; Macmillan, New York, 1959.
The Battle of the Nile, Batsford; Macmillan, New York, 1960.

WELLESLEY, A., *The Dispatches of the Duke of Wellington*, 13 vols., ed. Lt. Col. Gurwood, London, 1834–9.

WHEELER, H. F. B., and BROADLEY, A. M., *Napoleon and the Invasion of England: the story of the Great Terror*, 2 vols., John Lane, 1908.

WILKINSON, H., *The French Army before Napoleon*, Clarendon Press, Oxford, 1915.

WILSON, R., *Narrative of Events during the invasion of Russia by Napoleon Buonaparte and the retreat of the French Army*, 1812, ed. H. Randolph, London, 1860.

INDEX